Matilda Lees Dods

Handbook of Practical Cookery

Matilda Lees Dods

Handbook of Practical Cookery

ISBN/EAN: 9783744763882

Printed in Europe, USA, Canada, Australia, Japan

Cover: Foto ©Andreas Hilbeck / pixelio.de

More available books at **www.hansebooks.com**

HANDBOOK OF PRACTICAL COOKERY

DEAD GAME

THOMAS NELSON & SONS

LONDON, EDINBURGH & NEW-YORK.

HANDBOOK OF PRACTICAL COOKERY

New and Enlarged Edition

In which special prominence is given to the preparing of New Cakes,
Jellies, etc.; to very simple recipes for Cottage Cookery;
also to various modes of preparing food
for the Sick-room.

By

MATILDA LEES DODS,

DIPLÔMÉE OF THE SOUTH KENSINGTON SCHOOL OF COOKERY.

With an Introduction
ON THE PHILOSOPHY OF COOKERY.

London:
T. NELSON AND SONS, PATERNOSTER ROW.
EDINBURGH; AND NEW YORK.

1886.

PREFACE.

The question will naturally be asked, in connection with this volume, Why is such a work required at all? Is there not already an abundance of books devoted to and exhausting the various branches of the subject, from the monograph which discusses all the points and possibilities of cold mutton, to the "Complete Housewife," whose "common-sense" suggestions and elaborate instructions range over all possible topics, from the currying of a lobster to the management of a husband?

To such a criticism we should reply, that cookery is now accepted as both a science and an art. As a science it is, of course, subject to all the laws of natural development; while as an art it can also lay claim to the privileges of continued inspiration; and the disciples of to-day need not admit that all wisdom has died with the prophets who have taught in the past. In sober earnest, there has been, during the past few years, a much more general recognition of the fact that the work of cooking—upon which depends so much of the comfort and, in fact, the happiness of existence—cannot be successfully carried on in a hap-hazard or in a "hit-or-miss" fashion. The interests imperilled are too serious and the results of failures too grave. It requires and demands careful, persistent study, and should utilize also all possible ingenuity and creative power that can be pressed into service. Originality of conception, thoroughness of knowledge, and precision of method may be said to be as important for the practice of cookery as for the practice of medicine; and it is very evident that the more fully these are called into play for the former, the greater the prospect of getting rid altogether of the latter.

The due recognition, during the past decade, of the proper position of this branch of human knowledge has led to the establishment of institutions planned to give instruction in the principles of cooking, and to further its higher development as a fine art; and during the next few years we hope to see the number of such institutions largely increased. Having obtained a first class diploma from the Kensington School of Cookery, with this in my possession, and a definite purpose before me of doing what was in my power to further the knowledge of my fellow-women and the comfort of my fellow-men, I could no longer feel that my life was aimless, even though my work should have no higher "range" than that of the kitchen. In course of my work with classes I have found that there was quite a general demand for a book that should embody, with somewhat more comprehensiveness and completeness of detail than was possible in any single course of lectures, the whole range of instruction, and should give the particular application of the general principles,—a book that should be, not a mere stereotyped schedule of dinners, suppers, and breakfasts, nor a depressing list of semi-intelligible recipes, but one that should present a comprehensive insight into the general rules for the intelligent preparation of food, and at the same time clearly describe the several means and processes of arriving at desired results. In response to such demand this volume has been prepared. Nothing has been included in it of which the practical worth has not been thoroughly tested; and it is believed that the examples have been so selected that, although of necessity limited in number, they demonstrate the whole theory and practice of the culinary art, and will make the reader familiar with the most approved methods and the latest attainments therein.

The purpose of our work is now set forth, although, if the whole story were told, it might be proper to show how the original cook-book grew from an onion, the veritable

> "Piece of chalot
> Which she never forgot."

But this touches the romance of the whole matter, without which nothing, however prosaic, is complete. With such prose and such suggestions of romance as belong to my subject, these pages are now submitted to the interpretation of those to whom my book is most affectionately dedicated—the world-wide sisterhood of housewives and their husbands—trusting that through its instrumentality all may be convinced that, while Heaven still furnishes the food, the Promethean fire of knowledge has redeemed the cooks.

CONTENTS.

Directions for Carving,	xxiii
Philosophy of Cookery,	xxv
Soups,	9
Purées,	19
Oysters and other Shellfish,	23
Fish,	32
Meats—	
Roasts,	42
Boiled Meats,	46
Meat Dishes,	50
Cold-Meat Dishes,	67
Broiled and Fried,	76
Game,	80
Entrées,	87
Vegetables,	102
Salads,	119
Croquettes and Fritters—	
Croquettes,	126
Fritters,	131
Soufflés,	135
Puddings,	141
Sweet and Savoury Sauces—	
Savoury Sauces,	174
Sweet Sauces,	179

CONTENTS.

ICES, CREAMS, AND JELLIES—
- Ices, ... 181
- Creams, ... 184
- Jellies, ... 190

PIES AND PASTRIES—
- Pastries, ... 195
- Pies, ... 197

BREAD AND CAKES—
- Bread, ... 201
- Cakes, ... 207

BREAKFAST DISHES, ... 227

TEAS, COFFEES, AND CHOCOLATE, ... 242

MISCELLANEOUS DISHES, ... 243

SIMPLE MILK PUDDINGS, ... 261

SIMPLE PUDDINGS, ... 264

MEATS, ... 273

SICK-ROOM COOKERY, ... 281

KEY TO DIAGRAMS.

OX.

1 Shin.
2 Clod.
3 Neck.
4 Cheek.
5 Chuck Rib.
6 Middle Rib.
7 Fore Rib.
8 Sirloin.
9 Shoulder.
10 Brisket.
11 Thin Flank.
12 Rump.
13 Edge Bone.
14 Round.
15 Veiny Piece.
16 Mouse Buttock.
17 Leg.

SHEEP.

1 Shoulder.
2 Breast.
3 Back Ribs.
4 Best End Neck.
5 Scrag End Neck.
6 Head.
7 Saddle.
8 Leg.

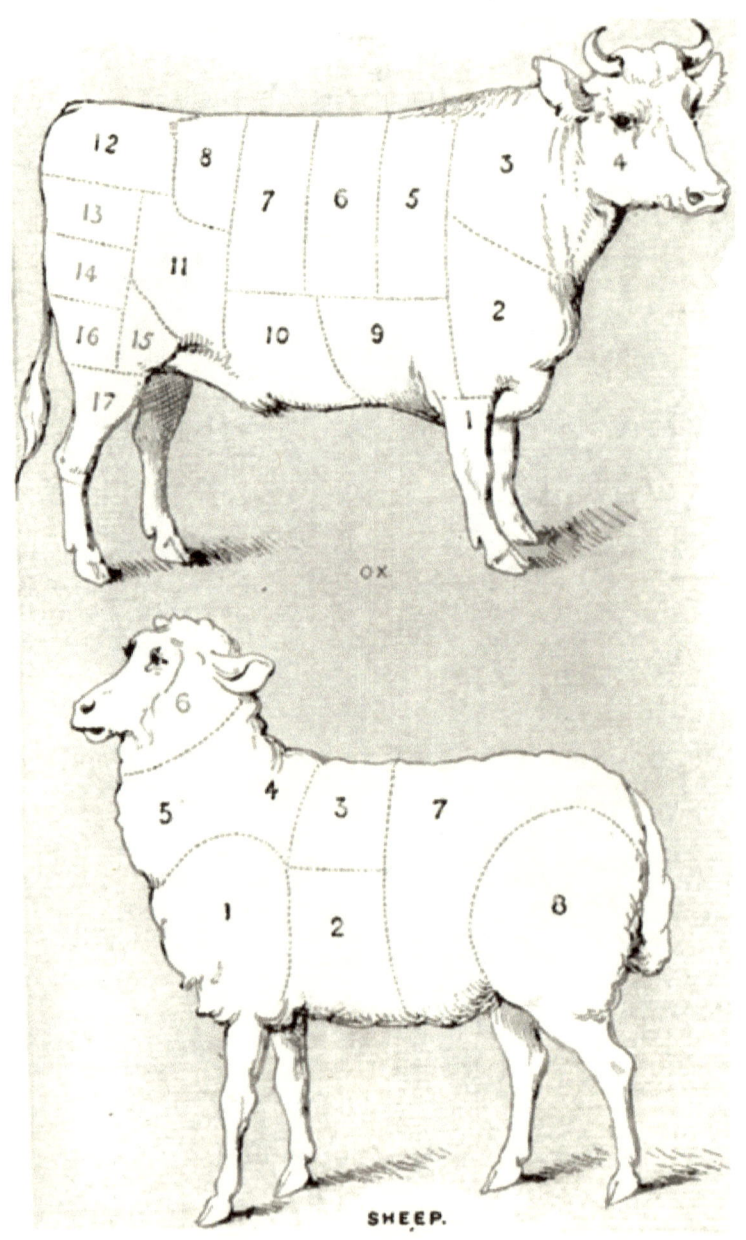

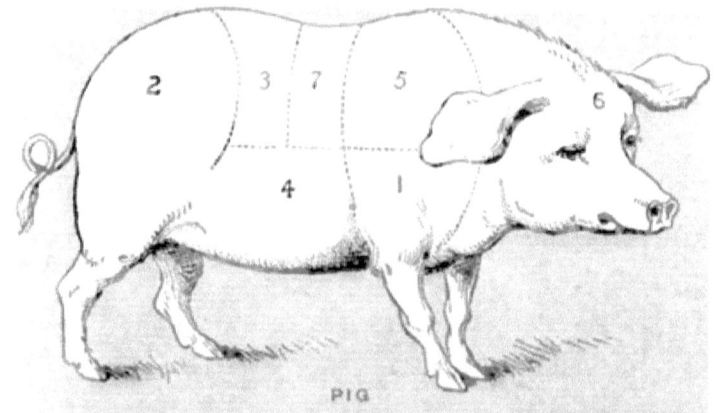

PIG

1 HAND. 2 LEG. 3 HIND LOIN. 4 SPRING. 5 SPARE RIB. 6 HEAD. 7 FORE LOIN.

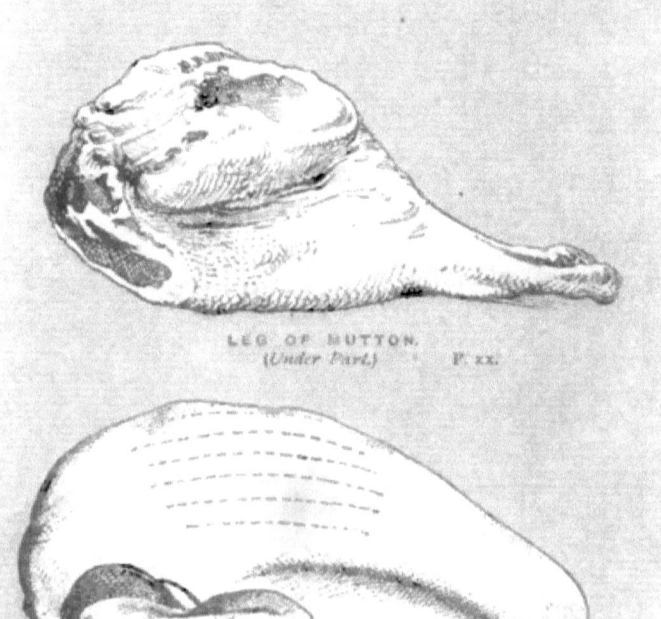

LEG OF MUTTON.
(Under Part.) P. xx.

BOILED TURKEY.
P. xxii.

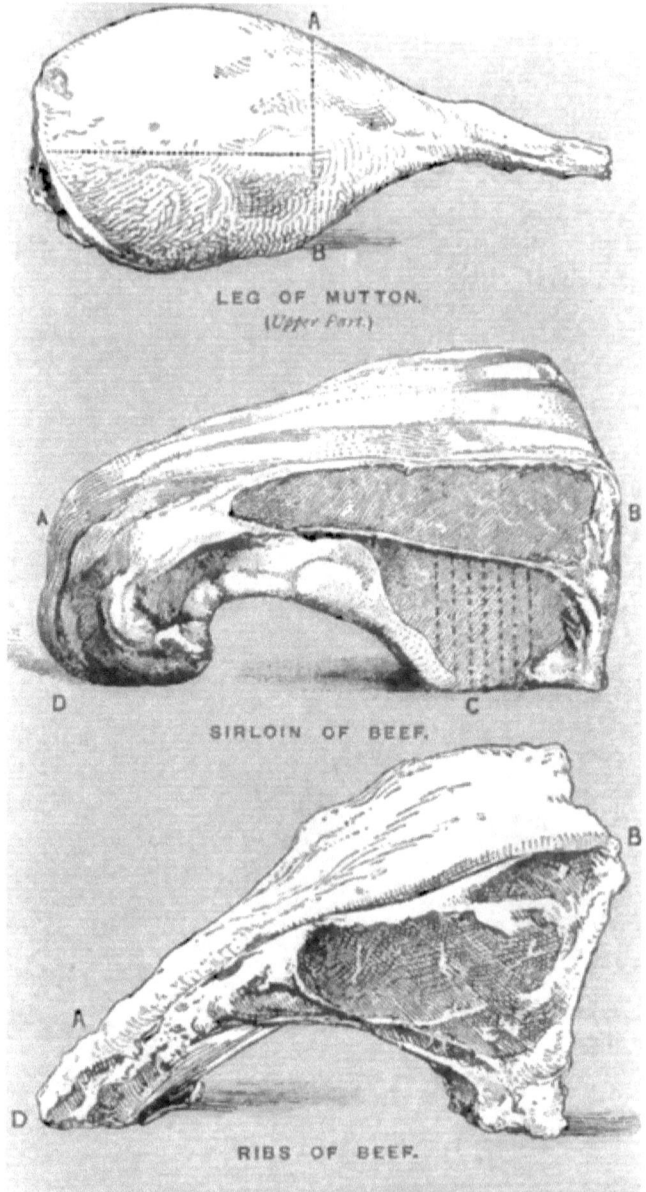

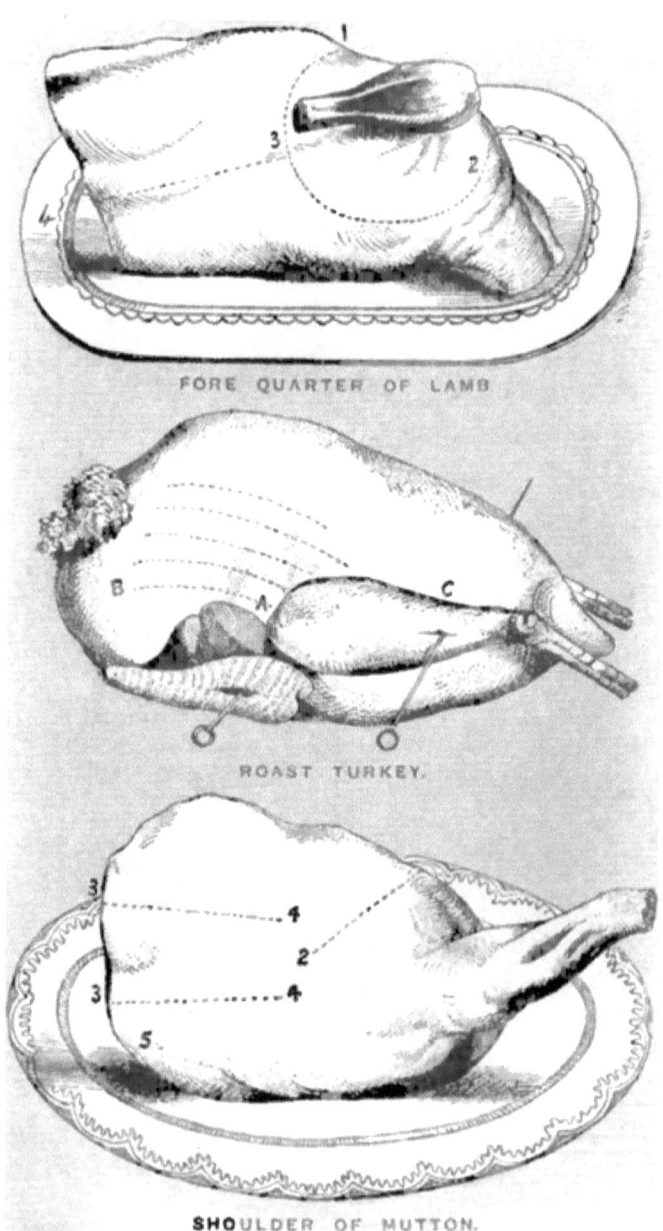

FORE QUARTER OF LAMB.

ROAST TURKEY.

SHOULDER OF MUTTON.

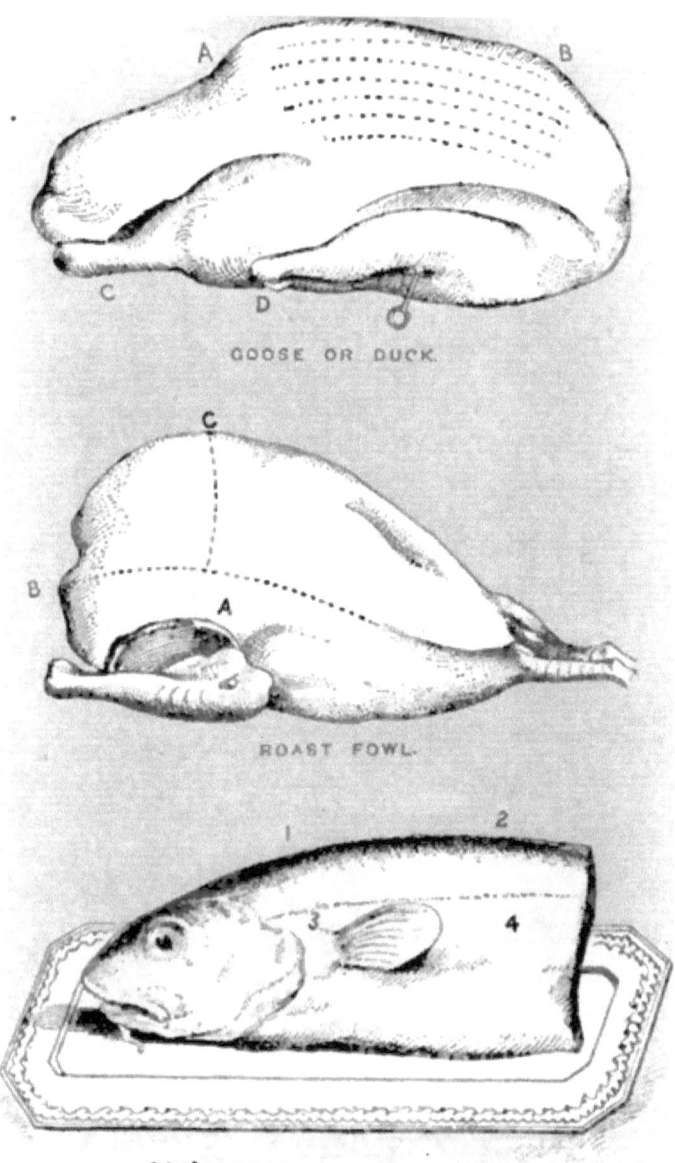

GOOSE OR DUCK.

ROAST FOWL.

COD'S HEAD AND SHOULDERS.

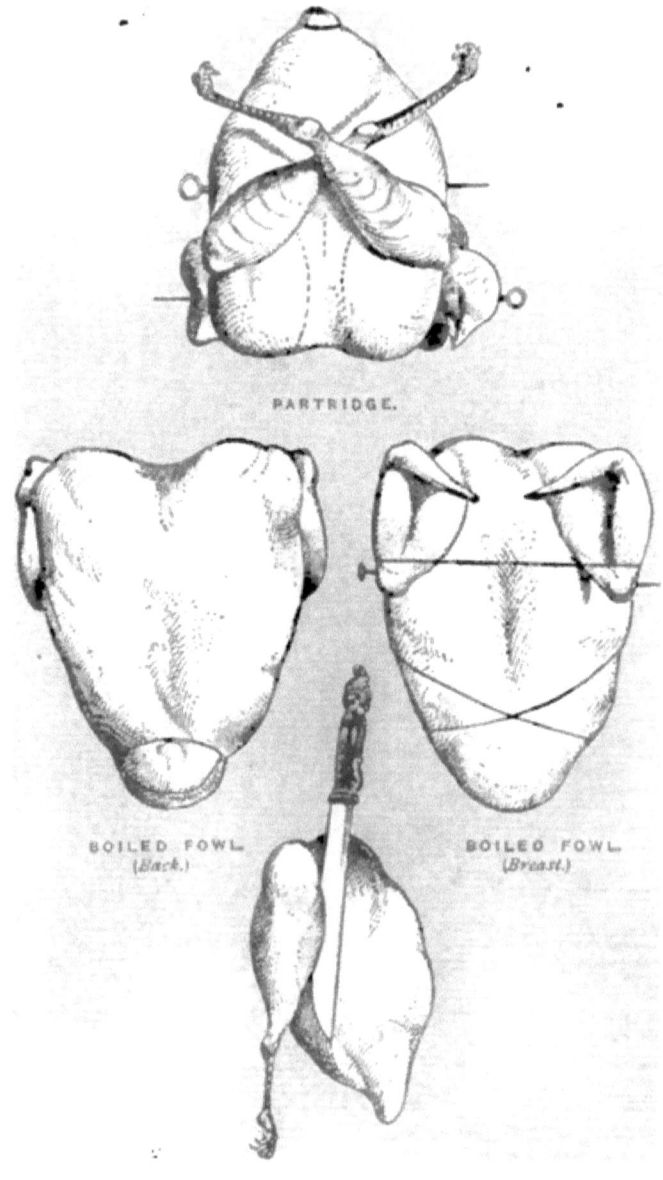

PARTRIDGE.

BOILED FOWL. (Back.) BOILED FOWL. (Breast.)

DIRECTIONS FOR CARVING.

SIRLOIN OF BEEF.

CARVE first in slices the under-cut as shown by lines in engraving. Carve upper part in slices from **A** to **B**, serving with each slice a little fat from **D**.

RIBS OF BEEF.

Carve from **A** to **B**. Serve with slices pieces of fat cut from **D**.

SHOULDER OF MUTTON.

Should be laid on dish skin side uppermost. The leaner parts ought to be cut straight to the bone from **1** to **2**. Delicate slices may be cut on each side of blade-bone from **3** to **4**. The "oyster cut"—the most tender—lies under the blade-bone. The fat ought to be cut in very thin slices. (See engraving, *Sheep*, 5.)

LEG OF MUTTON.

Under Part.

Place this joint with skin side next to the dish it is served on. Cut in slices fat and lean together.

Upper Part.

Place this joint on dish with skin side uppermost. Carve in straight lines from **A** to **B**.

FORE QUARTER OF LAMB.

Remove first the shoulder by placing the carving-knife at **1** and cutting round to **2** and **3**. Place the shoulder on one side, and cut in a straight line from **3** to **4**. Serve then ribs, or thin part of breast, according to choice.

ROAST TURKEY.

Cut long slices from both sides of the breast from **B** to **A**. The legs may then be removed and the thighs separated from the drumsticks. The wings ought then to be removed. The joint of the pinion will be found a little below **B**. Should the body be stuffed, an incision must be made at **C** to remove it.

BOILED TURKEY.

This differs from roast turkey only in the manner of trussing. (See directions for trussing boiled fowl.) For carving, follow directions given for roast turkey.

GOOSE OR DUCK.

Cut in slices from **A** to **B** on both sides of breast. To do this conveniently the neck end ought to be placed towards the carver. Should the legs be required, turn the fowl on its side, place the fork in the thin end of the leg at **C**, press the leg close to the body, insert the knife at **D**, turn back the leg, and the joint will then separate easily.

ROAST CHICKEN.

Place the fork firmly in the leg, insert the knife between the leg and body, and cut close to the bone. Turn then the leg back with the fork, and the joint will give way. Remove the wings in the direction from **A** to **B**, dividing the shoulder joint with the knife. Remove now the merry-thought by inserting the knife at **C** and following the bone with it. Divide now the breast from the carcass by cutting through the rib bones close to the breast.

BOILED CHICKEN.

Carved in the same manner as roast chicken. If either be large, the breast may be cut in slices, as directions for roast turkey are given.

ROAST PARTRIDGE.

Follow directions for carving chicken.

COD'S HEAD AND SHOULDERS.

Carve from **1** to **2**, taking the slices as low as **3**. Serve with each slice of the fish a piece of the sound which lines the back bone.

SALMON.

This and all short-grained fish ought to be cut lengthwise, and not across, portions of the thick and thin being served together.

HADDOCK.

This is served in same way as cod.

MACKEREL.

Mackerel are generally served in slices from head to tail, cutting close to bone.

PHILOSOPHY OF COOKERY.

MAN has been justly defined a cooking animal; and though his full definition is to be taken from something different and higher, yet assuredly he is the one only cooking animal in nature. He can in his lowest condition devour raw blubber, or maintain a stunted and pinched existence on the undressed fruits of the earth and on crawling insects, from which civilized man turns with abhorrence. And even the most pampered child of civilization and luxury, when pressed by the famine of shipwreck, or that which the desolation of war or pestilence occasions, can fall back upon the lowest capacities of his animal nature, and live for a season on such uncooked mockeries of food as shoe-leather and sawdust-bread, which the dainty Eskimo, fresh from his draught of whale-oil, and the Bushman, surfeited with locusts, would turn from with contempt.

But man is never, when he is free to choose, a willing eater of uncooked food. The more grateful fruits, indeed, which have been cultivated into richness by a process as elaborate and much more protracted than any which Cookery prescribes, are welcome to the most luxurious in their simplest condition; but they form a very small portion of the food by which the bulk, strength, and living energy of the frame are sustained. And even in those favoured regions of the globe where the cocoa-nut, the bread-fruit, and the banana grow together, and appear to exempt man from the necessity of doing more than plucking and eating, he is found roasting his bread-fruit, fermenting his cocoa-milk into spirit, and holding his fast-days and his feast-days as faithfully as if he had a lettered rubric to guide him. In truth, as the oldest of crafts was that of the gardener, or tiller of fields, so next to him come the women grinding at the mill, who figure in the most ancient historical records which sacred or profane literature has handed down to us; and as beyond the garden and tilled field the most famous of world-old workers was the hunter, so, awaiting his return from the chase, we find in constant alliance, all the earth over, the humble potter, whose broken cooking-vessels now encumber the sites of cities to which, four thousand or more years ago, forgotten Nimrods brought back the spoils of the spear and the bow.

The art of Cookery, as practised in modern times, is based, like all the other economical arts (though generally incognizant of the fact), on certain great laws of science, of which parts have been unsystematically and empirically applied to the arts in question. The profession of cook is one which, unreasonably enough, we are ready to profit by, but not disposed to honour greatly. Yet the most learned physicians and the most skilled chemists are ready to tell us that the ministers of the kitchen display (often no doubt unconsciously), in their processes and the results of these, a knowledge of the necessities and functions of the living body, and a command over the resources of practical chemistry, such as excite their interest and admiration.

An art, indeed, so ancient as that of Cookery could not fail to gather to itself much of the practical wisdom of the ages during which it has been followed; and this at least is certain, that we should not be alive to-day to read and write books about it had not our ancestors known pretty well how to cook food for themselves and their children. We must be content, in these days, to detect, if we can, the principles which lie at the bottom of the ancient empirical art, and, by announcing these, to make Cookery a science, the laws of which (comparatively few) may be taught easily to all, whilst experience is left to teach how best to apply them in practice. A perfect science of Cookery we shall not soon see, but one sufficiently extended to be of the highest value is already in our hands. We proceed to explain the laws which it acknowledges.

Three great ends are served by the food which we eat—namely, first, the growth of the body during early life; secondly, the supply of the waste of the body at all periods of life; and thirdly, the maintenance of the warmth of the body throughout our entire existence. We do not take food because we are conscious that it will serve those ends, but simply to allay the cravings of hunger and thirst, and to gratify the senses of taste and smell. But our natural appetites, if not perverted or over-indulged, are most certainly satisfied by those articles of food and drink which best serve the ends referred to. Hence the art of Cookery is not reprehensible for addressing itself mainly to the palate, however blamable may have been its efforts to tempt to over-indulgence, and its success in destroying the relish for simple fare. The epicure's motto, "We live to eat," is one which science as much as morality disowns. The cook's true motto is, "We eat to live;" and the fulfilment of it lies in supplying the kind and amount of food which shall best enable the eater to live an active, energetic manly or womanly life.

In seeking to obey this precept, the question which first comes before us is, "On what substances shall the cook exercise his or her art?" We are in the habit, in ordinary language, of referring to certain bodies, such as sugar, butter, arrow-root, calf's-foot jelly, as each of itself highly nutritious. But life could not be sustained on any one of these, unless for a short time, and deliberate trials in the case of the lower animals, as well as the undesired experiences of the famine-stricken, have fully proved that disease and death speedily follow restriction to a single edible substance, whatever it be.

And in entire conformity with this, we find that the simplest fare, sufficient if taken *alone* to support life, which nature has furnished to our hands, is after all very complex. A glance at those simplest pattern-diets which nature supplies and sanctions, and universal experience approves, will form the surest basis for a rational Cookery.

Of the pattern-diets referred to, there are four specially deserving notice—namely, milk, flesh, eggs, and bread.

Milk is at once the food and drink of the suckling, which, though unsupplied with any other nourishment whatever, grows in every part of its body. In milk, therefore, there must be everything which is needed to build up and repair the waste of bone, muscle, nerve, and all the other tissues of the wonderfully constructed human body. We may safely, therefore, affirm that an artificial diet containing all the substances present in milk will fully nourish the frame, and that, conversely, if any of them are absent, the nutritiousness of such diet will to that extent be diminished.

Flesh, including under that term the fat and lean, and all the juices of meat, is not largely employed as the sole article of food by any race of men. But that it can alone, or at least accompanied only by water, sustain animal life to the fullest, we see in the case of carnivorous creatures, such as the lion, which eat nothing else; and the Eskimos of the Arctic Regions, the Red Indians of the North American Prairies, and the Spaniards of the South American Pampas, sustain life for months together on flesh alone. Flesh thus, like milk, can supply the living body with all it requires for the sustenance and repair of every part.

Of eggs, the same may be said. For to hatch the egg of any bird, such as a hen, it is only necessary to keep it for a certain number of days at a particular temperature, and so placed that air shall not be prevented from entering through the pores of the shell. In due season the white and yolk of the egg (including a portion of the shell) are formed into a perfect little bird, which has been fully developed from the contents of the egg, or at least only with the addition of air and some earthy matter derived from the shell. An egg thus contains all that is requisite to form a perfect animal.

Lastly, bread (especially if made from the entire grain) can support for an indefinite period the life of man, though taken alone, or at least accompanied only with water.

It will surprise no one that the flesh of an ox, a sheep, a calf, or a pigeon, should admit of ready conversion into the flesh of man, and that it should serve alone for his full nourishment. But it does not so certainly appear that milk, or eggs, or bread should be equally serviceable as food. They certainly, however, are, though not in equal degree; and a determination of the substances which by their presence in them give them this feeding, life-sustaining power, will teach us what things must be present in all food. First, then, of milk. Besides water, it contains four things—namely, curd, butter, sugar, and mineral matters or salts. The curd, when dried, forms what is more familiar to us under the name of cheese. Butter does not essentially differ in character from fat or oil. The sugar of milk, though not identical with cane-sugar, much resembles it; and the mineral matters or salts are partly identical with those found dissolved in natural waters, partly with those which form the hard and solid part of the bones of animals.

Flesh, though it is so unlike milk in appearance, closely corresponds to it in composition. The lean portion of it, especially as seen in fowls or veal, but best of all in fishes, is a white, soft mass so like curd that in the case of the salmon it goes by that name, and it still more resembles it in chemical composition than it does in colour and consistence. There is no sugar in flesh, but there is fat, corresponding to the butter in milk, and there are the same mineral matters as occur in milk and bones.

Eggs still more resemble milk than flesh does. The white of a hard-boiled egg does not more recall to the eye the curd of milk than it corresponds to it in qualities and chemical constituents. The yolk of the egg is rich in fat or oil. A portion of the same kind of sugar as occurs in milk is found in it; and in white and yolk together occur the mineral matters present in milk, as well as in bones, blood, and flesh.

Finally, if we take the wheat-flour from which bread is baked, knead it into dough, and wash it in a stream of water as long as it comes off milky, we find that there is left a soft, sticky, tenacious body, which when dried resembles cheese, and, still more, the fibre of lean meat, or the flesh of white-fish thoroughly washed and dried. This may be properly enough called the *curd* of flour. Besides this, there are present in the flour a large amount of starch, a very small amount of fat, and the same mineral matters which have already been referred to as present in the other pattern-diets and in the bodies of animals. Flour or bread thus corresponds to skim-milk, for it has very little fat in it; and mankind accordingly have long ago come to the wise conclusion that "bread *and* butter" is much better than dry bread. It is devoid also of sugar; but then it abounds in starch, which has exactly the same composition as sugar, and, moreover, changes into it when taken as food into the stomach of a living animal, so that as an article of diet starch counts as sugar, though not possessed of a sweet taste.

It thus appears that in the simplest bill of fare which nature offers there is one standing ingredient familiar to all, as it occurs in curd of milk or white of egg; and the use of this never-absent constituent of food curious physicians have amply proved to be to form the important constituents of that river of life, the blood, and to build up through its instrumentality all the organs of the body. A second unfailing ingredient is a mixture of certain mineral matters or salts, of which we generally take little heed, unmindful of the fact that without them blood could not be formed, and that our limbs would be boneless, pulpy masses, like the bodies of jelly-fishes.

Those indispensable articles of diet rigidly provided, the other components of our food are dispensed with greater latitude. Sugar may be omitted, if starch is supplied, and the place of either may be taken by gum or succulent vegetable fibre. These four bodies, indeed, (namely, starch, sugar, gum, and fibre,) are so similar in composition, and are so easily changed into each other, that they may be regarded as forms of one substance, equally nutritious, though not equally acceptable to the palate.

Further, it appears that whilst milk has butter as well as sugar in it, eggs and flesh have little or no sugar, but abound in fat or oil, which is equivalent to butter; whilst, on the other hand, flour, which has very little fat or oil, is richer than any of the other kinds of food in starch, which is equivalent to sugar. It is manifest from this that butter may be omitted, if sugar is supplied in its place; only it is to be noticed that it requires about two and a half times as much sugar (or starch) to afford the same nutriment as one part of fat or butter would. Milk, the most perfect of pattern-diets, contains nearly equal weights of butter and sugar.

It may be noticed in addition, that when an animal, such as an ox, is supplied with a large amount of vegetable food, and is not required to take active exercise, it becomes very fat, even though there be little or no fat in its food, and the greater the amount of starch or sugar in its food, the fatter it becomes. The bee also produces all the wax (which is a kind of fat) for its honeycomb solely from sugar. We thus learn both that sugar (including starch, gum, and soft vegetable fibre) can replace fat in food, and also that sugar when eaten is changed into fat, and as such is deposited in the body of the animal eating it.

If, however, the same ox, which when stall-fed, and allowed little or no exercise, becomes loaded with fat, be taken from its stall, harnessed to the plough or the waggon, and kept at hard work, it rapidly grows lean, and, though fed as well as before, ceases to lay on fat. None of the swift-footed wild animals which are grass-eaters—such as the various tribes of deer, the quagga, the zebra, the goat, or the hare—exhibit much fat in their bodies; and all the active savage races of mankind, such as the Red Indians, are equally lean. The bee, when forming its wax, remains at rest in the hive; and the pig, which is to be made a prize-monster of fatness, must be penned in his stye.

It thus appears that the same starch or sugar which, when an animal is debarred from exercise, becomes converted into fat, does not, if it be allowed exercise, appear either as fat or as any other solid in its body; and further, that if it has been fattened, active motion rapidly causes the fat to disappear. Now, as active motion during a large part of each day is a condition of health in man, whilst a scanty endowment of fat is a mark of this health, it comes to be an important question, What service is rendered to him by the fat or sugar of his food, seeing that neither of them adds to his bulk or weight, unless in a trifling degree?

It is now universally acknowledged by chemists and physiologists that fat and sugar are the fuel of the living body, and, by being burned within it, maintain its warmth, as the coals burned in a furnace heat the walls of the furnace. That our bodies are warmer than the ordinary objects in their neighbourhood, every one is aware. Cloaks, blankets, flannels, and other articles of dress, have in themselves no power of communicating warmth to us; they simply prevent the chill and mobile air from robbing us of heat, which in some way is constantly developed within our bodies. The mode of its development appears now fully understood. It results from a true combustion occurring at every moment in every portion, however small, of our bodies. We are at first a little startled and, it may be, alarmed at being told that our bodies are continually undergoing *combustion*, with which word we connect the notion of flame and burning, the tortures of exposure to a red or white heat, and the destruction of living tissues which follows their exposure to such temperatures.

But the most inflammable bodies, such as charcoal, or sulphur, or phosphorus, admit of being burned in a chemist's vessels, so as to evolve, moment by moment, either a very large or a very small amount of heat, as may be desired; and the difference in the intensity of the heat thus generated is mainly determined by the quantity of air furnished in a given time to the burning combustible. It is of a very slow combustion, such as, if it occurred out of the body, would not occasion the evolution of light at all, that we are to think as occurring in our bodies. The fuel for this combustion is charcoal and hydrogen, the inflammable constituents of wood and coal and candles. Fat consists almost entirely of these inflammables; sugar and starch are less rich in them. To burn those bodies air is requisite, and when it burns them, it changes the charcoal into carbonic acid and the hydrogen into water; and this is one great, perhaps the chief reason, why we are constantly inhaling air by those important living bellows, the lungs. The air thus inspired dissolves in the blood, and is carried by the arteries which convey that blood to every part of the living frame. There is no point at which, if pricked, it will not bleed red blood; and wherever red blood is there is air, and wherever air is there is combustion. We are thus to conceive of our bodies as owing their heat, not to one single furnace blazing at the heart or the lungs, but, as it were, to an infinite number of tiny lamps, each giving out a very small quantity of heat, yet enough to keep warm its immediate neighbourhood. Now those lamps, though they burn very low in some diseases, are never extinguished as long as life lasts; and the chief reason of their continual burning is the unceasing supply of air which fans their flame. It is sufficient for the support of life that we take food at certain intervals, and we can occasionally fast for long periods without material inconvenience; but we cannot stop breathing, except for a very few minutes, without inducing a fatal result. Our living bodies are thus like furnaces *without dampers*, in which there is no provision for diminishing the draught of air, so as to economize the fuel when it is scarce. The mouth and nostrils are an ever-open furnace-door, by which air is continually entering the body; and it never leaves the body till it has taken from it so much of its charcoal and changed that into carbonic acid, and so much of its hydrogen and changed that into water. These pass away chiefly in the air we expire; for our throats serve the curious double purpose of acting as bellows-tubes to carry air to the lamps burning within us, and as chimneys to carry their invisible smoke away.

When a man accordingly is doomed, by shipwreck or siege, to perish by famine, he rapidly becomes emaciated, for the air which he cannot help breathing literally burns up his body, and changes it into invisible gases. To supply fuel for this inevitable and never-ceasing combustion is one of the two great objects for which food is taken. The body would perish of cold if the combustion were stopped; and hence it is maintained at all costs, so that if no food (that is, fuel) be supplied, one part of the body itself is burned to maintain the heat of the rest, and life is thus prolonged to the last.

It thus appears that in addition to that obvious reason for taking food—namely, the supply of materials out of which the bodies of the young may obtain the means of adding to their bulk and weight, and the bodies of the full-grown may be furnished with the means of maintaining their dimensions unchanged—there is the equally important though less obvious reason for taking it, that we must provide the body with the fuel necessary to maintain that warmth which is essential to vital action.

The two great ends of eating are thus, on the one hand, to strengthen our thews and sinews, to give solidity to our bones, and maintain the integrity of every organ; and, on the other, to secure at every moment, and at every point of the body, that genial glow of heat without which every sense would be sealed and every function paralyzed. All food serves to some extent both ends; but such substances as white of egg, curd of milk, lean flesh, and flour deprived of its starch, are mainly serviceable for the first of the ends referred to above—that is, the actual building up or maintaining in their integrity of the solids of the body, and are conveniently named the *flesh-producing* constituents of food, the word flesh being used in its widest sense. Fat, on the other hand, including butter and oil, and sugar, including starch, gum, and soft vegetable fibre, are of little service in adding to the mass of the body, but act as fuel for it, and are conveniently named the *heat-producing* constituents of food.

All the pattern-diets referred to contain both classes of constituents, though not in the same relative proportions; and those artificial mixtures on which the skill of the cook is exercised should contain both, unless separate dishes are provided containing the opposite kinds of food, as veal (which is almost entirely flesh-producing) in one, and rice (which is in greater part heat-producing) in another. Or, what comes to the same thing, in the course of every twenty-four hours each individual must take a certain amount of each kind of food, if health is to be preserved; and from the example which nature has set us, there can be no question that, as a general rule, it is better to take a mixture of both kinds of food, at least at the more substantial meals, such as breakfast and dinner, than to make one meal chiefly of the one kind, and another of the other. The proportions which should be maintained between the flesh-producing and the heat-producing constituents of food will vary with the age, sex, health, race, occupation, season of the year, and other conditions affecting the individual eater, so that no rule of universal application can be laid down. But the following table from Baron Liebig, with the commentary which follows it from Professor Gregory of Edinburgh, will show the principles which should guide us in arranging our meals:—

TABLE OF THE RELATIVE PROPORTIONS OF THE FLESH-PRODUCING TO THE HEAT-PRODUCING CONSTITUENTS IN DIFFERENT KINDS OF FOOD.

	Flesh-Producing.	Heat-Producing. Calculated as Starch.
Cow's milk contains for	10	30 = { 8.8 butter. 10.4 sugar
Pease	10	23
Fat mutton	10	27 = 11.25 fat.
Fat pork	10	30 = 12.5 "
Beef	10	17 = 7.08 "
Hare	10	2 = 0.03 "
Veal	10	1
Wheat-flour	10	46
Oatmeal	10	50
Rye-flour	10	57
Barley	10	57
Potatoes (white)	10	86
Potatoes (blue)	10	115
Rice	10	123
Buck-wheat	10	130

Here we see that milk and grain, the two best forms of natural food, contain, for 1 of flesh-producing, 3 to 5.7 of heat-producing matter. Fat meat has also 1 to 3 or 1 to 2.7, and agrees with pease and beans very nearly. Lean beef, hare, and veal have far too little heat-producing matter—only 1.7, 0.2, and 0.1 to 1 of flesh-producing matter. For this reason heat-producing matter should be added to lean meat, and also to pease and beans; but flesh-producing matter should be added to potatoes and rice.

"This explains the instinctive and universal use of beans and fat bacon, pork and pease-pudding (bacon containing very little flesh-producing matter), veal and ham, potatoes and rice with lean meat, and flour and butter with eggs. The best proportion for a working-man is about 5 of heat-producing to 1 of flesh-producing food; and for a child, 3 or 4 of the former to 1 of the latter. These proportions, which are those of grain and milk, are easily obtained in the mixtures above named.

"When the proportion of heat-producing matter is too small, then a large amount of flesh-producing matter must be used to supply heat, which is a great waste, since such matter is the worst source of heat. Thus, to obtain the same amount of heat we must use:—

Fat..	100 parts.
Starch...	240 "
Cane-sugar...	249 "
Honey...	263 "
Spirits at 50 per cent. of alcohol.....................	266 "
Fresh lean meat......................................	770 "

"Alcohol belongs to the heat-producing class; and, therefore, if properly diluted, and used as an addition to flesh-producing food, such as lean meat, cheese, eggs, or pease and beans, it is useful rather than hurtful. But if added to food already containing 5, 6, 10, or 15 parts of heat-producing for 1 of flesh-producing matter, it is hurtful, as reducing the proportions of the latter still further. Now, when the food contains too little flesh-producing matter, enormous quantities of it are required to supply the waste of the body. Thus, it will take 123 parts of rice to supply as much flesh as 33 parts of fat pork, or 125 of blue potatoes to yield as much flesh as 27 of lean beef."

The enormous quantities of rice which certain of the Hindu tribes devour startle those who for the first time see them at their meals; and withal they are so much less robust than the flesh-eating races that no rice-eater was enlisted by the East India Company as a soldier. The practice prevalent among the Irish peasantry before the great famine of living chiefly upon potatoes, which contain a very small proportion of flesh-producing matter, was equally wasteful, and opposed to the development of the full strength of the body. The practice also of giving young children large quantities of arrow-root (a variety of starch), especially when that is made into a jelly with water only, is equally injudicious; for a child, especially after being weaned, when it is growing every day more active, requires an increasing amount of the materials which strengthen the muscles and give solidity to the bones. But it is impossible that its limbs can acquire additional firmness and vigour from arrow-root, which consists of nothing but charcoal and water. Bread and milk, or any entire grain, such as oats, barley, or millet, boiled with milk, are the proper food for young children, till they are old enough to take animal food, which, however, may be safely and usefully given them as soon as they are able to run about.

The modes in which food is dressed by the cook appear at first sight endless, but after all may be reduced, in the case alike of animal and vegetable food, to two—namely, *roasting* and *boiling*.

Roasting may properly be held to include broiling, grilling, stewing, baking, and all other processes, however named, which consist essentially in exposing food to the action of heat, without the presence of any liquid but the juices which it naturally contains. The broiling of a steak is perhaps the simplest, as it is one of the oldest, most universal, most rational, and most wholesome modes of cookery. When successfully managed, it secures the two great ends of rendering meat more palatable and more digestible, at a trifling sacrifice of its nutritious juices. The first application of heat in roasting and broiling animal food should be considerable and rapid, so as to form an external wall or crust by hardening the skin and coagulating the substance identical with white of egg which is present in the flesh of all animals. In this way the juices are to a great extent retained within the meat, and increase its flavour, digestibility, and nutritiousness. When meat is stewed or baked in pans, a considerable heat cannot be rapidly communicated to it. The juices accordingly flow out, and the meat is left comparatively dry in the centre. As the juices, however, are retained in the pan, no nutritious matter is lost; but unless the meat is cut small, it is less digestible than when roasted.

When meat is boiled, with a view solely to cook it, the water should be heated nearly to boiling before it is put in, so that the crust may be hardened, and the white-of-egg-like substance coagulated quickly, otherwise the juices of the meat will to a great extent escape into the water, and the meat will be stringy and tasteless. When meat is boiled in soup, and both are to be used as food, the water should be used much colder, but not quite cold, if the meat is intended to retain some flavour. On the other hand, when the object is to make soup of the best quality, the meat should be chopped small, put on with the coldest water, and kept long simmering at a gentle heat before the water is made to boil. In this way the greatest amount of soluble nutritious matter will be transferred from the meat to the soup. Similar remarks apply to the cooking of fish and vegetables. The water should be used warm if the solids alone are to be used as food, but cold if the liquid is to be used as soup, and lukewarm if it is to be used as a sauce with, for example, fish.

Chemistry does not indicate any special additional directions as called for in the case of puddings and pastry; but it seems well to warn the reader that pastry, plum-pudding, suet-pudding, and calf's-foot jelly, though most proper supplements to a meal where very little animal food has been taken, should be partaken of very sparingly by those who have already feasted freely on soup, fish, and animal food. Pastry and flour-puddings are as nutritious as animal food, whilst they are much less digestible. A custard, a spoonful of rice-pudding, or a little fruit is the only thing which one who has satisfied his appetite with animal food should allow himself by way of dessert.

One mode of preparing food remains to be noticed—namely, salting it. Salt meat is the only meat that can in many places be procured, and it is relished by many who are not under the necessity of eating it. It is naturally regarded as differing from fresh meat only by being salt, and the sole inconvenience apprehended from its use is that of thirst. But salt meat differs greatly from fresh meat in quality, and, as the experience of all modern navies has too fatally shown, soon occasions disease in those who are restricted to its use. When meat is pickled by soaking it in brine, the juices of the flesh are washed out, and the meat is left very much in the condition in which it remains after it has been boiled in water to make beef-tea, only with the addition of a great deal of salt to it. Salt meat is thus very much less nutritious than fresh meat, and those who have the choice should never make it the principal article of their food; or if they do, they should consume along with it the soup of fresh meat, or eat largely of vegetables.

It has been unjustly said that "God gave us food, and the devil cooks;" but it is not with the cooks that the fault mainly lies of inducing disease by fostering *gourmanderie* and gluttony. The cook is only fulfilling his vocation when he makes every article of food grateful to the palate and more digestible. And the custom among the more wealthy ranks of assembling the guests around a dinner-table, at which the host and hostess sit as if they too were guests, whilst silent servants simply offer to all every dish in turn, throws upon each individual the responsibility of eating wisely or unwisely exactly as he pleases. That plentiful dyspepsias are the fruits of such feasts is certain; but it is hard to blame the cook, whose dishes were wholesome, and so mingled that a Liebig would have given them his chemical imprimatur. The fault has lain with the dyspeptic himself, and has chiefly consisted, not in his innocently eating a temperate meal of wrong things, treacherously disguised as dainties by the perverse ingenuity of the genius of the kitchen, but in his deliberately tasting too many wholesome dishes, and too much of each, forgetting that the cook makes every dish palatable, that each of the guests may find something suitable to his taste, not that each may eat of all.

On the other hand, when we consider how unwisely a large portion of the wages of the working-classes, and also of classes higher in social rank, is spent in the purchase of food, from ignorance of what is best to be purchased, and how much of this ill-chosen food is wasted or rendered ungrateful and unpalatable through defective skill in cookery, and how often the tavern is fled to as a welcome refuge from a comfortless home, and whole families go headlong to destruction, we cannot but wish that the fundamental principles of Cookery, which are few and simple, instead of being held things for the wealthy and the luxurious alone to consider, were regarded as things as essential to be taught, by precept and example, to every girl as how to handle a needle or a pair of scissors. The work to which this is an introduction aims at contributing to produce this laudable result.

A HANDBOOK OF COOKERY.

SOUPS—FIRST DIVISION.

Brown Stock.—For this stock there will be required material in the following quantities:—

Four pounds of the shin of beef, four young carrots, four Bermuda onions, one small turnip, one half-head of celery, one half table-spoonful of salt, one half tea-spoonful of white pepper-corns, one half tea-spoonful of black pepper-corns.

First, cutting all of the meat from the bone, remove the marrow, and break up the bone with a hammer.

Put the meat and bone together in a large sauce-pan, and pour over these five pints of cold water, placing the sauce-pan over the fire.

Bring the water now quickly to the boiling-point and skim off, when boiling, all of the scum that rises to the surface. Throw into the sauce-pan then the salt, which will bring any remaining albumen or scum to the top; when, skimming once more, add to the contents of the pan the carrot, turnip, and celery, all cut into very small pieces. Before adding the onion blanch it with boiling water, to draw from it the greenness which produces indigestion; having done which, put it together with the pepper-corns into the sauce-pan and allow all again to boil.

When this is done, draw the sauce-pan to the side of the

fire, cover it closely, and allow its contents to simmer slowly for five hours; at the end of which time the stock should be strained through a clean towel to remove the meat and vegetables, the juices and flavour of which have been extracted, and put away to cool for future use.

NOTE.—Water boils at a temperature of 212 degrees, and to boil meat in it for eating, or to prepare stock, the water having been first brought to the boiling-point, should be permitted to fall to a temperature of 160 degrees, to prevent the meat hardening.

A second stock can be made from the meat and bones used for the first, by covering them again with cold water, adding some fresh vegetables, and bringing all to the boiling-point; allowing the preparation to simmer slowly thereafter for four hours.

Clear Soup.—Material and quantities required :—

One quart of brown stock, the whites and shells of two eggs, and as much salt and pepper as can be held between the thumb and finger.

The stock must have been allowed to become quite cold, when it will have thickened and set. Then, dipping the corner of a towel in boiling water, wash the grease from the top.

Now put the stock into a sauce-pan and allow it to melt— a copper sauce-pan is preferable. Put the whites and shells of the two eggs into a small bowl, add to them half a gill of cold water and the salt and pepper.

When the stock has melted add the eggs so prepared, and with two forks whisk the whole briskly until it boils.

The instant the soup boils cover the sauce-pan closely and draw it aside from the fire, and allow it to simmer for ten minutes.

Then strain through a clean towel, taking care not to break the crust which the eggs have formed at the top in process of clearing, and it is ready to serve.

NOTE.—Macaroni and vermicelli soup are made from this clear soup by simply boiling the macaroni and vermicelli in water, put on cold, then putting them into the tureen and pouring the hot stock over.

Kidney Soup.—Quantities and materials are to be used as follows:—

Two ox kidneys, two quarts of second stock, two table-spoonfuls of Harvey's sauce, two table-spoonfuls mushroom catchup, one ounce of flour of rice, two ounces of butter, one grain of cayenne pepper and a little of black pepper and table-salt.

In preparing this soup, the kidneys have first to be well washed in cold water, then after being thoroughly dried in a towel, they must be cut into thin slices. The butter is next to be put into a dry sauce-pan and heated until smoke begins to arise therefrom, the pieces of kidney added and browned therein; the flour of rice must then be put into a basin and be made smooth with a little of the stock, when the Harvey sauce is to be added, also the pepper, salt, cayenne, and catchup; after which the rest of the stock is thrown into the basin, stirred until well mixed, and then the whole mixture poured over the kidney as prepared and placed in the sauce-pan.

Now, putting the sauce-pan over the fire, stir the contents until boiling to prevent the flour lumping, and skim carefully meantime. After this boiling-point is reached the sauce-pan must be drawn aside from the fire, tightly covered and allowed to simmer for two hours, when it is done.

NOTE.—In browning meats of any kind the stock should be poured over them cold, that the brown which has been obtained may not be washed away in the process.

Kidneys especially should be cooked over a slow fire to prevent them hardening.

Mock Turtle Soup.—The ingredients for this soup must be provided in the following quantities:—

One calf's head, five ounces of flour, five ounces of butter, one ounce of mixed spice, two Bermuda onions, two wine-glassfuls of sherry, five quarts of cold water, one lemon, one table-spoonful of mushroom catchup, one half table-spoonful of salt, and one tea-spoonful of pepper.

The method of preparation is: first soak the calf's head in

cold water for an hour, for the purpose of cleansing it of blood or such other remaining impurities as there may be; then after drying the same in a clean towel, put it into a large sauce-pan and pour thereon the five quarts of cold water. The sauce-pan is then placed over a quick fire, and being carefully cleared of scum as it boils, which it should do speedily, the onions, mixed spices, pepper, and salt must be thrown in at once. Having reached the boiling-point and the flavouring materials having been added, the whole should now be permitted to boil slowly until the meat will readily separate from the bones—a period of from two to five hours, to be determined by the age of the calf—when the tongue is to be removed and skinned, also the meat taken from the cheeks, and both cut into small pieces to be presently used.

The bones and head remaining in the sauce-pan must now be permitted to boil four hours, at the end of which the liquor should be drawn off and strained, and the small pieces of meat remaining in the sauce-pan must be collected, cut finely, seasoned with pepper and salt, to which add a little flour, and then combined with the two fresh eggs to give consistency to the mixture, rolled into small balls, and placed in the oven for five minutes in order that they may keep shape by being hardened.

Now taking a clean sauce-pan, let the butter be melted and the remainder of the flour stirred into it, when the liquor should be added and the whole stirred until it boils.

The pieces of meat from the cheek and tongue previously prepared must now be thrown in, and all allowed to boil for ten minutes. The lemon, thinly sliced, is to be placed in the tureen, together with the sherry and the balls and the catchup, over which the soup is to be poured, when it is ready for serving.

NOTE.—If the soup is not sufficiently dark in colour, a little caramel may be added, the instructions for the preparation of which are given on page 247.

Brown Soup.—Materials and quantities:—
Three pounds of shin of beef, two and one half quarts of

cold water, one ounce of butter, one ounce of flour of rice, one dessert-spoonful of mushroom catchup, one dessert-spoonful of Harvey's sauce, one tea-spoonful of whole black pepper, one tea-spoonful of whole white pepper, one dozen cloves, one half table-spoonful of salt, six drops of caramel, one carrot, one turnip, one half head of celery, and one onion.

In preparing this soup, the first thing to be done is the cutting of the meat from the bone, and the removing of the marrow. Then the marrow and the butter must be heated together in a large sauce-pan, and when the smoke arises from them, the meat and bone must be put into the same and browned, and the vegetables cut into very small pieces and browned also. To this add the water in its given quantity, and allow the whole to come quickly to the boiling-point, skimming carefully meantime. The salt, pepper, and cloves should now be thrown in, and the whole allowed to boil slowly for four hours, when the liquor should be strained and returned to the sauce-pan.

The flour of rice should now be put into a bowl and made smooth with the Harvey sauce and catchup, then added to the strained liquor in the sauce-pan, and boiled together with it for ten minutes to prevent the flour of rice tasting raw. Just before serving add the caramel, which does not require to be cooked, but is used for the purpose of giving the soup the proper colour.

Giblet Soup.—The quantities and ingredients required are:—

Two sets of giblets, three quarts of stock, two ounces of butter, one gill of sherry, two ounces of flour, one table-spoonful of lemon juice, one sprig of parsley, two bay leaves, one sprig of thyme, one grain of cayenne pepper, one half a salt-spoonful of salt, and an equal quantity of pepper.

The manner of making the soup is as follows:—

The giblets must be scalded and picked entirely clean of skin, and then cut into small pieces equal in size. When this is done, next melt the butter and brown the giblets to a pale brown in it. Then add to them the sherry and one gill of the stock, after which let it cook slowly until the liquor is reduced to one-half the quantity, when the remainder of the stock must be added, also the parsley, thyme, and bay leaves, and let all cook slowly together until the giblets are tender, the time of which depends upon whether the giblets are of chicken or fowl.

When the giblets are tender they should be removed and the liquor strained, which is to be thickened with a little flour, the flour first being made smooth with a little cold water, and then the whole is to be boiled one hour; after which the giblets must be returned to the liquor, the lemon juice, cayenne pepper, and salt also added, and all permitted to boil for five minutes. When it is done it should be dished very hot.

Hotch-potch.—The necessaries and measures for this soup are:—

A neck of mutton, six lamb chops, two quarts of cold water, six young carrots, four young turnips, one head of lettuce, one table-spoonful of parsley, one pint of green pease, one young cauliflower, one half table-spoonful of salt, one small tea-spoonful of pepper.

The neck of mutton must first be washed thoroughly in cold water. It then should be put into the sauce-pan and covered with two quarts of cold water, and placed over the fire: when the water boils, skim it, and add the salt, allowing it to boil for two hours thereafter. At the end of this time it must be strained, the lamb chops first cut in two and then added, the turnips quartered and added, and five of the carrots cut into thin slices and also added, and all allowed to boil together for three-quarters of an hour. After this put in the lettuce and the parsley, which have been chopped fine meantime; the pease and the cauliflower, the flower of which only is used; the pepper and the remaining carrot, which must be grated; and let all boil slowly for twenty minutes.

NOTE.—The heart of a young cabbage may be added to this soup by persons relishing the flavour of this vegetable.

Hare Soup.—One hare, two pounds shin of beef, four quarts cold water, one onion, one head of celery, one tea-spoonful whole white pepper, one tea-spoonful whole black pepper, one table-spoonful salt, two ounces flour of rice, one table-spoonful mushroom catchup, one table-spoonful Worcester sauce.

When the hare has been skinned, take the greatest care, in removing the entrails, to lose none of the blood.

Pour the blood into a large soup-pan, and add to it the water; also the beef (cut in small pieces), and bone, from which the marrow has been removed.

Wipe the hare well with a damp towel, to remove from it the hairs which may adhere to it.

Cut the hare into convenient pieces; put the pieces in the pan, and stir all over a slow fire till boiling.

When this liquor boils, add the onion, celery, salt, and pepper-corns; cover the pan closely, and allow all to simmer very slowly for two hours.

Remove then the back parts and legs of the hare, and continue to boil slowly the remainder for an hour and a half longer.

Cut all the meat from the back and legs into small square pieces, and put them on one side.

When the soup has boiled for three hours and a half, pour it through a hair sieve into a large bowl; rinse the pan with cold water, and return to it the strained liquor.

Mix now very smoothly in a bowl the rice-flour with the catchup and Worcester sauce. When well blended, add all to the soup, also the pieces of meat which were removed from the back and legs of the hare.

Return the pan to the fire, and stir all till boiling. Simmer ten minutes, and the soup is ready for serving.

NOTE.—A potato and carrot may be added with the celery, if desired. If the liquor is not constantly stirred when first put on the fire, the blood is sure to curdle, and the soup is never so nice.

SOUPS.—SECOND DIVISION.

White Stock.—For this stock there will be required :—One fowl, two pounds of veal, four quarts of cold water, one Bermuda onion, two leeks, one head of celery, two cloves, one half table-spoonful of salt, one tea-spoonful of whole white pepper.

To prepare this stock, the veal and the fowl must first be put into a large sauce-pan and covered with the water, when it should be brought quickly to the boiling point, that the scum may arise at once and be removed. When this is done, the salt must be thrown in, after which it must be skimmed again, and the vegetables thrown in, the cloves and pepper also, and then the whole left to simmer slowly three hours. At the end of this time it should be strained through a clean towel and allowed to cool.

NOTE.—The directions for clearing this stock are to be found under the heading "Clear Soup," on page 10, beginning "Put the whites and shells of two eggs," etc.

Tapioca Cream Soup.—For this soup provide :—One quart of white stock, two ounces of crushed tapioca, the yolks of four eggs, four table-spoonfuls of sweet cream, one half a salt-spoonful of salt, and an equal quantity of pepper.

The stock must first be brought to the boiling-point, and as it boils, the tapioca should be sprinkled in carefully to prevent its lumping, and when this is done, both allowed to simmer for twenty minutes. While the stock and tapioca are boiling, the egg-yolks, the cream, pepper, and salt should be put into a bowl and smoothly beaten together. Then let the boiling liquid cool a little,—two minutes will be sufficient,—after which put two table-spoonfuls of it to the mixture in the bowl, stir it together and pour the whole into the sauce-pan; put all over the fire for two minutes, stirring meantime to prevent boiling, when the eggs will have cooked without curdling, and it is ready for serving, which should be done very hot.

Turkish Soup.—Furnish for this:—

One quart of white stock, one half tea-cupful of whole rice, the yolks of two eggs, one table-spoonful of cream, one half salt-spoonful of salt, and an equal amount of pepper.

In preparing this soup, boil first the rice in the stock for twenty minutes. At the end of this time pass the whole through a wire sieve, rubbing such of the rice as may stick through with a wooden spoon; then stir it thoroughly to beat out such lumps as the rice may have formed, and return all to the sauce-pan. The yolks of eggs, cream, pepper, and salt must now be well beaten together and added to the stock and rice, and the whole stirred over the fire for two minutes, care being taken to prevent boiling after the eggs are put in, for reasons already given.

This soup should also be served very hot.

Soup à-la-Reine.—For this there will be required:—

One young fowl, one Bermuda onion, one and one-half quarts of cold water, one sprig of parsley, one bay leaf, one sprig of thyme, three gills of cream, one half a dessert-spoonful of salt, and one half tea-spoonful of white pepper, one half-dozen celery tops.

Begin the preparation of this soup by putting the fowl into a large sauce-pan and covering it with the given quantity of water. When this boils and has been skimmed, add the vegetables and the herbs, also the pepper and salt, and allow the whole to boil slowly for one hour. After boiling this length of time, the fowl must be taken out, the white meat cut from the breast, and put aside to be used later. This being done, return the fowl to the sauce-pan, and let it boil for two hours longer, then draw off the liquor and strain it through a sieve. Take now the white meat and chop it very fine, or pound it in a mortar, as may be most convenient, mix well with it the cream, pour the compound into the strained liquor, put the whole into a clean sauce-pan, and allow it just to come to the boiling, when it is ready for use.

NOTE.—By celery tops, the small tender leaves at the top of the stalk are meant, which are delicious as a flavouring agent.

Rabbit Soup.—Materials and quantities must be provided as follows:—

Two rabbits, three ounces of butter, two quarts of boiling water, one and one-half ounces of flour of rice, one grain of grated nutmeg, three Bermuda onions, one tea-spoonful of salt, one quarter of a tea-spoonful of pepper.

Preparatory to the making of this soup, the rabbits should be soaked for an hour in strong salt and water, for the purpose of draining out the blood and also taking from them the strong, wild, gamey flavour peculiar to them; then cut them into pieces convenient for the sauce-pan, and wash them well in boiling water to whiten the meat.

Now put them, so prepared, into the sauce-pan, and pour the two quarts of boiling water over them, adding the onions, pepper, and salt, and allow all to boil until the meat of the game will separate readily from the bone.

In a separate sauce-pan then melt the butter, stir into it the flour of rice, and strain the liquor from the rabbits into it. Add to this the nutmeg, and cook slowly for fifteen minutes, when it is ready for serving.

NOTE.—In departing from the usual mode of using either cold water or cold stock, as above, it is to be noted that the boiling water is here used to keep the meat from darkening, which it has a tendency to do.

If it should be desired, the small, nice pieces of meat may be added to this soup.

Mullagatawny Soup.—Materials and quantities:—One fowl, two quarts of cold water, two onions, two ounces of butter, two ounces of flour, one table-spoonful of curry-powder, one tea-spoonful of sugar, one half tea-cupful of whole rice, one dessert-spoonful of salt, one tea-spoonful of whole white pepper.

Begin this preparation by first covering the fowl with the two quarts of water, and bring it to boiling over a quick fire. When it boils up and has been skimmed, add the pepper-corns, salt, and onions, then boil slowly until the meat of the fowl becomes tender. Now, removing the fowl from the sauce-pan, cut the meat from the breast and legs, making the same into small pieces to thicken the soup with later, and return the bones and remaining fowl to the stock, when all must be allowed to boil for one hour longer, and then strained. The butter has then to be melted in a fresh sauce-pan, and the flour, curry-powder, and sugar added, with which put the strained stock and whole rice, and boil the whole for twenty minutes.

Just before serving, add the small pieces of chicken cut from the breast and legs, and send to table very hot.

Ox-tail Soup.—Ingredients to be used in the following proportions:—Two ox-tails, two quarts of second stock, ten cloves, one tea-spoonful of pepper-corns, one dessert-spoonful of salt, one large carrot, one turnip.

First cut the ox-tails into pieces about two inches in length, wash them well in cold water, put them together with the stock into a sauce-pan, and bring quickly to the boiling-point. When boiling, skim well and add the salt, also the pepper-corns and cloves secured in a piece of muslin or bag, after which allow it to boil slowly for two hours. Then the carrot and turnip should be cut into dice, or with a French cutter into balls, and added to the soup, boiled therein half an hour, when, removing the cloves and pepper-corns, the soup is ready for use.

PURÉES.—FIRST DIVISION.

Purée à-la-Condé.—For this will be required:—One pint of haricot beans, three pints of white stock, one carrot, one small turnip, one Bermuda onion, a bouquet garnée, two ounces of butter, one half pint of cream, two table-spoonfuls of tomato sauce.

The beans must have been soaked over-night in cold water, and when ready to begin the preparation of the purée, the water must be drained off, and the soaked beans put on to boil in the stock.

When the stock boils, the vegetables, the bouquet garnée, and the butter must be added, and these together allowed to boil for two hours, when it should be taken from the fire and passed twice through a fine sieve. The cream and the tomato sauce should now be put in, also the pepper and salt, of which one half salt-spoonful of each is sufficient, and the whole be brought to the boiling-point, great care being taken to take it from the fire the instant this point is reached, or the cream will curdle and the dish be spoiled.

Note.—To prepare a "bouquet garnée," tie a morsel of celery and a sprig of thyme into a bay leaf.

The small dry white bean, such as is commonly used for baking, may be used in making this purée.

Purée of Green Pease.—Take for this:—

One quart of shelled pease, one and one-half pints of white stock, one Bermuda onion, two ounces of butter, three table-spoonfuls of cream, one tea-spoonful of sugar, one half salt-spoonful of salt, and an equal amount of pepper.

Put first the pease, the onion, and the stock into a saucepan, and boil them together twenty or thirty minutes; after which pass the whole through a sieve, in order that the stock may become smoothly thickened with the pease and the skins removed. Add then to this mixture the cream, the butter, and the sugar, and let all be brought to the point of boiling, keeping in mind that the cream has been added and will curdle if permitted to remain upon the fire an instant too long.

Season now with the pepper and salt, and serve very hot.

Note.—The pease for this purée should be very young, in order that the colour of the dish may be a pretty bright green.

Tomato Purée.—For this provide:—

One quart of canned tomatoes, one and one-half pints of white stock, two ounces of butter, one ounce of flour, one tea-spoonful of sugar, one gill of cream, one half salt-spoonful of salt, and as much pepper.

In preparing this purée, begin with boiling the tomatoes

and the stock together for three quarters of an hour. Pass both then through a fine sieve, and while straining, melt in the sauce-pan the butter, into which stir the flour, and returning the strained liquor then to the sauce-pan, stir all together until it boils.

Now add the sugar, the pepper, and the salt, and pour the purée into the tureen; after which add the cream, which, if otherwise done, will be almost certain to curdle with the sour of the tomatoes.

PURÉES.—SECOND DIVISION.

Asparagus Purée.—For this there will be required:—

One bundle of asparagus, five ounces of butter, one and one half ounces of flour, three pints of white stock, one half pint of cream, one half salt-spoonful of salt, and the same quantity of pepper.

The asparagus has first to be treated by breaking off the tender tips and putting them aside, then blanch the remaining pieces in boiling water, drain them thoroughly, and place them in a sauce-pan with two ounces of butter and flour. Stir all together for five minutes, taking great care to prevent browning, then add the stock, and let all boil slowly, until the asparagus is tender. When this is accomplished pass the whole through a fine sieve, and returning it to the sauce-pan allow it to simmer for twenty minutes, after which add the remaining three ounces of butter. Boil the cream in a separate sauce-pan, and add just before serving. Have ready in a tureen the asparagus tips, having previously boiled them in salt and water, and pour over the purée as soon as the cream has been added.

Turnip Purée.—Materials to be used in the following quantities:—

One and one half pounds of turnip, one ounce of flour, three pints of white stock, three ounces of rice, three ounces of butter, one half pint of double cream, one half salt-spoonful of salt, and an equal quantity of pepper and sugar.

Blanch the turnips with plenty of boiling water to keep them white, then soak them in cold water for one hour. Melt in a sauce-pan two ounces of butter, stir into this the flour and two pints of the white stock. Stir the compound now until it boils, and then put in the turnips, pepper, salt, and sugar, having well drained and dried the turnips after taking them from the water. This must simmer until the turnips are tender, when it should be passed through a sieve and the remainder of the stock added, bringing all again to the boiling-point. The rice should now be washed well and boiled in two quarts of water for twenty minutes, when the water should be well drained from it, and the rice placed in the tureen, the purée poured over it, adding then the cream and the remaining ounce of butter, stirring all until the butter melts, when it is ready for immediate serving.

NOTE.—The turnips must be weighed after being pared, and should be pared thickly, as the outside is always bitter.

Potato Purée.—For this should be furnished: one pound of potatoes, one Bermuda onion, two leaves of celery, one and one half pints of whole stock, one gill of single cream, one ounce of butter, one half salt-spoonful of salt, and the same amount of pepper.

So provided, put into the sauce-pan the potatoes, pared and sliced, the celery, onion, and butter, stirring all over the fire for five minutes, taking care that they do not discolour. Add now one pint of stock, and let it boil slowly until the potatoes are cooked, then pass all through a sieve, using the remaining one half pint of stock hot, to prevent the gluten of the potatoes from stiffening and clogging in the sieve. The sauce-pan should then be well washed and the purée returned to it, the cream, pepper, and salt added, and stirred until it boils.

This should be served with fried bread or asparagus tips, arranging either in the tureen as before directed, and pouring the purée over.

Note.—By single cream, that is meant which arises in twelve hours. Double cream arises in twenty-four hours, and cream for butter in forty-eight hours.

General Notes on Purées.—These purées are intended to suffice for serving four persons; and the apparent inequality of liquids used will be found to correspond with the different lengths of time for boiling, which is, of course, the reducing process.

If it should happen that the purée is thickened unduly by boiling too quickly, this fault may be remedied by adding more of the stock while it is being passed through the sieve.

OYSTERS AND OTHER SHELLFISH.
FIRST DIVISION.

Oyster Soup à-la-Reine.—One quart of oysters, one pint of white stock, one half pint of cream, one and one half ounces of butter, one ounce of flour, one blade of mace, one grain of cayenne, one tea-spoonful of salt, and half as much pepper.

Drain first the liquor from the oysters, and putting the liquor over the fire, bring it to the boiling-point.

In a separate sauce-pan melt the butter, stir into it the flour, and pour in the stock. Add also the mace, pepper, cayenne, and salt, and let all boil for ten minutes, when the oysters should be added. Watch the oysters closely, and when the leaves begin to shrivel, pour the soup into the tureen, and add thereto the cream, which must have been made boiling hot.

Note.—The great difficulty to be surmounted in making this soup, is bringing the cream and liquor together without curdling, which is obviated by boiling each separately.

Fish Chowder.—For this are required one large haddock, weighing about two pounds, three Bermuda onions, one quarter pound pork, six potatoes, one table-spoonful chopped parsley, one dessert-spoonful chopped thyme, one-fourth of a can tomatoes, one dessert-spoonful of salt, one tea-spoonful of pepper, one half wine-glassful of Worcestershire sauce, two ounces of butter.

When the haddock has been cleaned and well washed, place it in a sauce-pan, cover it well with cold water, add a pinch of salt, place the sauce-pan on the fire, and when the water in it boils remove the haddock. Remove from the haddock all skin and bone, throw them into the water in the sauce-pan, and allow the water to boil for twenty minutes very slowly.

While the water is boiling, melt in a frying-pan the butter, and put into the same when hot the pork and the onions, cut into very thin pieces, and fry to a light brown.

Put this preparation into a sauce-pan with the potatoes boiled and mashed, and add the parsley, thyme, and tomatoes, Worcestershire sauce, pepper, and salt; pour over this the liquor (which has been boiling on the fish bones and skin) through a strainer, and allow all to simmer slowly thirty minutes. Just before serving add the pieces of haddock previously separated from the bone and skin.

Oyster Soup.—Procure one quart of oysters, one pint of milk, three ounces of butter, one grain of cayenne, one half tea-spoonful of salt, one salt-spoonful of pepper, one ounce of flour.

The oysters must first be strained, and the liquor brought to boiling-point, and then thoroughly skimmed.

Melt then the butter in a separate sauce-pan, add to it the flour, then the milk, and stir the mixture until it boil. Add now the pepper, salt, cayenne, and oysters, which, if large, should be cut into pieces; pour over this the boiling liquor, allowing all to cook for five minutes, when the oysters will begin to show their leaves. Serve very hot.

OYSTERS AND OTHER SHELLFISH.
SECOND DIVISION.

Fricassée of Oyster.—Procure for this:

Twenty-five oysters, two ounces of butter, one ounce of flour, yolks of two eggs, one tea-spoonful of lemon juice, one grain of cayenne, one grain of grated nutmeg, a piece of salt the size of a pea, one half a salt-spoonful of pepper.

Bring first the oysters in their own liquor to the boiling-point, and when this is reached strain them, and put the oysters, for the time, aside. Melt now, in a separate sauce-pan, the butter, and add thereto the flour, together with one tea-cupful of the strained liquor. Cook this for about two minutes, to give the mixture consistency, and then taking the sauce-pan from the fire, drop in the yolks of the eggs, one by one, stirring quickly until all is well mixed together. Add then the lemon-juice, pepper, salt, nutmeg, and cayenne, when the whole should be placed again over the fire, stirred briskly to prevent boiling, and allowed to become very hot. Just before serving drop in the oysters, and serve on buttered toast.

Fried Oysters.—Provide for this:

Twenty-five large oysters, two table-spoonfuls of flour, four table-spoonfuls of milk, four table-spoonfuls of cracker-dust, two eggs, four heaped table-spoonfuls of bread crumbs, one salt-spoonful of salt, one salt-spoonful of pepper, one salt-spoonful of grated nutmeg.

Put the oysters into a strainer and drain them thoroughly of their liquor. Then upon a plate mix together the flour, milk, pepper, and salt; into which preparation dip the oysters one by one, using a fork, and taking care not to mutilate the oyster. Place now upon a sheet of kitchen-paper the cracker-dust, and putting the oysters therein, lift the sheet of paper by its opposite sides, and roll them in the dust from side to side. The oysters should now be removed to a plate and left standing for half-an-hour, in order that the juices may drain out and harden the cracker-dust encasing them. Heat meantime in a stew-pan one pound of clarified fat, and when the blue smoke arises therefrom, throw in a peeled potato to keep it from burning. Upon a plate beat now the two eggs, dip the oysters one by one into them, then roll them in the bread crumbs, which have been made ready upon the kitchen-paper, and with which has been put the nutmeg, and drop them lightly into the hot clarified fat, letting them remain therein for three minutes. Before serving, put them for a moment upon a clean sheet of kitchen-paper, that it may absorb the extraneous fat.

NOTES.—It is important to avoid touching the oysters with the heated hands, as it makes them both tough and heavy.

Clarified fat and lard boil at about 500 degrees, which is more than double the heat of boiling water. At 375 degrees the blue smoke arises from these heated substances, which is the cooking-point, and boiling fat or lard will burn to a cinder instantly anything that is put into it.

The peeled potato prevents burning, as it furnishes an object for the fat to act upon, and so keeps it from growing hotter: a piece of hard bread will answer the same purpose.

A large quantity of fat is used in this recipe, but its extravagance is tempered by the fact that the same fat may be used over and over again until the heating property is exhausted.

The reason for allowing the oysters to stand for thirty minutes, after being rolled in the cracker-dust, is, that unless so permitted to harden, the egg with which the oyster is subsequently treated would not adhere, but merely draw the cracker-dust off, making it thus necessary to pack these substances on with the hands, and a heavy, soggy dish would be the consequence.

Fried oysters must be quickly cooked and as quickly served.

Recipe for clarifying fat on page 247.

Scalloped Oysters.—Provide for this one quart of oysters, six ounces of bread crumbs, three ounces of butter, one grain cayenne, one salt-spoonful grated nutmeg, one salt-spoonful mace, one wine-glassful sherry.

Bring the oysters to boiling-point, and drain from them their liquor. Melt in a small pan one ounce of the butter. When melted, skim carefully, and draw the pan on one side.

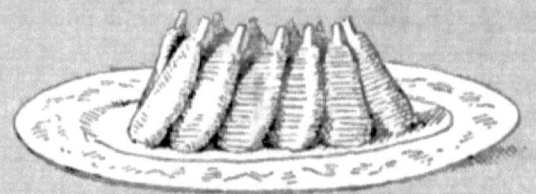

LOBSTER CUTLETS. P. 30.

FISH CAKES. P. 32.

FOWL AND EGG SAUCE. P. 42.

MACKEREL. P. 34.   SCALLOPED OYSTERS. P. 36.

Mix well with the bread crumbs the mace, nutmeg, and cayenne. Put in a deep dish alternate layers of the oysters and seasoned bread crumbs, and over each layer of oysters distribute small pieces of the unmelted butter. When the last layer of bread crumbs is sprinkled over the top, pour over the strained liquor, the sherry, and also the melted butter. Place the dish in a moderate oven, and bake for two hours.

Oysters à-la-Crème.—Materials and quantities as follows: Twenty-five large oysters, one dessert-spoonful of chopped parsley, one heaped table-spoonful of bread crumbs, three and one half ounces of butter, one and one half ounce of flour, a piece of onion half the size of a nutmeg, one gill of cream, one half salt-spoonful of grated nutmeg, one half salt-spoonful of pepper, a piece of salt the size of a pea.

The oysters should first be boiled in their own liquor for five minutes, after which strained, cut into rough pieces, and put upon a plate. Season them then with the pepper, salt, and nutmeg. Melt the butter now in a fresh sauce-pan, adding thereto the flour and the cream, and boil all together for two minutes. Take then the sauce-pan from the fire, put into it the oysters and the parsley and onion, chopped finely, as well. This mixture must now be put nicely into large, deep oyster-shells, the bread crumbs sprinkled over each, and put into a quick oven until browned over the top.

NOTE.—As the oysters used do not always furnish the proper shells for this preparation, it is well to select from time to time the shells from oysters used in other ways, and scrubbing them well, make a reserve of deep shells for this purpose.

Broiled Oysters.—There will be required for this twenty-five large oysters, two table-spoonfuls of flour, four table-spoonfuls of milk, four table-spoonfuls of cracker-dust, two eggs, four heaped table-spoonfuls of bread crumbs, two ounces of butter, and the juice of half a lemon, one half a salt-spoonful of salt, and an equal amount of pepper.

Drain thoroughly the liquor from the oysters, mix upon a plate the flour, milk, pepper, and salt.

Dip the oysters into this mixture, one by one, and, putting the cracker-dust upon a sheet of kitchen-paper, drop the oysters into the dust separately, and roll them from side to side by lifting the paper alternately at opposite corners. Return then to the plate, using a fork in the lifting, and let them stand for thirty minutes, that the dust may harden with the juice. Beat the eggs now until very light, and dip the oysters one by one therein, then into the bread crumbs; and having lightly greased the broiler, put them into it, and broil for five minutes.

In serving, put the butter upon them in small lumps, and squeeze over them the lemon juice.

NOTE.—Before beginning the preparing of oysters in this manner, it would be well to read the notes on fried oysters, page 25.

Oyster Croquettes.—Materials to be used in the following proportions: Twenty-five large oysters, one dessert-spoonful of chopped parsley, three and one half ounces of butter, one and one half ounce of flour, one gill of cream, one tea-spoonful of lemon juice, one egg, three heaped table-spoonfuls of bread crumbs, one half salt-spoonful of pepper, and a piece of salt the size of a pea.

The oysters should be boiled in their own liquor for five minutes, then strained, cut into rough pieces, and seasoned with the pepper and salt. The butter must then be melted in a fresh sauce-pan, the flour added, also the cream, and all cooked for two minutes. Remove the sauce-pan now from the fire, and put in the oysters, parsley, and lemon juice; after which mix all well together and turn out upon a plate, leaving it to cool for one hour.

When cool, form the mixture into small balls; beat the egg very light, and roll them in it; after which put the bread crumbs upon a sheet of kitchen-paper, roll each ball therein from side to side separately, and fry in hot clarified fat or lard for two minutes.

Put them as taken from the fat upon a piece of the kitchen-paper for a moment, to drain the grease off, and serve on a heated napkin garnished with sprigs of parsley.

OYSTERS AND OTHER SHELLFISH— SPECIAL DISHES.

Oyster Balls.—One dozen oysters, two ounces of veal, two ounces beef suet, one salt-spoonful powdered mace, one quarter tea-spoonful salt, one quarter tea-spoonful pepper, three table-spoonfuls bread crumbs, one egg.

Place the oysters and their liquor in a sauce-pan, place the pan over the fire, and just allow the liquor to come to the boiling-point. Strain the oysters from the liquor and chop them very finely. Remove the skin from the suet and chop it very finely. Chop very finely the veal. Place the oysters, veal, and suet in a basin; add the mace, pepper, and salt. Stir all well with a spoon, drop in the yolk of egg, stir again together.

Flour slightly a board, and roll the mixture into small balls, beat up the white of egg on a plate, roll each ball in it. Place on a sheet of paper the bread crumbs, and roll each ball in it. Half fill a sauce-pan with clarified fat, heat it over the fire until the smoke rises. Drop in one by one the balls and cook them for two minutes. Take them out one by one, and drain them for a second on a sheet of kitchen paper. Serve on a hot napkin and garnish with parsley.

Crab Pie or Deviled Crabs.—Provide two crabs, three ounces of butter, one ounce of flour, one gill of milk, one gill of cream, one tea-spoonful of anchovy sauce, one table-spoonful of bread crumbs, one salt-spoonful of pepper, one half salt-spoonful of salt.

First throw the crabs into boiling water, and boil them for quarter of an hour. Pick the meat then from the shells, taking care not to break the shells, as they are to be used as natural bake-pans for the pie. Cut the meat into irregular pieces, and put them in readiness for use; then, taking a fresh sauce-pan, melt two ounces of the butter, to which add the flour, milk, and cream, and boil all for two minutes.

The sauce-pan must now be taken from the fire, and the anchovy sauce, pepper and salt, and meat from the crabs added. When this is mixed thoroughly together, arrange it smoothly in the shells, sprinkle thickly with the bread crumbs, putting the remaining butter in small pieces on the top of each, and brown in a quick oven.

Lobster Cutlets.—Place in readiness one lobster, one and one half ounce of butter, one ounce of flour, one gill of cold water, one table-spoonful of cream, one half tea-spoonful of lemon-juice, one grain of cayenne, one salt-spoonful of salt, one salt-spoonful of pepper, one egg, three table-spoonfuls of bread crumbs.

The lobster should be put into boiling water for twenty minutes; after which the head must be twisted off, and the coral that runs down the back removed. Beat this coral with half an ounce of butter together in a mortar; and to make it perfectly smooth rub it through a wire sieve. Now melt in a sauce-pan the remainder of the butter, add thereto the flour and cold water, stir all until the water boil, and then allow it to boil two minutes.

Take it now from the fire, and add the coral, cream, pepper and salt, lemon-juice and cayenne. When this is done, cut the lobster into small convenient pieces, and mix them well with the contents of the sauce-pan. Turn all now out upon a plate, and set to cool for one hour. When cool, divide into five pieces, and form into cutlets similar in shape to cutlets of lamb. Dip them lightly into the egg, which must have been well beaten; roll them in the bread crumbs, which must have been placed upon kitchen-paper for the purpose, from side to side; and fry for two minutes in hot clarified fat or lard. When done, put them to drain for a moment upon a clean piece of kitchen-paper, and serve on a hot napkin garnished with the claws of the lobster.

NOTE.—The female lobster should be selected for this dish, as it alone furnishes the coral which gives both a delicious flavour and beautiful colour to the composition.

Curried Lobster.—One large lobster, one half pint second stock, one dessert-spoonful curry powder, one small onion, one salt-spoonful salt, one salt-spoonful pepper, one tea-spoonful lemon-juice, one dessert-spoonful cream or milk, one half ounce butter.

Remove all the meat from the lobster, cut it in small pieces, melt in a small sauce-pan the butter, and throw in the onion, which must first be soaked over night in boiling water, dried in a towel, and chopped very finely. When the onion takes a pale brown colour, stir in the curry powder and pepper and salt. Smooth out all the lumps in the powder, and add by degrees (stirring well meanwhile) the stock. When this boils, throw in the pieces of lobster, and cook all very slowly for half an hour or three-quarters. When ready to serve, draw the pan from the fire, and stir in the cream or milk and lemon-juice, and do not again allow it to boil.

Serve the curry on a very hot dish, and send to table with quarter of a pound boiled rice in a separate hot dish. Directions for boiling the rice will be found on page 237.

NOTE.—A little more than half of a pound of tinned lobster may be used instead of the fresh lobster.

Eel Pie.—Six eels, one half pound lean ham, one half pound suet, one tea-spoonful salt, one grain cayenne, one half tea-spoonful pepper, one salt-spoonful mace, one salt-spoonful nutmeg, the rind of half a lemon, one half tea-spoonful chopped parsley, one half tea-spoonful mixed herbs, one egg, one large sprig parsley, two cloves, half a bay leaf, one half tea-spoonful arrowroot, one half pint cream, one small bunch savoury herbs, one pint stock.

Skin the eels, cut them in pieces about two inches long, place the pieces in a sauce-pan, cover them with cold water, and boil them three-quarters of an hour.

Place in a separate sauce-pan the stock, add the parsley, the cloves, the half bay leaf and the bunch of savoury herbs, and half of the salt. Place this over the fire to boil for half an hour, then strain the stock and return it to the sauce-pan, allow it to boil till reduced to half a pint. Mix then in a basin, till very smooth, the arrowroot and cream; add them to the stock in the sauce-pan, and boil for ten minutes longer. Chop now very finely the lean ham and the suet, place them in a basin, add the remainder of the salt, the pepper, cayenne, mace, nutmeg, lemon peel, the savoury herbs, and bind all together with the egg.

Place this forcemeat in a pie-dish, lay in the pieces of eel, and pour over the stock and cream from the sauce-pan. Cover the pie-dish with puff paste. (See directions, page 195.) Place the pie-dish in a quick oven, and bake twenty-five minutes.

Fricassée of Lobster.—One lobster, one gill of cream, one gill and a half of milk, one half tea-spoonful salt, one quarter tea-spoonful pepper, one grain cayenne, one ounce and a half butter, the juice of half a lemon, one half ounce flour.

Plunge a lobster into a large pan of boiling water, and boil it for twenty minutes. Remove the meat from the lobster. Melt then in a sauce-pan the butter, add the flour, stir both well together; then add by degrees the milk and cream, stir till boiling; add the pepper, salt, and cayenne, then the meat from the lobster; cover the sauce-pan, draw it on one side, and let all simmer very slowly for ten minutes.

Take the pan from the fire, and put before serving on a very hot dish; stir in the lemon-juice.

FISH.—FIRST DIVISION.

Filet de Sole à-la-Maître d'Hotel.—Take for this two large soles, two ounces of butter, one half ounce of flour, four table-spoonfuls of cream, one half tea-spoonful of lemon-juice, one dessert-spoonful of chopped parsley, one half salt-spoonful of salt, one half salt-spoonful of pepper.

Begin this by reversing the usual rule for cleaning fish; skin the sole first, and then fillet it. To do this the skin must be loosened at the tail, the fish being held firmly to the table with a dry towel, and with the disengaged hand the skin quickly torn off. This process must be repeated, as the sole has two distinct sides to be relieved of skin. Make then an incision straight down the back with a sharp knife, and pressing the knife as closely as possible to the backbone, separate the flesh from it, removing the four fillets. Roll each fillet separately, in the fashion of a rolled jelly-cake; place them side by side in a slightly greased tin; squeeze over each a little of the lemon-juice, to preserve their colour; cover them with a piece of greased kitchen-paper; and bake in a brisk oven ten minutes. While the fillets are baking, cover the heads and skins of the fish with cold water, and boil for five minutes. Then melt in a small sauce-pan the butter, add to it the flour, and one gill of the liquor obtained by boiling the heads and skins; boil all for two minutes, stirring meantime, when it must be taken from the fire, and the cream, pepper, and salt added.

Put the fillets now into a flat dish, pour this sauce around them, and sprinkle over each fillet a little of the chopped parsley; and serve.

NOTE.—Large flounder may also be prepared after this recipe with the same result.

Boiled Cod-fish.—Provide four pounds of cod, middle cut, one large table-spoonful of vinegar, one half table-spoonful of salt.

The cod-fish should be purchased the day before it is desired to serve, and permitted to lie over night in salt. When ready to boil, fill the fish-kettle two-thirds full of boiling water, add to this the vinegar and salt, place the fish into the drainer, and plunge it into the boiling water, where it must remain for thirty minutes, boiling rapidly.

Serve upon a dry napkin, garnished with parsley, and with it oysters or egg sauce.*

NOTES.—If the cod should be of more than ordinary thickness, it must boil a few minutes longer, that it may become done through.

This recipe may be used in boiling all large fish except salmon. Salmon must be treated with this difference: it should be put to boil in *tepid* instead of boiling water, and thoroughly skimmed as it boils up.

For boiling small and fresh-water fish, use *cold* water; and the

* See "Sauces," page 174.

instant the boiling-point is reached, remove the fish. In this way small fish may be prevented breaking in the kettle.

If not provided with a fish-kettle which has the plunging drainer, it is better to wrap the large fish in a single layer of coarse towelling.

Sole au Gratin.—This requires one small sole, two heaped table-spoonfuls of bread crumbs, one table-spoonful of chopped parsley, two small mushrooms, one ounce of butter, a piece of chalôt the size of a bean, two table-spoonfuls of second stock, one salt-spoonful of salt, one salt-spoonful of pepper.

First the bread crumbs must be put into a dry tin, and browned to a pale brown in the oven. Sprinkle half of them, when prepared, upon a small baking-tin, also having chopped one of the mushrooms, and half of the chalôt finely; scatter this with half of the parsley over the bread crumbs.

Skin now the sole,* and cut away the head, fins, and tail. Place the fish over the preparation in the baking-tin; sprinkle over it the remaining bread crumbs, chopped mushroom, chalôt, and parsley, also the pepper and salt; put over all the butter, in small pieces, and bake in a quick oven ten minutes. Serve on a hot dish, with the stock heated and poured around.

NOTE.—If the chalôt or small French onion is not to be procured, a bit of the common onion may be substituted.

Broiled Mackerel.—Prepare one mackerel, two ounces butter, one half salt-spoonful of pepper, one half tea-spoonful of salt.

Split the mackerel, when cleaned, directly through the backbone with a strong sharp knife. Grease the broiler slightly, place the fish between its leaves, and broil over a quick, clear fire for ten minutes. When done, remove quickly from the broiler, dress with the butter, pepper, and salt, and send it to the table as hot as possible.

The dish may be garnished with lemon quarters, and a sprig of parsley at either end.

NOTE.—All classes of broiling fish may be treated after this recipe.

* See directions for skinning sole, page 32.

Stuffed Haddock.—Provide one large haddock, two ounces of beef suet, three table-spoonfuls of bread crumbs, one tea-spoonful of chopped thyme, one dessert-spoonful of chopped parsley, one egg, one salt-spoonful of salt, one salt-spoonful of pepper.

The haddock must be thoroughly dried after cleaning, and the tail and fins cut off, leaving the head. Make a stuffing by mixing two table-spoonfuls of the bread crumbs with the parsley, thyme, pepper, and salt, into which drop the egg, to give the dressing consistency. Pack this stuffing snugly into the stomach of the fish, sew the sides together with needle and thread, place it in a greased baking-pan, damp it over with milk or egg, sprinkle over it the remainder of the bread crumbs, and bake three quarters of an hour in a moderate oven, taking occasion to baste from time to time with the drippings.

NOTE.—To bake evenly, the fish should stand in the pan in the position which it naturally takes in the water; and this may be accomplished by placing a long skewer first through the tail of the fish, next through the centre of the body, and lastly through the head. A strong cord passed in the same manner through the fish and drawn taut will serve the purpose.

Salmon and trout may be done also after this recipe.

Fried Smelts.—One dozen smelts, two table-spoonfuls of flour, two eggs, four table-spoonfuls of bread crumbs, one tea-spoonful of salt, one tea-spoonful of pepper.

Take first the flour and the bread crumbs, and place them upon separate sheets of kitchen-paper. Mix with the bread crumbs the salt and pepper; when the fish have been thoroughly prepared, dip them one by one into the flour, for the purpose of drying them. Beat now the eggs until very light, and roll the fish one by one therein; place them then into the bread crumbs, rolling each from side to side until well covered. Throw the fish thus prepared into smoking-hot clarified fat or lard, and cook for five minutes. Garnish with parsley, and serve in a folded napkin.

NOTE.—All pan fish, including brook trout, may be treated in this way.

White-bait is cooked by simply being thrown into hot lard just as taken from the water, and cooked for two minutes.

Broiled Haddock.—One haddock, one half ounce suet, one half ounce flour.

Wash well, and scrape the haddock after it is cleaned. Dry it well in a towel. Sprinkle over then the flour. Rub well the gridiron with the suet. Place the gridiron over a clear fire, and when it is hot place on the haddock, and broil it for ten minutes, turning it once. Place it on a napkin folded on a hot dish, and garnish it with parsley. Send to table, in a sauce tureen, a little shrimp sauce.*

Sole in Jelly.—One sole, one half pint shrimps, one ounce gelatine, six pepper-corns, one blade mace, one tea-spoonful salt, one pint cold water. Soak the gelatine for half an hour in one gill of cold water.

Wash and clean the sole, but do not skin it. When the gelatine has soaked half an hour, place it in a small pie-dish, add the sole, pepper-corns, salt, and mace, pour over the remainder of the cold water; place the pie-dish in a moderate oven for half an hour. In the meantime pick the shrimps carefully. Dip a mould in cold water, and lay in the bottom of it a layer of the shrimps. Remove the skin from the sole, and divide it in pieces about an inch in size. Put a layer of the pieces over the shrimps in the mould. Continue to put those layers until all is used up. Pour now over the sole and shrimps the liquor in the pie-dish through a strainer. Put the mould on one side till cold and set, then turn out the shape on a flat dish, and garnish with parsley.

Sole à-la-Normandie.—One large sole, two whitings, two eggs, the rind of a lemon, one table-spoonful bread crumbs, one quarter tea-spoonful pepper, one tea-spoonful salt, one dozen button mushrooms, one ounce butter, one half ounce flour.

Wash well and clean the sole, remove the black skin; with

* Directions for which see page 177.

a sharp knife make an incision down the back to the bone. Remove the bone, taking care to break the fish as little as possible. Take the skin from the whitings; take the fish from the bone. Place the bones in a sauce-pan with the skin, and cover them well with cold water. Place the pan over the fire, and let the water simmer for half an hour. Take now the pieces of whiting in a mortar and pound them; add the eggs, half the pepper and salt, all of the bread crumbs, and pound all well together. Add the lemon rind, and then stuff the sole with this. To hide the incision, put down the back a row of mushrooms. Grease well a dripping-tin; put on the sole, and cover it with a sheet of greased paper; place the tin in the oven for twenty-five minutes. While this is baking, roll into small balls the remainder of the stuffing; place them in a small pan of boiling water, and boil them slowly for five minutes. Melt in a separate sauce-pan the butter; add the flour, then by degrees three gills of the water in which the bones were boiled. Stir till boiling, and boil two minutes. When the sole is cooked enough, place it on a hot flat dish; take the balls from the water and place them round; pour round the sauce, and the dish is ready for use.

NOTE.—If desired, at the last minute the yolks of two eggs may be added to the sauce.

FISH.—SECOND DIVISION.

Fish à-la-Russe.—Provide for this one half pound of flour, one quarter of a pound of butter, one tea-spoonful of yeast-powder, three eggs, one half tea-cupful of boiled rice, one pound raw fish, one gill of cold water, one half tea-spoonful of salt, one salt-spoonful of pepper.

Put the flour upon a mixing-board, and with it a little salt and the yeast-powder, rubbing all together. Make this into a light dough with the cold water and the white of one egg whipped to a stiff froth. Knead the dough lightly, and roll out as thinly as possible. Spread upon this paste one-third of the butter, fold it in three layers, and again roll out thinly. Spread upon it the second part of butter, and repeat the process of folding and rolling. Now spread on the last piece of butter, and refold it in the same manner.

Roll the crust once again into a square; place in the centre of it the boiled rice, two of the eggs, which must have been hard boiled, also the fish; sprinkle over this the remaining salt and the pepper; wet the edges of the crust with the yolk of egg, fold it over squarely, brush the entire surface over with the yolk of egg, and place it first in a quick oven for ten minutes, when it should be changed to a cooler part of the oven, to prevent its browning too quickly, and allowed to bake three quarters of an hour.

NOTE.—The quantity of water given cannot be imperative, for the reason that the amount to be used is determined by the amount of gluten in the flour, which is never equal in different brands.

Any kind of fish may be used for this preparation, so long as it is of a kind to be boned and skinned; but fillets of sole, flounder, or haddock will be found most satisfactory.

Fish Cakes.—For these will be required one pound of cold boiled fish, one pound of raw potatoes, two ounces of butter, two eggs, four heaped table-spoonfuls of bread crumbs, one grain of cayenne, one tea-spoonful of salt, one half salt-spoonful of pepper.

Separate the skin and bone from the flesh with two forks, and put the fish, cut into irregular pieces, into a large bowl. Boil the potatoes, putting a little salt into the boiling water; place a sieve over the bowl containing the fish, put the potatoes while hot into the sieve, and rub them through over the fish with the back of a wooden spoon. The pepper, salt, and cayenne should now be added; drop in also the yolks of the eggs and the butter, mix together thoroughly, and form the mixture into round flat cakes.

Beat then the whites of the eggs sufficiently to break the albumen, dip the cakes therein, place the bread crumbs upon a sheet of kitchen-paper, and roll the cakes separately in it. They must now be thrown into hot clarified fat or lard, and cooked for three minutes, when they may be transferred to a sheet of kitchen-paper, to remove any particles of fat that may have clung to the surface. Serve garnished with parsley and very hot.

NOTE.—When fresh fish is not available, salt cod or other fish may be substituted, leaving out of course the salt, and picking the salt fish to shreds, and washing through numerous waters, until sufficiently freshened. When salt fish is used, it should be carefully dried after freshening, by putting it into a clean towel, and wringing until moisture will no longer exude.

Turbot à-la-Crême.—Materials as follows: One pound of cold boiled turbot, two ounces of butter, one ounce of flour, one ounce of grated cheese, one half pint of milk, one gill of cream, one salt-spoonful of grated nutmeg, one half salt-spoonful of pepper, one half tea-spoonful of salt.

Remove the bone and skin of the fish, and place it upon a flat dish, cut into irregular pieces. Melt in a sauce-pan the butter, stirring in the dry flour, to which add by degrees the milk, stirring constantly, to prevent the flour from lumping, until it boils. When boiling, add the cream, and a little of the pepper and salt; allow all to cook for two minutes, after which pour the mixture over the pieces of fish in the flat dish. Sprinkle over this the grated cheese, the remainder of the pepper and salt, and the nutmeg; place the dish into a moderate oven, and bake for ten minutes.

NOTE.—Turbot done in this manner must be prepared in the dish in which it is to be sent to the table, as it cannot be moved.

Salmon Pie.—For this will be required two pounds of salmon, one-fourth pound of bread crumbs, one table-spoonful of chopped parsley, two ounces of butter, two eggs, one gill of cold water, one tea-spoonful of pepper, one tea-spoonful of salt.

First mix well together the chopped parsley, bread crumbs, the pepper and the salt, and put a layer of this into the bottom of a flat dish. The salmon must then be cut into thin slices, and a layer of it put next to the bread crumbs and parsley. In this way alternate layers must be placed in the dish until all of the material is used; then beat until very light the two eggs, add to them the water, and pour this mixture over the dish already arranged. Place upon the top of this the butter in small pieces, and bake in a moderate oven three quarters of an hour.

NOTE.—Flounder, haddock, and halibut may also be done in this way.

Potted Halibut.—For this provide two pounds of halibut, one tea-spoonful of salt, one tea-spoonful of black pepper, one half tea-spoonful of spice for potted meats,* one half tea-cupful of vinegar, one half tea-cupful of Bass ale, one tea-spoonful of tarragon vinegar, one ounce of butter.

Lay the fish in layers in a deep dish, putting between each layer a little of the spice and pepper and salt; press the contents well down in the dish, then mix well together the vinegar, Bass ale, and tarragon vinegar, and pour this composition over the halibut. Place the butter in small pieces over the top, and bake in a moderate oven for thirty minutes.

Kedgeree.—For this will be required one pound of cold boiled fish, two ounces of butter, two eggs, one tea-cupful of rice, one tea-spoonful of curry powder, one salt-spoonful of salt, one half salt-spoonful of pepper.

Boil the eggs for ten minutes, and the rice for a quarter of an hour. Chop the eggs into irregular pieces, and removing the skin and bone of the fish, melt the butter in a sauce-pan, and add thereto the hard-boiled eggs, the fish, and rice. Stir all now together over the fire until it is very hot, taking care that the mixture does not burn, it being very dry and apt to spoil, since the only moisture in it is the butter.

---

* The spice for potted meats is composed of the following ingredients, thoroughly mixed: One ounce of ground cloves, one ounce pulverized mace, one ounce of Jamaica pepper, one ounce of grated lemon-rind, one-fourth ounce of cayenne, one grated nutmeg.

Add, just before serving, the curry powder, pepper, and salt; and piling it very high in the middle of a hot dish, garnish the preparations with a little fresh parsley, and serve very hot.

NOTE.—Instead of garnishing this dish with sprigs of parsley, the parsley may be chopped and sprinkled over the top.

Stewed Cod Fish.—Have in readiness for this two pounds cod fish, three gills white stock, three table-spoonfuls bread crumbs, one tea-spoonful flour of rice, one salt-spoonful mace, half table-spoonful lemon juice, one glassful sherry, one grain cayenne.

Begin by cutting the cod fish into slices one inch and a half thick; place into a fish-kettle of boiling water in which has been placed a large pinch of salt.

Boil the fish slowly for five minutes, then drain well from it the water. Heat in a stew-pan the white stock, add to it the bread crumbs, and stew for five minutes.

Place in a small bowl the flour of rice, make it very smooth with a little cold water, add to it the mace, cayenne, sherry, and lemon juice, stir all into the hot stock, and boil two minutes. Place into this mixture very carefully the pieces of fish, and cook very gently five minutes. When ready to serve, take the fish very gently from the stew-pan, and placing it on a hot dish, pour the sauce over.

NOTE.—A dozen oysters may be added to this, according to taste; or, if preferred, a table-spoonful of essence of anchovies.

Salmon Pudding.—Provide for this one pound salmon (cold boiled), eight table-spoonfuls bread crumbs, one tea-spoonful anchovy paste, one gill cream, four eggs, one tea-spoonful salt, one grain cayenne.

Take one table-spoonful of the bread crumbs, place it on a small baking-tin, place the tin in a moderate oven, and allow the crumbs to take a pale-brown colour. Grease well with a little butter a small mould. When this is done, throw into it the browned bread crumbs, and shake the mould from side to side, so as to get a thin layer of crumbs on the greased surface.

Chop very finely the cold salmon, from which must first be removed all bone and skin, mix it well with the remaining seven table-spoonfuls of bread crumbs, also the anchovies.

Add now the seasoning, and moisten all with the cream and the eggs, well beaten. Press this mixture firmly and smoothly into the mould, and twist over a piece of buttered paper.

Have in readiness on the fire a sauce-pan half filled with boiling water; place into this water the mould, and boil for one hour.

NOTE.—Tinned salmon may be used for this dish; and if desired, the anchovy paste may be omitted.

MEATS.—FIRST DIVISION.

ROASTS.

Roast Beef.—Six pounds of sirloin beef, one half table-spoonful of salt, one salt-spoonful of pepper, one ounce of butter, one half ounce of flour, one half pint of second stock.

Put the meat into a *dry* oven-pan, and then into a hot oven for ten minutes, that the albumen may form, closing up the pores of the beef, and confining thus the juices.

Allow the oven then to cool a little, and continue roasting with a moderate heat, giving fifteen minutes to each pound of meat, and fifteen minutes over—which is one hour and three-quarters for a roast of this size. As soon as the fat is discharged from the meat into the pan, basting or moistening with this natural gravy should be commenced, and continued at frequent intervals during the entire time of roasting. At the end of the specified roasting time, take the meat from the oven, put it on a hot platter and sprinkle over it the salt. Pour the grease now out of the oven-pan, as it is not to be used for the gravy, and put the stock into the pan, both that it may become brown and partake of the flavour of the roast; then melt in a fresh sauce-pan the butter, stir into it the dry flour, add the pepper and a little salt, also the stock, and let all boil for two minutes. Serve in a sauce-boat with the roast.

Note.—Veal, lamb, and mutton may all be roasted by the same directions as for roasting beef. Mutton takes the same time to do, and veal and lamb require twenty minutes for each pound of meat, and twenty minutes longer.

The same sauce may be used for veal and mutton, but for lamb only mint sauce is proper; to prepare which see Sauces, page 173.

Roast Turkey.—One turkey, two ounces of butter, one ounce of flour, one half pint of second stock, two tea-spoonfuls of salt, one tea-spoonful of pepper, four ounces of beef-suet, seven ounces of bread crumbs, one egg, one table-spoonful of chopped parsley, one heaped tea-spoonful of chopped thyme.

After the turkey has been cleaned and singed, chop from it the claws, and dipping the feet into boiling water, draw off the skin. Slit them also through with a sharp knife, that by severing the tendon the leg may not draw up in an ugly manner when exposed to the heat. Twist the tip of the wings behind the shoulders, then pass a skewer through the under part of the wing, through the top part of the leg, straight through the body,—through the top part of the other leg, and through the under part of the other wing, which brings the skewer in a straight line across the fowl. Take now another skewer and put it through the skin of the fowl at the side, at a point that will permit the fastening down of the legs, by running the skewer over them, through the skin at the base of the breast, and again into the skin of the bird on the opposite side.

Having thus trussed the turkey, the dressing must now be prepared. Chop the suet finely, and mix with it the bread crumbs, the parsley, and thyme, also half of the pepper and salt. To bind this together drop in the egg, and then stuff the preparation into the turkey through the incision at the neck; and when it is full, fold the skin together, and fasten by sewing through with a needle and thread.

Put the bird now into a dry baking-tin, and distribute one ounce of butter in small pieces over the breast, after which place it in a quick oven, and allow it to roast twenty minutes for each pound, and twenty minutes additionally.

While the turkey is roasting, the neck and giblets should be put on to boil, first being well covered with cold water; and when the turkey is done, the giblets, etc., should be taken from the water and chopped very finely. Place the roast now upon a hot platter, pour the grease out of the baking-tin, and substitute for it the liquor made by the boiling of the giblets. In a small sauce-pan then melt the butter, stir into it the flour, add to it the liquor from the baking-tin, also the chopped giblets, season all with the remainder of the pepper and salt, and let the whole cook for two minutes. Serve in a gravy-boat along with the turkey.

NOTE.—Chickens, ducks, and geese may also be prepared and roasted in this manner, the stuffing for ducks and geese being different only in the addition of two Bermuda onions, chopped fine, and one **tea-spoonful** of sage to the seasoning of this given amount of dressing.

Roast Pork.—One small loin of pork, three table-spoonfuls of bread crumbs, one Bermuda onion, one half teaspoonful of chopped sage, one half tea-spoonful of salt, one half tea-spoonful of pepper, one ounce of chopped suet, one table-spoonful of dripping.

First separate each joint of the loin with a chopper, and then make an incision with a knife into the thick part of the pork in which to put the stuffing. Prepare the stuffing by mixing the bread crumbs together with the onion, which must have previously been finely chopped. Add to this the sage, pepper, salt, and suet, and when all is thoroughly mixed, press the mixture snugly into the incision already made in the pork, and sew together the edges of the meat

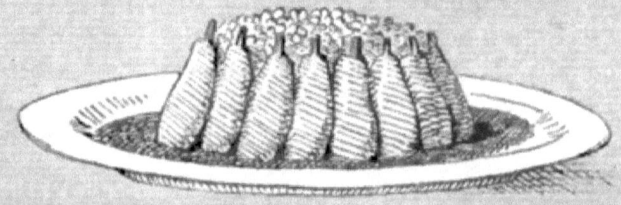

WINDHAM CUTLETS.   P. 58.

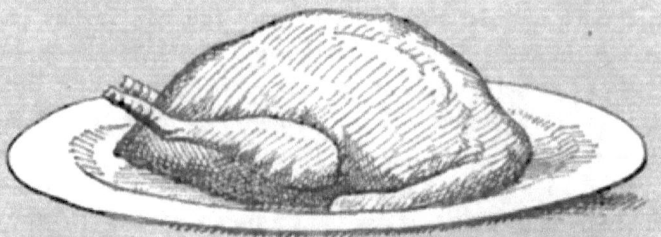

ROAST TURKEY.   P. 13.

KIDNEYS.   P. 76.

with needle and thread, in order to confine the stuffing. Grease well a sheet of kitchen-paper with the drippings, place the loin into this, making an envelope of the paper, and securing it with a wrapping of twine. Put to bake in a dry baking-pan, in a brisk oven, basting immediately and constantly as the grease draws out, and roast a length of time, allowing twenty minutes to each pound of meat, and twenty minutes longer.

This should be served either with apple-sauce or apple-fritters. See pages 177, 133.

NOTE.—The sage powders, that may be purchased in small packages, can be used in all cases where chopped sage is required.

Roast Bullock's Heart.—One bullock's heart, three ounces of chopped suet, three ounces of bread crumbs, one table-spoonful of chopped parsley, one dessert-spoonful of mixed powdered herbs, one gill of milk, two ounces of drippings, one Bermuda onion, one pint of cold water, one ounce of butter, one ounce of flour, one table-spoonful of mushroom catchup, one tea-spoonful of pepper, one dessert-spoonful of salt.

The stuffing for this must first be prepared by mixing together the suet, bread crumbs, parsley, and powdered herbs. Bind this with the gill of milk, and season with the pepper and salt. The heart must now be made ready by thoroughly washing it in several waters, and cutting off the "deaf ears" or valves closing the arteries. Make the cells of the heart now into one large one by cutting away the partitions, place into this the stuffing, and greasing a sheet of kitchen-paper, tie it over the top, in order to secure the stuffing.

Dry whatever moisture there may be upon the outside of the heart with a dry towel, and place it together with the drippings in an oven-tin, and allow it to bake briskly, twenty minutes for each pound, and twenty minutes longer, basting meantime.

While the heart is roasting, the "deaf ears" must be

washed, put into a sauce-pan with the pint of cold water, adding also the onion sliced, and the whole allowed to simmer slowly for one hour.

When the heart is roasted, strain the liquor from the "deaf ears," melt in the sauce-pan the butter, stir into it the flour, and add to this the strained liquor, also the catchup, pepper, and salt, and allow all to cook for two minutes, when the paper should be removed from the heart, and placing it upon a hot platter, serve with the sauce poured around.

NOTE.—A sheep's heart is delicious done in the same way, the preparation being that the quantity of stuffing must be made according to the size of the heart.

GENERAL NOTE.—The above processes have been termed "roasting," but are in reality baking; roasting proper only being done by reflected heat before an open fire. Meat is more nourishing done upon the spit than in the oven, for the reason that the unwholesome vapours are dissipated when exposed to the air, and preserved when confined to an oven.

MEATS.—SECOND DIVISION.

BOILED MEATS.

Boiled Leg of Mutton.—One leg of mutton, two ounces of butter, one ounce of flour, one and one half gill of milk, one salt-spoonful of salt, one salt-spoonful of pepper, two heaped table-spoonfuls of capers.

Put over the fire a large sauce-pan of water, and bring it to the boiling-point. If the mutton be newly killed, beat it with a rolling-pin to soften the fibre, but it is better to have hung it a week if the weather permits. Plunge the meat into the boiling water and allow it to boil up once, then draw the sauce-pan aside from the blaze of the fire, cover it closely, and allow it to simmer slowly; how slowly may be determined by keeping the water bubbling easily at one side until it is done, which will be according to the weight of the leg,—allowing fifteen minutes for each pound, and fifteen minutes longer.

Fifteen minutes before the mutton will be done, prepare the sauce by melting in a sauce-pan the butter, and stirring into this the dry flour. When the flour and butter are thoroughly mixed, add one gill and a half of the liquor that the mutton is boiling in, also the milk, pepper, and salt, cook all two minutes to swell the grains of the flour. Then take the mutton up and place it on a large hot platter, pour over it the sauce, adding just before doing this the capers, in order that their colour may not be lost by standing in the hot liquid.

NOTE.—The plunging of the mutton first into boiling water is for the purpose of hardening the albumen and confining the juices of the meat; it is then allowed to cook slowly, that the fibre may not toughen, which rapid boiling would inevitably bring about.

Boiled Corned Beef.—Six pounds of corned beef, twelve ounces of flour, five ounces of beef-suet, one half tea-spoonful of baking-powder, one salt-spoonful of salt, one dozen small carrots, one half pint of cold water.

Place over the fire a large sauce-pan, two-thirds full of cold water, and put into it the meat. Bring this quickly to the boiling-point over a hot fire, and when it boils, skim thoroughly.

When the albumen has all been displaced and the scum all taken off, draw the sauce-pan aside from the blaze, and allowing fifteen minutes to each pound of meat, and fifteen minutes over, let the beef boil gently until done.

Meantime the carrots should be well washed and thinly scraped, and three-quarters of an hour before the meat will be ready for serving, throw them in to cook with it.

When this is done, mix next, in a large bowl, the suet, finely chopped, and flour; add to this the baking-powder and salt, and knead into a dry dough with the water. Divide this dough into six or eight pieces, roll each piece into a small ball, and throw them one by one into the boiling liquor with the beef twenty minutes before serving.

NOTE.—The dropping in of the balls of dough cools the boiling liquor, and care should therefore be taken to wait an instant between the putting in of each one, that the liquid may boil up; otherwise the balls will burst, making a very ugly combination.

Beef-suet should be used, unless the dish prepared is designed for the sick, as it mixes most readily with other materials. For the sick, mutton-suet should always be used, as it is easier of digestion, being thinner in the fibre, although more difficult to manipulate.

Boiled Fowl : Egg Sauce.—Two fowls, three ounces of butter, one and one half ounces of flour, one half pint of milk, one half pint of cream, two eggs, one salt-spoonful of salt, one salt-spoonful of pepper.

After the fowls have been cleaned and singed, the legs must be chopped off at the first joint and pocketed, which is done by pressing the bones inward until entirely sheathed in the skin. Take then a trussing-needle, threaded from a ball of twine, put the points of the wings behind the shoulders, and passing the needle through the under part of the first wing at the point of the joint, on through the thick part of the leg at the top, thence straight through the body, through the other leg and wing at the corresponding point, draw the thread after, carefully forming a straight line across the fowl; then, turning back, put the needle through the upper part of the wing, through the skin of the neck and the upper part of the remaining wing, drawing the thread again after, and tying the two ends of the twine, which now approach each other, into a secure knot.

Thread the trussing-needle now anew, and putting it through the fowl at the tail, just over the back-bone, pass it over one leg, through the skin at the base of the breast, and over the other leg, bringing the ends of the twine again together, where they must be tied very tightly.

When both fowls have been trussed, grease two sheets of kitchen-paper, and tie one over the breast of each fowl. Have then in readiness a large sauce-pan of boiling water, plunge the fowls therein, and allow the water to boil up. When boiling cover the sauce-pan closely, and drawing it aside from the blaze of the fire, allow the fowls to simmer slowly, from an hour to an hour and a quarter, until the chickens are tender.

While this is being accomplished, put two eggs into boiling water, let them boil for ten minutes, then taking them from the fire, throw them at once into a bowl of cold water, that they may cool quickly, and the coating of the yolks preserve their colouring. When the eggs are quite cold, remove the shells and chop the whites into irregular pieces, preparatory to making the sauce.

Five minutes before the fowls are to be removed from the boiling, put into a small sauce-pan the butter, and melting it, stir therein the flour, adding by degrees the milk, stirring meantime until all boils, when the cream must be thrown in, also the pepper and salt, allowing the whole to cook together for two minutes.

Remove now the fowls from the sauce-pan, take the papers off from the breasts, and cut out the strings, and place them upon a large hot platter, pouring over the breast of each the sauce; to which must be added at the last moment the whites of eggs, in order that they may not discolour with standing. Before serving, hold a wire sieve over the upturned breasts of the chickens, and rub the yolk of the eggs through upon them.

NOTES.—The length of time given for boiling is for very young fowl; for older ones the time must be increased, to what length will be determined by the period at which the meat becomes tender.

The object of trussing is to keep the fowl in proper form, and give it a plump, neat appearance, when brought to the table.

The greased paper is put over the breast for the purpose of keeping the meat white, and, by absorbing the grease with which it is saturated, tender.

Boiled Beefsteak Pudding.—Two pounds of steak from the round, two sheep's kidneys, one pound of flour, six ounces of beef-suet, one tea-spoonful of baking-powder, one dessert-spoonful of salt, one half tea-spoonful of pepper, one half pint of cold water, one dessert-spoonful of mushroom catchup, one dessert-spoonful of Worcestershire sauce.

First mix well on a plate the salt and pepper, leaving out a little of the salt, which will be required for the crust; after which cut the steak and kidney into inch-square pieces, and roll them about on the plate, until thoroughly seasoned.

Now chop the suet finely, and put it upon a mixing board, together with the flour; add to this the baking-powder and the remaining salt, and knead all into a light dough with the cold water. Cut off a third part of the dough, and reserve it for the covering of pudding, and rolling the remainder until about one quarter of an inch in thickness, grease a quart bowl, and line it therewith. Put now loosely into this crust-lined bowl the steak and kidney, and having poured over the top the catchup and Worcestershire sauce, fill it to within an inch of the top with cold water. The remainder of the crust should then be rolled out to the exact size of the bowl, and put over the meat, pinched firmly together with the lining crust around the edge.

Dip a towel in hot water, flour it slightly, and tie it tightly over the top of the bowl to prevent any of the juices escaping, and putting all into a large sauce-pan of boiling water, allow it to boil for two hours and a half.

If served in the bowl, a napkin may be arranged to cover the ware, and the whole be carried to table on a round china or silver plate. If it is to be transferred to another dish for serving, one should be selected for the purpose, into the bottom of which the round of the upper crust will fit nicely, and care be exercised not to break the paste in turning it out.

MEATS.—THIRD DIVISION.

MEAT DISHES.

Beefsteak Pie.—Three pounds of round steak, one dessert-spoonful of salt, one half tea-spoonful of pepper, one table-spoonful of Worcestershire sauce, one half pint of second stock, one pound of flour, one half pound of butter, two tea-spoonfuls of baking-powder, three gills of cold water.

The steak must first be cut into pieces three inches square; into each piece put a little of the pepper and salt, and then roll each separately into a roll. Put these rolls loosely in the bottom of a deep pie dish, pour over them the Worcestershire sauce, the catchup, and the stock. Place upon a mixing board the flour and baking-powder with a little salt, mix all well together, and knead into a light dough with the cold water. Roll this dough out as thinly as possible, and dividing the butter into three pieces, spread one piece upon the dough. Fold the dough into three layers, and again roll out, and repeat this process until the butter is all used. When this is done, roll it out to a size a little larger than the top of the pie dish and a half an inch in thickness. Rub the top of the pie dish with cold water, and cutting some narrow strips from the dough, line the edge therewith, and wetting this strip of lining also with cold water, cover the remaining dough over the top, when the edges should be pressed together with the thumb, and the whole evenly cut around with a knife. The pie should then be brushed over with a little egg or milk, as may be most convenient, a hole cut into the top to permit the steam escaping, and the pieces of crust that have been cut off at the edges cut and arranged ornamentally over the surface, to conceal the hole as much as possible without covering it. Put the pie to bake in a quick oven for half an hour, to raise and cook the crust, then cooling the oven a little, allow it to bake slowly an hour longer, or until the steak is quite tender, which may be ascertained by inserting a skewer or a fork.

NOTE.—If the crust should appear to be browning too much or too rapidly in the baking, it may be protected by covering it with a sheet of greased kitchen-paper.

Hot-pot.—One and one-half pound of lean mutton, two pounds of raw potatoes, one and one-half ounce of flour, one dessert-spoonful of salt, one half tea-spoonful of pepper, one salt-spoonful of grated nutmeg, one table-spoonful of catchup, one ounce of butter, one half pint of cold water.

When the potatoes have been pared, put them into cold water, and allow them to come to the boiling-point, which being reached, they are at once to be taken out. Slice then enough of the potatoes to cover the bottom of a good-sized vegetable dish, putting them in in layers, after which cut the mutton into small, convenient pieces, roll each piece into a mixture made of the flour, pepper, salt, and nutmeg, and put them into the dish in layers alternating with the layers of potato, until the contents are level with the top. The remaining potatoes should be cut in half and arranged over the top, leaving the round sides up. Melt the butter and brush it over the top of the potatoes to prevent their hardening in the oven, pour the catchup and water in at the side of the dish, and bake in a moderate oven for an hour and a half.

NOTE.—Potatoes should never be used without being put first into cold water and then brought to the boiling-point. This draws out the greenness, which produces indigestion, and is exceedingly injurious to some stomachs.

Stewed Beef.—Four pounds of stewing beef, two carrots, two turnips, one onion, one half ounce of flour, one ounce of butter, three gills of second stock, one half table-spoonful of Worcestershire sauce, one half table-spoonful of catchup, one tea-spoonful of salt, one half salt-spoonful of pepper.

The butter must first be melted in a sauce-pan, and when the smoke arises therefrom, put into it the beef, and brown well on both sides. While the beef is browning, put into a bowl the flour, and make it smooth with a table-spoonful of the stock; add then the catchup, Worcestershire sauce, with the pepper and salt, and the remainder of the stock. Stir all until thoroughly blended, and pour the mixture over the browning beef. Stir the liquor around the meat until it boils, skimming the grease from the top as it arises, and adding then one carrot and one turnip sliced; also the onion. Draw the sauce-pan now aside from the blaze of the fire, and allow it to simmer slowly for two hours; meantime, half an hour before the time for cooking expires, cut the remaining carrot and turnip into fancy shapes with a vegetable cutter, throw them into a small sauce-pan filled with boiling water, and cook them until quite tender. When the meat is done, place it upon a large hot platter, strain over it the gravy, and taking the prepared carrot and turnip from the water, drain, and garnish with them the stew.

Haricot of Mutton.—One half dozen mutton chops, one half ounce of butter, twelve button-onions, one ounce of flour, two turnips, one carrot, one tea-spoonful of salt, one half salt-spoonful of pepper, one pint of second stock.

Trim the fat from the chops, and melting the butter in a sauce-pan, slice into it one of the onions.

When the blue smoke arises from the heated butter, put into it the chops, and brown them to a nice pale brown. When this is done, take out of the pan the chops, and pour off the grease, after which put the flour into the pan, the grease still adhering to which will be sufficient to prevent its lumping; add to it the stock, and stir all until it boils, when it should be skimmed to remove such particles of the onion and grease as may arise, and the chops returned to the pan. All should now be permitted to stew for half an hour gently, when the button-onions must be added; also the carrot, cut in fancy shapes; and the turnips, which must have been quartered; the pepper and salt; and the whole allowed to stew for half an hour longer, when it is ready to serve.

Arrange the chops for serving in a circle upon a hot platter, fill the vegetables into the centre, and pour the sauce around from the outer edge.

NOTE.—By "button-onions" is meant onions of the size of a button,—the smallest onions procurable.

Blanquette of Veal.—Three pounds of fillet of veal, one and one-half pint of white stock, one table-spoonful of lemon juice, one table-spoonful of sherry, one table-spoonful of chopped parsley, yolks of two eggs, one table-spoonful of cream, one tea-spoonful of salt, one half salt-spoonful of white pepper, one half ounce of flour.

Begin by cutting the veal into small regular pieces about four inches square, place it then into a copper or porcelain-lined sauce-pan, and pour over it a pint of boiling white stock. Whatever of impurity there may be in the meat will at once arise to the surface; therefore it must be immediately skimmed, and allowed thereafter to simmer very slowly for one hour.

While the meat is thus cooking, put the flour into a bowl, wet, and make it smooth with a table-spoonful of the cold stock; add to it the pepper, salt, lemon-juice, and sherry, and the remainder of the stock; and pouring this into the sauce-pan, let the whole cook together for twenty minutes longer.

Just before serving, put the yolks of the eggs into a bowl, together with the chopped parsley; beat these until thoroughly blended, when the cream must be added; and when the sauce-pan containing the veal has been removed from the fire and allowed to cool for two minutes, pour into it this mixture, and stir all quickly, to prevent the eggs curdling, which they are liable to do by coming in conjunction with the cream and lemon-juice.

This should be served very hot.

NOTE.—A copper or porcelain-lined sauce-pan is here specified because a common sauce-pan in which anything else has been cooked, unless especially scoured for this purpose, will unfailingly discolour the veal.

Fricassée of Chicken.—One young fowl, one ounce of butter, one and one-half ounce of flour, one carrot, one Bermuda onion, one and one-half pint of second white stock, one tea-spoonful of salt, one half salt-spoonful of white pepper, one blade of mace, one gill of cream, one dozen of small mushrooms.

First disjoint the chicken, and throwing it into cold water let it remain therein for twenty minutes. Put the pieces of meat into a copper or porcelain-lined sauce-pan, and pour over them the whole of the stock, boiling. As it boils skim it well, add the pepper and salt, also the carrot and onion, and allow all to cook as slowly as possible for half an hour, at the expiration of which the pieces of fowl must be taken out and the liquor strained.

Put the mushrooms now into the emptied sauce-pan, cover them with cold water, and let them boil for five minutes, when they should be poured out and strained, and the sauce-pan thoroughly cleansed.

Melt then in the sauce-pan the butter, add to it the flour, and by degrees the strained stock; and when this boils, add the mace, the flour, and the mushrooms, and allow all to cook together for twenty minutes longer.

Remove now the mace, and at the last moment add the cream. Serve on a large hot platter.

NOTE.—If the canned mushrooms are used, they will be found already prepared; but if the fresh ones are preferred, or are found more convenient, they must be skinned before using.

Rolled Shoulder of Mutton.—One shoulder of mutton, three ounces of butter, one tea-spoonful of salt, one salt-spoonful of pepper, three table-spoonfuls of bread crumbs, one and one-half ounce of chopped suet, one table-spoonful of chopped parsley, one egg, one gill of cold water.

It is desirable that the mutton should be boned by the butcher, but should this office fall to the cook, it is easiest done by placing the mutton with the skin side to the table, and with a sharp knife making an incision that will enable the bone to be firmly taken hold of. Proceed then very carefully to separate the bone from the flesh, exercising caution not to break the outer skin.

When this is accomplished, prepare the dressing. Begin this by mixing in a bowl the pepper, salt, bread crumbs, and suet. Add to this the chopped parsley, and bind all together with the egg. Place this dressing into the shoulder where the bone has been removed, and roll the meat into a neat roll, tying it loosely around with twine, as the bread in the stuffing swells, and room must be allowed for this.

Now melt the butter in a sauce-pan. When it is hot, put in the shoulder, cover it closely, and allow it to cook for one hour and a half. During this time of cooking the meat should be frequently basted, and turned occasionally, that it may brown evenly on all sides.

When ready for serving, put the meat upon a large hot platter, pour the grease out of the sauce-pan, and pour in its stead a gill of cold water. Stir the water well around, and scrape with the spoon the bottom of the pan, that all of the browned juices may be collected; and when this liquor boils, pour it over the mutton, and serve at once.

Windham Cutlets.—Five mutton cutlets from the back rib, one gill of second stock, one carrot, one turnip, one small piece of celery, one onion, one pound of mashed potatoes, yolks of two eggs, one ounce of butter, one half ounce of flour, one and one-half gill of cold water, one half table-spoonful of Worcestershire sauce, one half table-spoonful of catchup, six drops of caramel, one tea-spoonful of salt, one half tea-spoonful of pepper, one pint of green pease.

Trim all of the fat from the cutlets, and leave a half an inch of the bone bare at the top of each one. Place them then in a copper frying-pan, and slice over them the carrot and turnip, onion and celery, adding also the pepper and salt. Pour over all the second stock, and put the pan over a slow fire, allowing the contents to cook for twenty minutes, turning the cutlets meantime in order that they may cook evenly through. While they are cooking, rub the potatoes through a sieve to make sure that they are perfectly smooth, when they must be put into a sauce-pan, the yolks of egg dropped into them, and stirred over the fire until the eggs are rendered dry by the action of heat.

When the cutlets are ready, take a fifth part of the potatoes so prepared, and flattened with a knife upon a mixing-board to the thickness of a quarter of an inch, and roll in this one of the cutlets, leaving the bone bare as a handle. Envelop each of the cutlets in its blanket of potato prepared in this way; and when this is done, lay all of them upon a baking-tin, lightly greased, brush them over with a little milk or egg, and brown them in a very quick oven.

While they are browning, stir into the frying-pan the butter, place it over the fire, and add thereto the flour, when the cold water should be put in, and all stirred until boiling. Put then with this the catchup, Worcestershire sauce, and caramel, and allow the whole to cook for two minutes.

Arrange the cutlets now in a circle upon a hot platter, fill into the centre a pint of boiled green pease, and pour the brown sauce around the whole through a strainer, to keep out the vegetables that have been used to flavour it.

NOTES.—In preparing the potato envelope, a little flour should be sprinkled over the board to prevent sticking.

If, by any accident, the oven should not be hot enough to brown the cutlets quickly, this may be done by holding over them a heated fire-shovel, as leaving them long in the oven dries out the potatoes, and so spoils the dish.

The sauce is made in the frying-pan in preference to a fresh one, in order that it may partake of both the flavour of the vegetables and of the juices of the meat, which adhere to the pan in the process of cooking.

Mutton Soubise.—Five mutton chops, three table-spoonfuls of bread crumbs, one egg, two Spanish onions, one ounce of flour, one half-pint of milk, one salt-spoonful of salt, one half salt-spoonful of pepper, two ounces of butter, one ounce of clarified fat, two carrots, one turnip.

First throw the onions into boiling water to draw out the greenness, and then allow them to stand in the soak overnight. When ready to prepare the dish, throw the onions again into boiling water, and let them boil in it for half an hour. Cut the carrot and turnip into small balls with a French vegetable-cutter, and throw these also into boiling water, letting them boil for twenty minutes. Prepare the cutlets then by trimming the fat off and dipping them into a well-beaten egg, when the bread crumbs should be put into a sheet of kitchen-paper, seasoned with a little pepper and salt, and the cutlets rolled from side to side therein until well covered. After the cutlets have been rolled thus in the bread crumbs, the coating should be pressed on firmly and smoothly with the blade of a knife; and when the clarified fat has been heated in a frying-pan until the blue smoke arises from it, the cutlets should be dropped one by one therein, and cooked for seven minutes, turning them once in the pan while frying.

While the cutlets are cooking, the onions should be taken from the boiling water and chopped very finely. Put them then into a dry sauce-pan, and mix them together with an ounce of flour, add by degrees the milk, pepper, and salt, when the sauce-pan must be placed over the fire and its contents stirred until the milk boils. When boiling, add the butter, letting all cook together for two minutes.

The cutlets should now be arranged in a circle upon a hot platter, the turnip and carrot filled into the centre, and the soubise poured around the whole.

Ragout of Rabbit.—One rabbit, one quarter of a pound of bacon, one tea-spoonful of mixed dried herbs, six small mushrooms, one very small onion, one tea-spoonful of salt, juice of one-half of a lemon, two ounces of flour, one table-spoonful of Harvey's sauce, one wine-glassful of sherry, one gill of stock.

The rabbit must first lie for an hour in strong salt and water, after which it should be cut into convenient pieces and dried thoroughly in a towel.

The bacon should then be cut into dice, and, putting it into a stew-pan and over a hot fire, fried until it is brown. Take out now the browned bacon, and substituting the pieces of rabbit therefor, fry these also until brown, sprinkling in the flour as they cook, which helps them to a fine colour.

While the meats are browning, the mushrooms and onion should be chopped exceedingly fine, almost to a powder, and this sprinkled over the browned rabbit, also the salt, pepper, and herbs. Stir all well together, then squeeze over it the lemon-juice, adding also the Harvey's sauce, sherry, and last of all the stock.

Cook slowly for one hour, stirring constantly meantime, as the perfection of this preparation lies in preserving its exceeding dryness without letting it burn.

NOTE.—Only a young rabbit is suitable for this dish, as an old one requires too long for the cooking.

The bacon is used for this preparation because of the fine flavour which it imparts, but butter may be substituted for it in cooking the rabbit, if more convenient or desirable.

Stewed Kidney.—One pair of ox-kidneys, one ounce of butter, one and one-half ounce of flour, one half ounce of flour of rice, three gills of second stock, one tea-spoonful of salt, one half tea-spoonful of pepper, one dessert-spoonful of mushroom catchup, six drops of caramel.

Begin by washing the kidneys thoroughly in cold water. Dry them well in a towel, and cut into very thin slices. Prepare upon a plate the flour, pepper, and salt, into which dip each piece separately; and melting the butter in a frying-pan, when the blue smoke arises brown the kidney therein.

As the pieces of kidney become brown, remove them from the butter into a stew-pan, and when all are thus transferred, put the stock into the frying-pan, and stir until it boils. When boiling, pour the stock over the kidney in the stew-pan, and let all cook over a very slow fire for an hour and a half. At the end of this time, put the flour of rice into a bowl, moisten it with the catchup, add the caramel, and pouring this into the stew-pan with the kidneys, cook all together for half an hour longer. Serve in a covered dish.

Braised Fillet of Veal.—Three pounds of fillet of veal, one quarter of a pound of fat bacon, one and one-half pint of stock, one carrot, one turnip, one head of celery, one tea-spoonful of whole white pepper, one tea-spoonful of salt.

Cut the bacon into thin strips about two inches in length and one-third of an inch in width. Place next the fillet upon a board, and with a sharp knife take off the skin, then threading a larding-needle with the bacon, lard the top of the fillet with it as thickly as possible. When the veal is larded, cut the vegetables into small pieces and put them into a braising or ordinary copper stew-pan. Pour over them then the stock, add to this the pepper-corns and salt, and lay the fillet upon the vegetables, which should be arranged thickly enough to lift the meat quite above the stock. Place the braising-pan now over a quick fire, and baste the fillet constantly until the stock boils. Cover the fillet then with a sheet of greased kitchen-paper cut to the size of the braising-pan, close the lid of the pan, and place it in a quick oven, where it must remain for an hour and a quarter. While in the oven, the lid of the pan and the paper covering should be raised and the fillet basted at frequent intervals with the stock.

At the expiration of the hour and a quarter, remove the fillet to a hot platter and put the braising-pan over a quick fire, until the stock is reduced to half the quantity, when it should be poured through a strainer around the meat and all hurried quickly to the table.

NOTE.—The secret of successful larding lies in cutting the strips of bacon long, and taking a deep, long stitch with the larding-needle.

Browned Rabbit.—One rabbit, six thin slices of bacon, one laurel leaf, one sprig of thyme, one table-spoonful of chopped parsley, one table-spoonful of flour, one and one half glasses of brandy, one tea-spoonful of salt, one salt-spoonful of pepper, one gill of stock.

Cut the rabbit in neat joints, and sprinkle over them the flour. Place in a frying-pan the bacon, and cook it slightly on both sides; take them out of the frying-pan and place them in a stew-pan. The pieces of rabbit must now be placed in the frying-pan and browned to a nice light brown. As each piece browns, remove it and place it in the stew-pan; add the thyme, laurel leaf, and parsley. Pour now into the frying-pan the stock, pepper, and salt, and stir all over the fire till boiling. When boiling, pour this over the rabbit in the stew-pan, add the brandy, and allow all to simmer very slowly for one hour.

Remove the pieces of rabbit, place them on a dish, and strain the gravy over.

Rabbits Stewed in White Sauce.—Two young rabbits, one pint white stock, two onions, the rind of half a lemon, one gill of cream, one ounce of butter, half an ounce of flour, the juice of half a lemon, one tea-spoonful of salt, one salt-spoonful of pepper.

Cut the rabbits in small neat joints; do not use the heads or necks. Place the pieces in a basin, and cover them well with boiling water; allow the rabbits to soak for one hour. Place the stock in the sauce-pan, and allow it to boil; take the pieces of rabbit, one by one, from the water in which they have been soaking and add them to the boiling stock. Draw the pan on one side, add the pepper and salt, also the rind of lemon and the onions, and allow all to simmer very slowly for two hours. Melt now in a small sauce-pan the butter, add the flour, and, when well mixed, pour in by degrees the cream; stir all together till boiling, then take the pan from the fire. Remove now the pieces of rabbit from the larger sauce-pan and place them on a hot dish. Add the flour, butter, and cream to the stock, stir all over the fire till boiling; draw the pan from the fire, add the lemon-juice, shake the pan a little, and pour all quickly over the pieces of rabbit.

Curried Rabbit.—One rabbit, one and one-half ounce of butter, one dessert-spoonful of curry-powder, six mushrooms, one table-spoonful of flour, three gills of stock, one gill of cream, two onions, one tea-spoonful of salt, one salt-spoonful of pepper.

Skin the onions, place them in a basin, cover them with boiling water, and let them soak over night.

Cut the rabbit in neat joints, and roll each piece in the flour. Take the onions from the water, dry them well, slice them very thinly; melt in a stew-pan the butter, and when the smoke rises from it, put in the pieces of onion and brown them to a pale brown. Pour the butter now into a basin through a strainer, so as to keep out the pieces of onion. Pour the butter back into the stew-pan, heat it again, and put in the pieces of rabbit to brown; when they are browned, sprinkle over the curry-powder, pour over the stock, and stir all till boiling. Skim well, and then add the browned onion, salt, and pepper. Draw the pan on one side, and allow all to simmer very slowly for one hour and a half. Just before serving add the cream. Serve in the centre of a dish with a wall of boiled rice round.*

Rabbit Pie.—One rabbit, two eggs, one quarter pound bacon, one half pint of stock, six forcemeat balls, one tea-spoonful of salt, one half tea-spoonful of pepper.

Cut the rabbit in small neat pieces, place the pieces in a basin with a large tea-spoonful of salt, cover them with cold water, and let them soak for two hours. Boil the eggs for ten minutes, remove the shells, cut them in slices. Slice very thinly the bacon, and place it in a pie-dish. Take the pieces of rabbit from the water, dry them in a towel, and lay them on the top of the bacon in the pie-dish; lay round the sides the forcemeat balls,† sprinkle over the salt and pepper, pour over the stock, and over all place the slices of egg. Cover the dish with flaky crust, directions for which see page 195.

Veal Pie.—Two pounds fillet of veal, five ounces of bread crumb, three ounces of suet, one tea-spoonful chopped parsley, one tea-spoonful dried herbs, two eggs, two ounces lean ham, one tea-spoonful of salt, one half tea-spoonful of pepper, one grain cayenne, one half pint of stock.

Remove all skin from the suet, place it on a board, and chop it very finely. Wash well the parsley, put it in the corner of a towel, wring it very dry, then chop it finely also; chop finely the ham. Place now in a basin the bread

---

* See directions for boiled rice on page 237.
† Directions for forcemeat balls, see page 65.

crumb, add the suet, parsley, and ham; season with the salt, pepper, and cayenne; add now the herbs, stir all well together, and bind with the eggs. Cut now in pieces about four inches square the veal; roll into each piece an equal quantity of the stuffing, place the rolls in a pie-dish, and pour over the stock. Cover the pie-dish with rough puff paste, directions for which see page 197.

Pigeons and Tomatoes.—One pair of pigeons, one quarter pound bacon, one half quart tin of tomatoes, one gill cream, one ounce butter, one ounce flour, one gill stock, one tea-spoonful salt, one salt-spoonful pepper.

Draw and wash thoroughly the pigeons; cut off the heads and necks, also the toes at first joints. Twist the wings behind the shoulders. Thread a trussing-needle with twine, pass the needle through the under part of the wing, then through the top of one leg straight through the body, through the top of the other leg, then through the under part of the remaining wing. Turn the pigeon on its breast, pass the needle through the top of the wing, through the skin at the neck, then through the top of the remaining wing. Tie the two ends of the twine closely together; cross the legs at the bottom of the breast, then tie them tightly together. Cut now in small square pieces the bacon, place the pieces in a stew-pan, place the pan over the fire until the bacon takes a pale-brown colour. Place then in the pan the pigeons, and brown them all over; add now the tomatoes, salt, pepper, and stock, and allow all to cook very slowly for an hour and a half. Remove the pigeons, and pass the tomatoes and stock through a coarse wire sieve. Melt in the stew-pan the butter, add the flour, and stir both well together; pour in then the tomatoes and stock, stir all till boiling, skim well, add the pigeons, cook slowly ten minutes longer, and at the last moment before serving add the cream.

Duck with Green Pease.—One young duck, one pint of green pease, one tea-spoonful of salt, one half tea-spoonful of pepper, one half pint of stock, two ounces of butter.

Draw and truss the duck. Melt in a large stew-pan the butter, and when it smokes place in the duck breast downwards. When both sides of the breast are browned turn it over, and brown the legs and back; this takes about twenty minutes. Add then the stock, and when it boils skim it well; add the pepper and salt, and allow this to cook for three-quarters of an hour very slowly. Add then the pease, and cook all twenty minutes longer.

Turkey Stuffed with Chestnuts.—One turkey, four ounces of butter, one ounce of flour, three gills of stock, one dessert-spoonful mushroom catchup, one dessert-spoonful Worcester sauce, one half tea-spoonful of salt, one half salt-spoonful of pepper, one quarter pound bread crumb, one table-spoonful chopped parsley, one gill of milk, the yolks of four eggs, thirty chestnuts, one salt-spoonful grated nutmeg.

Place in a baking-tin the chestnuts, place the tin in the oven, and bake the chestnuts for half an hour; remove the skins, keeping the chestnuts as whole as possible. Soak in a basin for half an hour the bread crumb and milk, then melt in a sauce-pan two ounces of the butter, add the soaked bread crumb, also the chopped parsley, nutmeg, pepper, and salt. Stir over the fire until very hot, then drawing the pan from the fire, drop in one by one the yolks of egg. Stir all well together, then add the chestnuts. Again place over the fire and stir all till a firm paste. Draw, singe, and truss the turkey; put the above stuffing into the crop before folding the skin over the neck. Place the turkey as close to the fire as possible for the first fifteen minutes, then allow it to cook more slowly for an hour and a quarter, basting frequently during this time. While the turkey is roasting, place the giblets in a small pan of cold water; put the pan on the fire and boil them slowly for three-quarters of an hour. Take them from the water, and placing them on a board, chop them very finely. Melt now in a small sauce-pan the remainder of the butter, stir in the flour, add by degrees the stock, and stir all till boiling. Add the catchup and Worcester sauce, also the chopped giblets, and boil slowly five minutes.

When the turkey is cooked take it from the fire, place it on a very hot dish, remove the twine, and send the sauce to table in a small tureen.

NOTE.—Directions for trussing, see page 48. Good beef dripping is best to baste the turkey with.

Browned Calf's Head.—One calf's head, one tablespoonful chopped parsley, one half dessert-spoonful lemon-thyme, two table-spoonfuls bread crumb, one quarter pound bacon, one lemon, the yolk of one egg.

Soak the calf's head in sufficient cold water to cover it for two hours. Wash it well, place it in a large sauce-pan, cover it well with cold water. Place the pan over a very hot fire, and when the water boils skim it well. Allow the water then to boil very gently for one hour and a half. Take the head from the water, dry it well with a clean towel, place it on a flat dish, and score it with a sharp knife. Dip an egg-brush in the yolk of egg and brush the head well over, sprinkle over the thyme and parsley, also the bread crumb. Place the dish in a brisk oven and bake the head for twenty minutes. While it is baking, cut the bacon in very thin slices, roll each slice up and put it on a small baking-tin. Place the tin in the oven and bake the bacon for ten minutes. When the head is nicely browned, arrange round it alternately the rolls of bacon and pieces of the lemon thinly sliced.

Forcemeat Balls.—Three ounces of ham, three ounces of suet, five ounces of bread crumb, one tea-spoonful of lemon-juice, one tea-spoonful of chopped parsley, one half tea-spoonful of salt, one salt-spoonful of pepper, two eggs, one grain of cayenne.

Place the ham on a board and chop it finely, remove the skin from the suet and chop it finely also; place both in a basin, mix them well together, then add the salt and pepper, the cayenne and eggs. Place over the basin a wire sieve, rub the bread crumb through, then stir all to a consistency; add last of all the lemon-juice.

Roll this mixture into small balls about the size of a large nutmeg. Have in readiness some clarified fat; when the smoke rises drop them in one by one and allow them to cook for seven minutes.

Dressed Lamb's Head.—One lamb's head, three ounces of butter, two ounces of flour, one table-spoonful mushroom catchup, one table-spoonful Worcester sauce, one tea-spoonful salt, one half tea-spoonful pepper, one table-spoonful bread crumb, the yolk of one egg.

Wash well the lamb's head, also the lights, heart, and liver. Saw through the skull of the head, and place the head, liver, lights, and heart in a large pan of cold water. Place the pan over a very hot fire, and when the water boils skim it well; draw the pan on one side, and allow all to simmer very slowly for one hour. Take the head from the pan of water, split it open and lay it on a baking-tin, brush the cheeks over with the yolk of egg, and sprinkle over the bread crumb.

Place now on a board the heart and lights, and chop both very finely; grate the liver on to a plate with a carrot-grater, or rub it through a wire sieve. Melt now in a sauce-pan the butter, stir into it the flour, add by degrees three gills of the liquor in which the head was boiled, stir all till boiling, then add the catchup and Worcester sauce, also the chopped lights, and heart, and the grated liver. Draw the pan on one side, and cook all slowly twenty minutes. While this is cooking, place the baking-tin into the oven and bake the head twenty minutes. When ready, place the head on a hot dish and pour the contents of the sauce-pan round.

Minced Collops.—Two pounds steak from the round, one ounce of dripping, one and one-half ounce of flour, one half pint cold water, one table-spoonful mushroom catchup, one tea-spoonful salt, one half tea-spoonful pepper.

Place the steak on a board and chop it very finely, melt

in a stew-pan the dripping; when the smoke rises from it, place in the chopped steak, and with the back of a wooden spoon constantly stir it until well browned. By degrees as the steak browns sprinkle over the flour, which enables the steak to brown more quickly. When browned add the catchup, stock, pepper, and salt. Stir all till boiling, and allow all to simmer very slowly for half an hour.

Mutton Cutlets.—Four or five mutton cutlets, four table-spoonfuls bread crumbs, one egg, one tea-spoonful salt, one quarter tea-spoonful pepper, two ounces clarified fat.

Procure the cutlets from the best end of the neck; cut all the bones an equal length. Trim the cutlets neatly, leaving half an inch of the bone bare. Place a sheet of kitchen-paper on the table, and rub through a wire sieve on to it the bread crumbs. Mix with the bread crumbs the pepper and salt. Beat well on a plate the egg, dip one by one the cutlets into it, then roll them in the bread crumbs. Smooth each cutlet neatly with a knife, dip each one a second time in the beaten egg, and roll each a second time in the bread crumbs. Heat in a frying-pan the clarified fat. When it begins to smoke place in one by one the cutlets, and cook them for four minutes on each side. Serve in a circle on a hot dish; pour round a brown sauce, directions for which see page 176.

MEATS.—FOURTH DIVISION.
COLD-MEAT DISHES.

Rissoles.—Three-quarters of a pound of cold roast beef, one table-spoonful of chopped parsley, one tea-spoonful of salt, one half tea-spoonful of pepper, one salt-spoonful of grated nutmeg, one table-spoonful of milk, one egg, twelve ounces of flour, four ounces of butter, one tea-spoonful of baking-powder, one and one-half gill of cold water, three ounces of vermicelli.

Chop the cold meat very finely, the fat and lean together, place it into a bowl with the pepper, nutmeg, and nearly all of the salt, and stir together with the milk. Put the flour now upon a mixing-board, rub into it the butter, add the baking-powder and remaining salt, mixing all into a firm dough with the cold water. When the dough is mixed, knead and roll it out to about a quarter of an inch thickness, cut it then into rounds with a biscuit-cutter, beat the egg until very light and brush the edges of the rounds with it. Put now into the centre of these rounds as much of the minced meat as the crust can be made to cover, gather up the edges of the dough over the meat and pinch them firmly together.

When the rounds are all filled, roll them separately into the beaten egg, crush the vermicelli to a powder, put it upon a sheet of kitchen-paper and roll the rissoles by turns in this, until thoroughly blanketed with the powder.

Cook now in hot clarified fat for five minutes, putting in only a part of the rissoles at a time, as the fat will be too much cooled by plunging all in at once.

When taken from the fat, drain the rissoles upon a clean piece of kitchen-paper, and serve them in a hot napkin, garnishing with sprigs of parsley.

NOTE.—When clarified fat or lard is used for frying, care must be taken that what is used for fish and sweets be kept distinct.

Curry.—Three-quarters of a pound of cold mutton, two ounces of butter, one onion, one half ounce of flour, one dessert-spoonful of curry-powder, one apple, one half pint of second stock, one half tea-spoonful of salt, one half tea-spoonful of pepper.

Melt first the butter in a sauce-pan, and brown in it to a very pale brown the sliced onion. Stir into this the curry-powder and flour, and when all is thoroughly mixed, add to the mixture by degrees the stock.

Stir now carefully until boiling, and when this point is reached grate the apple and add it also.

Put on then the lid of the sauce-pan, and allow all to simmer slowly for ten minutes; in the meantime, cut the mutton into slices, drop it slice by slice into this boiling sauce, and allow it to cook just long enough to heat the meat through, when the sauce-pan must at once be removed from the fire and the preparation served.

NOTE.—The great fault in preparing cold meats for a second serving lies in losing sight of the fact that the meat is already cooked to a turn, and allowing it to remain too long exposed to the drying and toughening action of heat in the second preparation.

Cold Boiled Mutton with Tomato Sauce.—Three-quarters of a pound of cold mutton, one pint of cold stewed tomatoes, two ounces of butter, one half ounce of flour, one half tea-spoonful of pepper, one half tea-spoonful of salt, one tea-spoonful of sugar, one grain of cayenne, one gill of second stock.

First cut the mutton into slices, place them neatly into the bottom of a flat vegetable dish, and season each piece lightly with the salt, pepper, and cayenne. Melt then the butter and make it hot, when half should be poured over the meat; and into what remains stir the flour, adding to it, when smooth, the stock. When this mixture boils add to it the sugar, the remainder of the seasoning and the tomatoes, and let all cook for two minutes, that the tomatoes may become very hot, when the sauce should be poured over the mutton and the whole covered tightly until taken to the table.

NOTES.—It should be remembered that all highly-seasoned dishes, particularly those in which pepper predominates, should be served very hot.

When cold tomatoes are not in the larder, either fresh or canned ones may be prepared for the above use.

Corned Beef Hash.—One pound of chopped corned beef, three-quarters of a pound of boiled potatoes, two ounces of butter, one gill of stock, one tea-spoonful of pepper, one half tea-spoonful of salt, one Spanish onion.

Before chopping the meat trim away and remove all the skin and gristle, that all substances likely to present hard lumps may be taken out. Chop then the potatoes, taking care that they do not become too fine or a mashed paste, and mix them together with the meat in the chopping-bowl. Chop the onion then finely, and brown it to a pale brown in the butter; when brown, add to it the stock, and, when this is hot, the chopped corned beef and potatoes; season all with the pepper and salt, and stir over the fire until very hot.

Serve this hash banked up in a hot flat dish, with a piece of butter let into a hole made by the print of a spoon-bowl in the top.

NOTES.—Cold roast beef may also be used in this way, and pieces of cold beef-steak as well; and a delicious, juicy hash can be made after this method, for those who enjoy rare meats, by substituting raw steak minced for the cold cooked meats.

Potatoes are best for this use that are a little underdone, as when hard they mince without mashing, and so retain their character.

Cornish Pasties. — Three-quarters of a pound of cold beef-steak, one half pound of raw potatoes, one Spanish onion, one salt-spoonful of pepper, one tea-spoonful of salt, one pound of flour, four ounces of beef-suet, one tea-spoonful of baking-powder, one half pint of cold water.

Cover the potatoes in a sauce-pan with cold water, and bring the water to the boiling-point, and when this is reached take out the potatoes and cut them into small square pieces. Put the pieces upon a plate and shred over them the onion, add to these the steak, which must also be cut into small square pieces, and sprinkle over all the pepper and nearly all of the salt.

Toss these all now together with a fork, then place the suet upon a board and chop it very finely, mix well with it the flour, baking-powder, and the remainder of the salt, and make these into a light dough with the cold water.

Cut the dough then into six or eight pieces, roll each piece out round and to a quarter of an inch thickness, brush the edges of the rounds with a little cold water, and put into each an equal part of the meat mixture, gather up the edges of the crust and pinch them firmly together, brush each over with a little egg or milk, and bake them in a quick oven three-quarters of an hour.

Shepherd's Pie.—One pound of cold roast beef, one Spanish onion, one and one-half ounce of butter, one half ounce of flour, one pound of mashed potatoes, one table-spoonful of catchup, one half gill of cold water, one tea-spoonful of pepper, one tea-spoonful of salt.

Mince the meat very finely, and melt then in a sauce-pan half an ounce of the butter, throw into it the minced meat, and brown it well, keeping the meat moving all the time to prevent its lumping. While this is doing sprinkle the flour in by degrees, both to help the browning and to thicken the composition. Add then the pepper, salt, and water, and stir all until boiling, when the onion must be sliced and put in. Draw the sauce-pan now to one side of the fire, in order that it may keep hot without cooking, and taking another sauce-pan, melt in it the remainder of the butter, add to it the gill of milk, and when this boils throw into it the mashed potatoes, and stir all together until the potatoes are very hot.

Place then into a pie dish a layer of the potatoes, add the catchup to the minced meat and cover the potatoes with a layer of it, and so alternating the meat and potatoes, fill all into the dish, leaving a last layer of potato at the top. When this is done dip a knife into milk and smooth this top covering with the blade of it, and place it in a moderate oven for half an hour to bake, watching that the potatoes at the top brown handsomely.

NOTE.—Veal, mutton, or cold beef-steak may be used for this pie as well as the roast beef.

Sausage Rolls.—One half pound of cold pork, four leaves of sage, and one half salt-spoonful of pepper, one grain of cayenne, twelve ounces of flour, four ounces of butter, one egg, one and one-half gill of cold water, one tea-spoonful of baking-powder, one tea-spoonful of salt.

The pork must be chopped very finely, also the sage leaves, which are to be well mixed with the meat. Season this with the pepper, half of the salt, and the cayenne. Put now the flour upon a mixing-board, and rub into it the butter, add to it the baking-powder and remaining salt; and making a little well in the centre of this mixture, drop into it the yolk of the egg, pour over it the water, knead all lightly together, and roll the dough so formed out to the thickness of a quarter of an inch. Cut this paste into pieces four inches long and three wide, beat the white of the egg slightly, and brush the edges of the paste with it.

Put now into each of these pieces a portion of the chopped pork, gather together the edges of the crust around it and pinch them firmly together. Brush each one over with a little of the egg, place them into a lightly-floured baking-tin, and put them to bake in a hot oven for half an hour.

Veal Balls.—One half pound of cold veal, eight table-spoonfuls of bread crumbs, two table-spoonfuls of chopped parsley, one tea-spoonful of mixed dried herbs, one half salt-spoonful of pepper, one tea-spoonful of salt, one salt-spoonful of grated nutmeg, two eggs.

Put six table-spoonfuls of the bread crumbs into a bowl, and chopping the veal finely, mix it therewith. Season this with the pepper and salt, adding the nutmeg, also the parsley and herbs, after which the whole must be thoroughly mixed together. To give this consistency, drop in the yolks of the two eggs, saving the whites separate upon a plate.

Roll the mixture now into small balls, using an ounce of flour upon the hands to prevent sticking. Beat the whites of the eggs then slightly, roll the balls therein, and placing the remaining bread crumbs in a paper roll them also in it. Throw them now into smoking clarified fat for four minutes, when they should be taken out and put to drain on kitchen-paper, after which pile in orderly manner upon a hot napkin for serving.

Cold Turkey with White Sauce.—One half pound of

cold turkey, two ounces of butter, one ounce of flour, one half tea-spoonful of white pepper, one half tea-spoonful of salt, one half pint of milk, one gill of cream, one salt-spoonful of grated nutmeg.

The turkey must first be boned, the skin having been removed, and the fragments then cut into small even pieces. Melt in a copper or porcelain-lined sauce-pan the butter, mix well with it the flour, and add by degrees the milk, stirring all until it boils. When boiling put in the cream, pepper, salt, and nutmeg, also the pieces of turkey, taking great care not to break up the meat in the process, and let all simmer together very slowly until the turkey is heated through.

Serve very hot on a small platter, with sippits of toast or fried bread.

NOTES.—Cold veal or chicken may also be used in this way.

A copper or porcelain-lined sauce-pan should always be used in the preparation of white meats, as anything but a very bright vessel is sure to cause them to discolour.

Minced Chicken with Potato Wall. — Three-quarter pound of cold chicken, two ounces of butter, one half ounce of flour, one table-spoonful of Worcestershire sauce, one half gill of second stock, six drops of caramel, one pound of potatoes, one table-spoonful of cream, one egg, one half tea-spoonful of salt, one half salt-spoonful of pepper.

Begin with chopping the cold chicken very fine, melt then in a sauce-pan one ounce of the butter, and when this is hot put into it the cold chicken and brown thoroughly; add to this the flour and the stock, stirring all until it boils, when it must be seasoned with the pepper and salt, and the Worcestershire sauce and caramel thrown in; then covering the sauce-pan, draw it aside from the fire, that it may keep an even heat but not cook.

The potatoes must now be boiled and rubbed through a wire sieve while hot, and when so floured return them to the sauce-pan, add the cream, the remainder of the butter and the egg, and stir all well over the fire until the butter is melted and the egg dry.

Arrange the potato mixture then in a circle upon a hot platter, leaving a round hole in the centre, smooth it with a knife, and place in the centre the minced chicken and serve.

Note.—If it is desired, the potato wall may be browned before the chicken is put in; but if this is done at all, it must be done in a very hot oven, otherwise the potato will dry out and become tough and heavy.

Cold Meat Shape.—One pound of cold meat, two ounces of macaroni, one tea-cupful of bread crumbs, one ounce of butter, one egg, one table-spoonful of stock, one tea-spoonful of salt, one half salt-spoonful of pepper.

Chop the cold meat very finely, put it into a basin when done, and season with the pepper and salt. Wash the macaroni well in cold water, and boil it for half an hour. Drain it then thoroughly, and cut into inch lengths, when it must be mixed together with the chopped meat and bread crumbs, and separating the butter into small pieces, mix that in also. Bind all now together with the egg and the stock, and when thoroughly mixed together, pack the mixture into a well-greased basin or bowl, and steam the contents for one hour.

Notes.—The macaroni must be put on the fire in cold water and boiled rapidly.

By steaming it is meant that the bowl or basin, covered with a piece of kitchen-paper, should be placed in a sauce-pan within which is sufficient water to reach half-way up its sides, and allowed thus to cook in its own steam. Any kind of cold meat except pork can be used for this preparation.

Savoury Hash.—Three quarters of a pound of cold meat, one Spanish onion, one ounce of butter, one ounce of flour, one tea-spoonful of salt, one half salt-spoonful of pepper, one dessert-spoonful of catchup, one dessert-spoonful of Harvey's sauce, one half pint of second stock, one carrot, one turnip.

Clean and chop fine both the carrot and turnip, when they must be put to boil in a small sauce-pan with boiling water until tender, which will take about twenty minutes. While these are cooking, melt the butter in a separate sauce-pan, brown in it the onion sliced; then cutting into slices the cold meat, roll them in the flour, and placing these slices in the butter with the onion, brown them slightly also. Pour over this now the stock, the Harvey's sauce and catchup, stir all together gently until the stock boils, and season with the pepper and the salt.

When the pieces of meat have become thoroughly heated through, arrange them in a flat dish, and pour the gravy over. Strain the water carefully from the turnip and carrot, lest by after-draining it impoverish the gravy, and pile them high upon the top of the pieces of meat when it is ready for serving.

NOTES.—Cold roast beef or cold beef-steak is best for this dish, but any other cold meat may be used.

[The weighing of the cold meats is given merely in order to fix proportions.]

Cold Chicken.—One-half of a cold chicken, four table-spoonfuls of bread crumbs, one egg, one ounce of butter, half an ounce of flour, one gill of milk, one gill of cream, one salt-spoonful of salt, one salt-spoonful of pepper.

Place on the fire to heat a sauce-pan half filled with clarified fat, and while it is heating, beat the egg on a plate until very light. Cut the chicken or turkey into neat pieces, and dip them in the beaten egg, taking care that each piece gets well covered.

Place on a sheet of paper the bread crumbs, season it with a little salt and pepper, lift one by one the pieces of fowl, place them on the crumbs, and roll the paper from side to side so as to get the fowl well covered with the crumbs.

When the fat in the sauce-pan is hot enough, throw the pieces of fowl one by one into it, and the instant each piece takes a pale-brown colour, remove them, and lay them for a second on a sheet of paper, to strain from them the grease.

Place the fowl now on a hot dish, and melt in a small pan the butter. When melted, stir in the flour; and when both are well mixed, add by degrees the milk. When this mixture boils, add the cream, and cook for two minutes longer. Add to this sauce the remainder of the salt and pepper, pour it over the browned fowl, and serve very hot.

NOTE.—Before frying the chicken, it would be well to glance at the directions for frying given in page 26.

Minced Cold Veal.—One pound of cold veal, rind of one lemon, one gill second stock, one gill milk or cream, one salt-spoonful grated nutmeg, one half tea-spoonful salt, one salt-spoonful pepper, two ounces bread crumbs, one of butter.

Mince very finely the cold veal, season it with the grated lemon rind, nutmeg, pepper, and salt.

Place the seasoned veal in a stew-pan, pour over it the milk or cream and stock, place the sauce-pan on the fire, stir well the contents until boiling; then all must cook slowly ten minutes.

Pour the mixture then into a pie-dish, sprinkle over the bread crumbs, and place over the top the butter in small pieces. Place the pie-dish in a hot oven or before the fire, and brown the top quickly.

NOTE.—Underdone veal is best for this; beef may also be re-cooked in the same manner.

MEATS.—FIFTH DIVISION.
BROILED AND FRIED.

Broiled Kidneys with Maître d'Hotel Butter.—Six sheep kidneys, two table-spoonfuls of bread crumbs, three ounces of butter, one half tea-spoonful of salt, one half salt-spoonful of pepper, one dessert-spoonful of chopped **parsley,** one tea-spoonful of lemon-juice.

The kidneys should first be washed, and the thin outer skin torn entirely off them. Separate them then through the back opposite the seam with a sharp knife, cutting them almost through in order that they may be spread out flatly; when, melting one ounce of the butter, each kidney should be dipped therein, a skewer passed through each leaf, and the kidney straightened thereon, and sprinkling over each of them a little of the bread crumbs, put them upon a gridiron, and broil over a very hot fire.

While the kidneys are broiling, put together the chopped parsley, lemon-juice, and butter, and rub all together with the point of a knife blade. Take the kidneys when done quickly from the broiler, arrange them upon a dish of buttered toast, sprinkle over each a little pepper and salt, and place in the centre of each a little of the maître d'hotel butter.

Broiled Beef-steak.—One porter-house steak, two ounces of butter, one tea-spoonful of salt, one salt-spoonful of pepper.

The steak should hang for one week in the ice-box before using; and before broiling, place it upon a board and beat it with a round rolling-pin sufficient to soften the fibre without mutilating it or crushing out the juices. Put it then upon a gridiron, and at first over the hottest part of the fire, that the pores of the meat may be immediately closed; then turning constantly to prevent burning, broil from seven to ten minutes according to the thickness of the steak; and when done, remove it from the iron to a very hot platter, put the butter in pieces over the top, and press it in with the point of a knife blade, sprinkle over all the pepper and salt, and serve in its own gravy, of which the butter will have drawn out sufficient from the steak without adding water.

NOTE.—To this gravy may be added a table-spoonful of Worcestershire sauce if desired.

Mutton or lamb chops may be broiled also in this way.

Broiled Chicken.—One young fowl, two ounces of butter, one tea-spoonful of salt, one half salt-spoonful of pepper.

The fowl must first be split down the back, washed thoroughly in and out with cold water, and as thoroughly dried in a clean towel. Grease then slightly a broiler, season the chicken, inside and out, by rubbing on the pepper and salt, and putting the fowl in it, place to broil over a strong clear fire. As soon as the juices begin to draw out, commence turning, and turn constantly thereafter until the meat is done, which may be determined by running a skewer into the breast, and when this draws out easily, the chicken will have been sufficiently cooked. Serve on buttered toast, distributing butter also in pieces over the fowl, and send it to table very hot.

NOTE.—Unless a very young spring chicken is used for broiling, it will be better that the fowl should have a slight preparatory cooking by steaming, which may be done by putting the chicken into the broiler; and laying this over a baking-pan of boiling water, then covering it with a plate, set all into the oven for about twenty minutes.

If the broiling fire smokes in the least, throw upon it a handful of salt, which will at once clear it, and prevent the fowl tasting smoky.

Pork Sausages.—One pound of pork sausages, one and one-half pound of raw potatoes, one table-spoonful of cream, one ounce of butter, one tea-spoonful of salt, one half salt-spoonful of pepper.

Put the potatoes pared into a sauce-pan, cover them with cold water, and bringing them quickly to the boiling-point over a brisk fire, throw in the salt. Boil them now rapidly until they begin to break on the surface, when they will be half cooked, and the water should be strained carefully off them, the sauce-pan closely covered, and drawn to the side of the fire, that they may finish cooking in their own steam. When a skewer will go into them readily, set the potatoes for a moment, with the sauce-pan uncovered, full over the fire, that the dampness of the steam may dry off, and while hot, mash them finely, adding the cream, pepper, and butter, after which again cover them closely in order that they may keep hot while the sausages are being prepared.

Prick through the skin of the sausages now with a fork in various places, that they may not burst with the steam that will be generated in them under the action of heat, and placing them in a cold frying-pan, put them over a moderate fire, that the fat may draw out in which to cook them, and fry for ten minutes.

Take up then the potatoes, and fill them into the bottom of a small hot platter, and smooth them down with a knife blade that has been dipped in milk to a flat bed about an inch in thickness, and across this bed arrange the sausage lengths at regular intervals.

NOTE.—If the gravy from the pan is used at all, it must be served by itself in a gravy-boat.

Liver and Bacon.—One half pound of calf's liver, one half pound of bacon, one half ounce of flour, one half pint of second stock, one dessert-spoonful of mushroom catchup, six drops of caramel, one salt-spoonful of salt, one half salt-spoonful of pepper.

Having been very carefully washed, the liver must be cut into thin slices and dried in a towel. Next slice the bacon thinly, and cut off the rind; when it must be put into a frying-pan, placed over a moderate fire, and cooked for five minutes, turning it once meantime.

Take the bacon now from the pan, arrange it upon a hot platter, and place in the warming-oven to prevent its cooling.

In the grease drawn from the bacon put then the slices of liver, and fry for ten minutes, turning them once while frying. Remove the liver from the frying-pan to the platter containing the bacon, and stir into the pan the flour, into which stir the stock also, when the flour has become well saturated with the grease and browned.

Stir this mixture until it boils, when the catchup, pepper, salt, and caramel must be added, and the whole poured over the liver and bacon.

NOTE.—Sheep's liver may be used for this dish; but when it is used, it should be parboiled before frying.

Fried Chicken with Chives.—One young fowl, two dozen chives, two ounces of flour, two ounces of butter, one half tea-spoonful of salt, one half salt-spoonful of white pepper.

First prepare the chives by cleaning and cutting the green tops into thin rings; throw them then into boiling water to soak for five minutes, and while they are soaking joint the chicken and wash it lightly in cold water. Season the flour with the pepper and salt, and dip into it each piece of the fowl, and throw them into hot clarified fat, letting them fry for ten minutes. While the fowl is frying remove the chives from the boiling water, and dry them in a towel. Melt now in a frying-pan the butter, and fry in it the chives, taking care that they do not burn; then removing the joints of chicken from the fat, drain them for a moment upon a sheet of kitchen-paper, when they must be placed upon a hot platter, and the chives distributed over them.

MEATS.—SIXTH DIVISION.
GAME.

Jugged Hare.—One hare, one large onion, six cloves, two wine-glassfuls of port wine, two table-spoonfuls of mushroom catchup, the rind of one lemon, one dessert-spoonful of salt, one half tea-spoonful of pepper, three ounces of butter, one ounce of flour, ten forcemeat balls.

Cut in small, neat pieces the hare, dredge over each piece a little flour. Melt in a frying-pan two ounces of the butter; when the smoke rises from it, place in the pieces of hare, and brown them to a nice brown. As each piece is browned put it in a large brown jar; when all are put in add the lemon-rind, pepper, salt, and stock. Stick into the onion the cloves, add it also, put on the cover of the jar, and tie over it a strong piece of brown paper. Place the jar in a pan of boiling water, and allow the water to boil for four hours. At the end of this time place the remainder of the butter on a plate, add to it the flour, and with the point of a knife mix both well together.

Ten minutes before serving the hare, add the forcemeat balls, the port wine, catchup, also the butter and flour.*

Haunch of Venison.—Six pounds of venison, five ounces of butter, one half pint of claret, one half pint of cold water, one and one-half ounce of flour, six drops of caramel, one tea-spoonful of salt, one half tea-spoonful of pepper.

* Directions for Forcemeat Balls, see page 65.

Cover the venison with a double sheet of greased kitchen-paper, and secure it against slipping with a wrapping of twine. Place the meat in a roasting-pan, distribute over it upon the paper two ounces of the butter in small pieces, and putting the pan into a hot oven, roast the venison for one hour, basting from time to time as the butter melts.

At the end of this time cut the twine, and, removing the paper, rub over the meat the remainder of the butter.

Pour into the roasting-pan half of the claret, and allowing the venison to remain in the oven three quarters of an hour longer, baste it constantly with the wine and butter gravy.

Transfer the venison to a hot platter, and skim the top off the gravy in the pan. Stir into the gravy when skimmed the flour, and scrape down into it with a cooking-spoon all the brown juices that may have adhered to the pan. Add to this the remaining water and claret, season with the pepper and salt, and pouring the gravy then from the roasting-pan into a small sauce-pan, place this over the fire, and bring its contents quickly to the boiling-point, when, dropping in the caramel, all should be stirred quickly together, and the **gravy** should then be poured very hot around the venison.

Roast haunch of venison is usually served with an accompaniment of red currant jelly.

Boudins.—One half partridge, one ounce butter, one ounce flour, one gill stock, six truffles, two eggs, one table-spoonful cream, one tea-spoonful salt, one quarter tea-spoonful pepper.

Remove from the partridge all skin and bone, chop it finely, then pound it in a mortar. Melt in a sauce-pan the butter, stir well into it the flour, then add by degrees the stock; continue to stir until the mixture boils, then take the sauce-pan from the fire. Add now the salt and pepper, also the cream and the pounded partridge; mix all thoroughly together, then drop in the yolks of eggs. Return the sauce-pan to the fire, and stir all together until the yolks of eggs are set. Turn the mixture out on a plate, and let it get quite cold. While it is cooling, wash well the truffles and place them in a sauce-pan, cover them with cold water, and boil them ten minutes. When boiled, chop the truffles finely, and add them to the cold mixture. Divide the mixture into small pieces, roll each into a pear shape, dip them in the whites of eggs, roll them in the bread crumbs, and fry to a pale brown in hot fat.

Jugged Hare.—One hare, two table-spoonfuls of flour, three ounces of butter, one Bermuda onion, six cloves, one half pint of brown stock, one tea-spoonful of salt, one half salt-spoonful of pepper, one dessert-spoonful of mushroom catchup, one dessert-spoonful of Worcestershire sauce.

When the hare is caught, skin and clean it; dip a towel in boiling water, and wipe it carefully over to remove the loose hairs. Dry the animal then thoroughly, and cut it into convenient pieces.

Put the flour upon a plate, and roll each piece of meat until entirely covered in this. Melt in a frying-pan the butter, and placing the pieces of hare into it, fry each one until brown upon both sides.

Place now in a stone jug or jar the stock, catchup, and Worcestershire sauce; season these with the pepper and salt, and then pack the pieces of hare with this mixture into the jug. Cover the jug to confine the steam, and placing it in a large sauce-pan of boiling water, let it cook therein for three hours.

While the hare is being jugged, a large platter should be covered with a flaky crust (see page 195), and this baked in the oven half an hour; and when the hare is done, the pieces thereof should be taken from the jug and placed upon the prepared platter, and such gravy as may have gathered in the jug should be poured over all.

NOTE.—If a stone jug be not available for this use, a stone jar of suitable size may be substituted.

Roast Pheasant.—One pair of pheasants, one quarter of a pound of butter, one tea-spoonful of salt, one half tea-spoonful of pepper, six table-spoonfuls of bread crumbs, one table-spoonful of chopped parsley.

ROAST PHEASANT. P. 82.

TIMBALES. P. 92.

CHAUD-FROID OF CHICKEN. P. 94.

PARTRIDGE PIE.

When the pheasants have been plucked, singed, and drawn, chop off the claws, and dip them into boiling water in order that the skin may be pulled easily from them. Which do. Twist then the point of the wings behind the neck, pass a skewer through them at the first joint, piercing the top of both legs and straight through the body in the process, to hold the bird in proper form for roasting and serving. Tie the legs together just above the claws; after which prepare the dressing by placing the bread crumbs into a bowl, together with the chopped parsley, pepper, and salt, and knead all together with two ounces of the butter.

Stuff the breast of each bird with this dressing, sew together the incision at the neck, when this is done, with a needle and piece of thread, and place the pheasants side by side in a roasting-pan; distribute the remaining butter in small pieces over the breast of each, and putting the pan in a moderate oven, roast the birds therein for an hour and a half, basting them constantly with the butter as it melts.

Serve the pheasants upon a hot platter, and with bread and brown sauce sent to the table in separate gravy-boats.

NOTE.—Bread and brown sauces, see page 176.

Partridge Pie.—One brace of partridges, one pound of fillet of veal, one table-spoonful of chopped parsley, three gills of brown stock, four ounces of butter, one dessert-spoonful of salt, one-half tea-spoonful of pepper.

Pluck, draw, and singe the partridges; after which split each in halves. Put into each half a piece of butter, sprinkling them also with a little pepper and salt. Place then in the bottom of a deep pie-dish the fillet of veal, sprinkle over it the chopped parsley, and putting the halves of partridge upon this, line the edge of the dish with a strip of puff paste (see page 195); pour over all the stock, and cover over all a blanket of the paste rolled to half an inch in thickness. Bake the pie in a quick oven for an hour and a half.

NOTE.—If desired, half a pound of lean bacon may be placed upon the veal as a flavouring ingredient.

Roast Grouse.—Two brace of grouse, one half pound of butter, one dessert-spoonful of salt, one tea-spoonful of pepper.

The birds should hang in a cool place at least three days after being shot, when they should be plucked, singed, and drawn, and wiped outside and inside with a clean cloth.

Sprinkle them each then thoroughly inside with the pepper, divide the butter into four equal parts, and place one of these inside each as well.

Place the birds then side by side in a baking-pan, and putting this into a quick oven, let all bake for half an hour.

When the grouse are roasted, arrange some slices of buttered toast upon a platter; place the birds upon these, and pouring over them the gravy from the pan, serve very hot.

Bread sauce should be served with roast birds. (See page 176.)

Wild Ducks.—One pair of wild ducks, one quarter of a pound of butter, one tea-spoonful of salt, one half tea-spoonful of pepper.

Carefully pluck, draw, and singe the fowls; wash them slightly, and dry them in and outside with a towel. Sprinkle inside of each the pepper and salt, spread the butter well over the breasts, and placing them side by side upon a dripping-pan, bake in a very quick hot oven fifteen minutes. The blood should follow the knife when carved, if the duck be properly cooked.

Cut into slices some cold boiled hominy, fry them to a light brown in butter, and arranging these upon a platter, serve the fowl upon this with an accompaniment of currant jelly.

NOTE.—Canvas-back duck, now sent largely to this country from Baltimore, ought to be cooked in the same way as our English wild duck.

Larks.—Six or eight larks, one quarter pound of fat bacon, one dessert-spoonful of salt, one tea-spoonful of pepper.

When the birds are plucked, singed, and drawn, they should be carefully cleansed inside and out with a dry towel.

Cut the bacon then into very thin slices, and folding one of these slices over the breast of each bird, securing it there with a wrapping of twine, string the birds upon a spit with the breasts all turned the same way, and broil over an open fire for twenty minutes.

Serve upon a hot platter, garnished with fresh sprigs of parsley or with water-cresses.

Woodcock on Toast.—Two brace of woodcock, four ounces of butter, one tea-spoonful of salt, one tea-spoonful of pepper.

When plucked and singed the woodcock should be drawn, cutting out the neck, but leaving the head, which must be drawn around, and the long bill passed through the legs, wings, and body as a trussing skewer.

Season each by rubbing a little pepper and salt inside, string them upon a spit, rub over each breast a portion of the butter, and broil the birds over an open fire for twenty minutes.

The livers should now be boiled for five minutes, pounded in a mortar or chopped very finely; and this paste being spread over two slices of butter toast, the toast should be placed upon a hot platter, and the woodcock served thereon.

NOTE.—Quail and snipe may be served and prepared as prescribed for woodcock.

Pigeons with Green Pease.—One pair of pigeons, one pint of shelled green pease, two ounces of butter, one gill of stock, one tea-spoonful of salt, one half tea-spoonful of pepper.

Pluck, singe, draw, and wash the pigeons slightly in cold water; twist the tips of the wings behind the shoulders, and threading a trussing-needle with fine twine, pierce with it the first joint of the wings, passing through the upper portion of the legs and straight through the body in doing so.

Return the needle then through the tips of the wings, piercing through the skin of the neck in passing, and bringing the twine thus to its point of departure, draw it taut, and tie the ends firmly together.

The claws should now be chopped off, and crossing the legs, tie them neatly together; after which, melt in a stewing-pan two ounces of butter, and when the smoke arises therefrom, put the pigeons into it breast downwards, and allow them to cook slowly for one hour, turning them from time to time to prevent burning, and in order that they may brown evenly.

At the end of the hour, the butter in which the pigeons have cooked must be drained off, and the stock poured over them, in which they must be allowed to cook for five minutes.

Put then in with the pigeons the pease, season them with the salt and pepper, and let all cook very slowly for twenty additional minutes.

At the end of this time remove the pigeons from the stewing-pan, cut and draw out the trussing-strings, and arranging the birds upon a hot platter, pour the pease and the reduced stock around them. Serve very hot.

Stewed Wild Pigeons.—Four wild pigeons, one quart of stock, one ounce of flour, one tea-spoonful of salt, six cloves, one blade of mace, one Bermuda onion, one half tea-spoonful of peppercorns, one table-spoonful of mushroom catchup, eight drops of caramel.

When the pigeons have been plucked, singed, and drawn, they must be cut into quarters, first splitting them through from breast to back, and then separating these halves into wing and drumstick quarters.

Place these quarters into a stew-pan, cover them with the stock, and when this boils up, skim the surface carefully; throw in the mace, peppercorns, cloves, chopped onion, and salt; when, covering the sauce-pan, draw it to one side of the fire, and allow its contents to simmer very slowly until the pigeons become tender, the length of time for which depends entirely upon their age.

Put the flour now into a bowl, beat it smooth with a little cold water, add to this the catchup and caramel, and pouring this mixture into the sauce-pan with the pigeons, stir all together until boiling again, when it must continue to boil for ten minutes, and the pigeons then should be transferred to a deep platter, and the sauce from the sauce-pan strained over them.

MEATS.—SEVENTH DIVISION.

ENTRÉES.

Kromesquies Russe.—One quarter of a pound of raw bacon, one quarter of a pound of cold turkey, two ounces of cold tongue, one ounce of butter, four ounces of flour, one gill of milk, one half tea-spoonful of salt, one half tea-spoonful of pepper, one salt-spoonful of grated nutmeg, one dessert spoonful of salad oil, one gill of tepid water, white of one egg.

Cut the turkey and the tongue into small equal pieces, melt in a sauce-pan the butter, stir into it one ounce of the flour, and add to this by degrees the milk, and stir all until boiling. When boiling, allow the mixture to cook for two minutes, when the sauce-pan must be drawn aside from the fire, and the turkey and tongue thrown into it.

Season all now with the pepper and salt, add to it the nutmeg, and turn the entire contents of the sauce-pan out upon a plate, and allow it to become cold.

While this is cooling, put into a bowl three ounces of the flour, pour into the centre thereof a dessert-spoonful of salad oil, and throwing over this the gill of tepid water, beat all well together.

Place upon a plate the white of egg, and whip it to a very stiff froth; mix the egg lightly with the contents of the bowl, exercising care not to break the froth; after which the bacon must be sliced very thinly, and cut into pieces about three inches square.

When the turkey and tongue compound has grown very cold, roll a little of it into each piece of bacon; then dipping each little bacon-roll into the batter in the bowl, drop them into hot clarified fat, of which there should be enough to cover them, and fry for five minutes.

Drain them when done upon a sheet of kitchen-paper, pile them high upon a hot napkin, and serve garnished with sprigs of parsley.

Notes.—By tepid water is meant two parts of cold and one part of boiling water.

When hot clarified fat is not convenient, lard may be substituted for this as for other frying purposes.

Curry with Boiled Rice.—Two pounds of veal, two ounces of butter, one Bermuda onion, two dessert-spoonfuls of curry-powder, one apple, three gills of stock, two table-spoonfuls of cream, one half of a lemon, one half tea-spoonful of salt.

First melt the butter in a small sauce-pan, and add to it the onion very finely chopped. With an iron spoon toss the onion about in the pan until it comes to a pale brown colour; then strain from it the butter, and put the onion aside upon a plate until it is required.

Return the butter to the sauce-pan, and when again hot throw into it the veal, which first must have been cut into small square pieces. Brown the meat well upon all sides, and when this is done, stir in the curry-powder, and draw the sauce-pan aside from the fire.

Dry then in a towel the apple, and grate it with a carrot-grater over the veal in the sauce-pan. Return the sauce-pan to the fire, add to its contents the salt and the stock, stir all until boiling, and then put in the browned onion.

After the onion has been thrown in, draw the sauce-pan again aside from the blaze of the fire, and leave all to simmer uncovered for two hours, for the purpose of reducing the sauce.

Just before ready for serving, stir in the cream, squeeze over it the lemon-juice, and dish up at once.

This should be served with boiled rice, which must be prepared as follows :—

Take three quarters of a pound of dry rice, and putting it

into a strainer, wash thoroughly with running water. When washed, throw the rice into a large sauce-pan two-thirds filled with boiling water, into which has been put a dessert-spoonful of salt. Cover the sauce-pan tightly until the water boils up, when the lid should be taken off, and the rice left to boil very rapidly for fifteen minutes. At the end of fifteen minutes take out of the pan a kernel of the rice, and if it flours by rubbing between the thumb and finger, it is sufficiently cooked; but if not yet done—the length of time required depending upon whether the grain be or be not freshly gathered—it must be kept boiling a few minutes longer, keeping in mind the fact that rice must be boiled quickly, otherwise it will be transformed into a starchy jelly.

Throw the rice when done into a colander, that it may be thoroughly drained of water, and serve very hot with the curry, but in separate dishes.

NOTES.—The reason for browning the onion separately from the meat is that the veal requires so much longer time to brown than the onion, that the vegetable would be reduced to a crisp before the meat could be done.

Lean mutton, rabbit, and chicken may also be curried in this way.

Rissoles of Veal.—One pound of fillet of veal, one quarter of pound of suet, one pound of bread crumbs, one half pint of milk, two eggs, one salt-spoonful of powdered mace, one tea-spoonful of salt, one half tea-spoonful of pepper, one ounce of butter, one half ounce of flour, one half pint of white stock.

Remove the skin from the veal, chop it very finely, after which pound it well in a mortar.

Put into a bowl three quarters of a pound of the bread crumbs, pour the milk over, and allow the crumbs to soak therein for ten minutes; then pouring the bread crumbs from the bowl into a towel, twist the ends of the towel in the hands, and press from them as much of the milk as may be.

Mix the bread crumbs with the pounded veal, season the mixture with the mace, pepper, and nearly all of the salt; drop into it then the yolks of egg, and beat all together with the finely-chopped suet.

Roll the compound then into small balls, dipping each into the beaten whites of egg, and then into the remaining bread crumbs; after which they must be thrown into hot clarified fat and fried for ten minutes.

While the rissoles are frying, melt the butter in a small sauce-pan; stir into it the flour, then add by degrees the stock, stirring all until it boils, when it must be seasoned with the salt, and allowed to cook for two minutes.

Drain the rissoles, when fried, upon a sheet of kitchen-paper, and serve upon a hot platter with the sauce poured around.

Beef Olives.—One and one-half pound of round steak, four table-spoonfuls of bread crumbs, one dessert-spoonful of parsley, one egg, one ounce of butter, one dessert-spoonful of mushroom catchup, one dessert-spoonful of Harvey's sauce, one half ounce of flour, six drops of caramel, one half pint of second stock, one tea-spoonful of salt, one half tea-spoonful of pepper.

Put the sprigs of parsley into cold water, wash it well, picking the stalk from it, and then dry thoroughly by wrapping it in a towel and wringing the water therefrom. Place it upon a board, chop very finely, and mix with it the bread crumbs. Drop into this the egg, seasoning all with the pepper and salt, and mix the whole well together.

The fat must now be trimmed from the steak and cut into little pieces, and the steak itself cut into squares four inches in size.

Into each of the pieces of steak put an equal part of the fat and bread-crumb dressing; make them into rolls, and tie around them a piece of twine.

Heat the butter now in a sauce-pan, and brown the rolls therein.

While the rolls are browning, put the flour into a bowl,

and make it smooth with a table-spoonful of stock; and when smooth add to it the catchup, caramel, and Harvey's sauce; after which the remaining stock should be put in cold, and pour all over the browned olive-rolls, stirring until the liquid boils.

When boiling, skim, and then covering the sauce-pan, allow the whole to simmer slowly for an hour and a half.

At the end of this time take up the olives, and cutting the strings therefrom, pour over them the gravy from the pan.

Fricassée of Sweet-Breads.—One pair of sweet-breads, two ounces of butter, one half ounce of flour, one egg, two table-spoonfuls of cream, one tea-cupful of white stock, one dessert-spoonful of chopped parsley, one salt-spoonful of grated nutmeg, one half tea-spoonful of salt, one half salt-spoonful of pepper.

Let the sweet-breads lie for an hour in iced water, preparatory to cooking; at the end of which they should be put into a sauce-pan, covered with cold water, and placed over the fire, where, when boiling, they should be left for five minutes.

Take them then from the fire, and throw them into a basin of cold water to whiten; after which draw off the outer casing, and cut them into thin slices.

Melt in a sauce-pan the butter, stir into it the flour, and add the stock; when all must be stirred until it boils. Put into this the sliced sweet-breads, season all with the pepper and salt, adding the nutmeg; and covering the sauce-pan, let the whole simmer slowly for three quarters of an hour.

Just before the sweet-breads are ready for serving, beat up the egg until very light, mix well with it the cream and chopped parsley, and moving the sauce-pan off the fire, stir this mixture in with the sweet-breads, and stir all together for two minutes, taking care that it does not boil.

This should be served immediately, and very hot, that the eggs may not get heavy.

Larded Sweet-Breads.—One pair of sweet-breads, two ounces of fat bacon, one half pint of stock, one half tea-spoonful of salt, one half tea-spoonful of pepper, one lemon, four drops of caramel, one half ounce of flour.

The sweet-breads must be first thrown into boiling water, boiled for five minutes, and then put into iced water for half an hour.

Cut the bacon into thin strips two inches long and one-third of an inch in thickness, and when the sweet-breads have been taken from the water and dried thoroughly in a towel, thread the strips of bacon into a larding-needle, and lard the sweet-breads thickly, making a deep long stitch, as the flesh of the sweet-bread is so apt to break.

When larded, place the sweet-bread into a stewing-pan, and pour over it the stock boiling-hot.

Cook them slowly for half an hour, when they must be put into a slightly-greased baking-tin, set into a hot oven, and baked for fifteen minutes.

While the sweet-breads are cooking, stir into the stock in the sauce-pan half an ounce of the flour; add to it the caramel, and let all cook for two minutes, when it should be seasoned with the pepper and salt.

When the sweet-breads have baked the fifteen minutes, take them from the oven, and putting them upon a small hot platter, pour around them the sauce from the pan, and garnish with the lemon, sliced.

Vol-au-Vent of Sweet-Breads.—Six ounces of flour, six ounces of butter, yolk of one egg, one tea-spoonful of lemon-juice, one half gill of cold water, one gill of milk, one half tea-spoonful of salt, one half salt-spoonful of pepper, one grain of cayenne, one pair of sweet-breads.

First put the flour upon a mixing-board, make a little well in the centre thereof, and drop into it the egg and half of the lemon-juice, adding by degrees the cold water, kneading all meantime firmly together, and when kneaded, roll out thinly.

Into the centre of the rolled paste put five ounces of the

butter, fold the edges together until the butter is covered, and, flouring a rolling-pin, roll out as thinly as possible. Fold the crust now into three layers, and roll out again; and repeat this process of folding and rolling seven times, when it should be put into the ice-box, and left long enough to become chilled through and firm.

Take the sweet-breads, first thoroughly washing them, and putting them into a sauce-pan, cover with cold water, and bringing the water to the boiling-point, allow them to boil in it for five minutes; when they should be again thrown into cold water, rewashed, and cut into small pieces.

Now put the butter and milk into a sauce-pan over the fire, and when the milk boils, put into the pan also the pieces of sweet-bread; season them with the cayenne pepper and salt, and let all simmer slowly for three quarters of an hour.

When the crust has become cool and firm in the ice-box, take it out, and placing it upon the mixing-board, roll it out to about a third of an inch in thickness. Cut out two vol-au-vent with the vol-au-vent cutter, or a biscuit cutter if the first be not convenient; cut in each a smaller circle, about one inch from the edges, half way through the crust; and placing both upon a baking-tin, bake in a hot quick oven for twenty minutes.

When done, remove the crust from the inner circle by slipping in a knife-blade and splitting it asunder; scrape out the centre of the vol-au-vent, in order to make a hollow in which to pack the sweet-breads; put into each equal parts of the sweet-bread; sprinkle over the meat the remainder of the lemon-juice; cover over it the little baked circle previously split out; garnish with fresh sprigs of parsley, and send to table in a hot napkin.

NOTES.—The difficulty in making the vol-au-vent paste lies in its becoming heated in rolling, and the butter, which is used in excessive proportion, running in consequence. This may be prevented by putting it to cool between rollings, and taking a little longer time for its preparation.

It is really puff-paste that is used for the vol-au-vent, and the crust should rise in baking at least three inches.

MEATS.

Chaud-froid of Chicken.—One young fowl, two ounces of butter, two ounces of flour, one half pint of milk, one gill of cream, one salt-spoonful of salt, one salt-spoonful of white pepper, one quart of second stock, one half ounce of gelatine, one table-spoonful of vinegar, one sprig of parsley, one gill of cold water, whites of three eggs, one half tea-spoonful of black pepper.

This dish requires two days for its preparation, and therefore its use must be anticipated.

Melt first the gelatine in half of the cold water, and let it stand for ten minutes; put then the stock into a copper or porcelain-lined sauce-pan, add to it the vinegar, parsley, black pepper, and half of the salt; place it over the fire, and when tepid put into it the gelatine.

Beat the whites of the eggs well in a bowl, with which mix the remainder of the cold water; pour this into the stock, and whisk all together until the stock boils, using either two forks or an egg-whisk.

The instant the stock boils cover the sauce-pan and draw it aside from the fire; let it simmer here slowly for twenty minutes, when it should be strained into a basin through a clean towel.

Let this preparation stand over night, as it will not cool through and set in shorter time.

Clean and wash also the fowl; then plunging it into boiling water, let it cook until a skewer will pierce easily into the breast, when it must be immediately taken out, and it also allowed to stand over night to become thoroughly cooled.

Having prepared the material in the above manner, upon the day the chaud-froid is to be used cut first the wings and legs from the fowl and trim them neatly; cut also two fillets from the breast, taking care not to break the crisp grain of the meat. Melt now in a porcelain-lined or copper sauce-pan the butter, stir into it the flour, add by degrees the milk, and stir all until boiling, when the mixture must be seasoned with the white pepper and salt, the cream added, and stirred carefully until it has boiled for two minutes.

Take the sauce-pan from the fire, and put with its contents a dessert-spoonful of the cold jelly; draw the skin off the pieces of fowl, and dip them into this sauce, when they are to be placed in a sieve, and left about thirty minutes to cool.

When the sauce is quite cold upon the pieces of fowl, arrange them neatly into the bottom of a flat dish, chop roughly the jelly and scatter it around, and garnish the dish either with fresh sprigs of parsley, or with parsley finely chopped and sprinkled over.

NOTES.—Small pieces of cold turkey may be made up in this way into a most delicious entrée.

A leek or onion may be used to flavour the sauce, being put in if used, with the parsley.

Chicken Croquettes.—One half of a cold chicken, six mushrooms, one gill of stock, two table-spoonfuls of cream, one half tea-spoonful of salt, one half tea-spoonful of pepper, one salt-spoonful of grated nutmeg, two eggs, six table-spoonfuls of bread crumbs, one ounce of butter, one ounce of flour.

The skin must first be taken from the cold chicken and the bones removed, when the meat should be chopped very finely, and the mushrooms, having been also well washed and chopped, must be mixed therewith.

Melt the butter in a sauce-pan, stir into it the flour, add by degrees the stock, stirring until it boils, and then put into it the cream. Season with the pepper and salt, flavour with the nutmeg, and let all cook briskly for two minutes. When this has cooked, remove the sauce-pan from the fire, stir into it the chopped chicken and mushrooms, and pour all out upon a plate to cool.

When quite cold, separate into equal parts, and form the compound with the hands to something near the shape of a pear; beat the eggs well upon a plate; roll each croquette therein, and placing the bread crumbs upon paper, roll each also in this; and throwing them into hot clarified fat, fry for two minutes.

When done, take them from the fat, drain upon a piece of paper, and if the pear-shapes are a success, thrust into the small end of each a clipping of parsley stalk, for the purpose of increasing the likeness by furnishing stems.

Quenelles of Veal.—One pound of fillet of veal, two ounces of butter, two ounces of flour, one half pint of second stock, two eggs, one gill of cream, one tea-spoonful of lemon-juice, one half tea-spoonful of salt, one half tea-spoonful of white pepper.

Mix together in a sauce-pan one ounce of butter and one ounce of flour; add to these one gill of stock, and stirring all until boiling, let it boil for two minutes thereafter. Turn out this mixture after the two minutes upon a plate, and let it get cold.

While this is cooling, put the veal upon a board, and removing the outer skin, chop it very finely; after which put into a mortar and pound thoroughly, when it must be rubbed through a wire sieve, which will bring the meat to the smoothness of a paste.

Then put into the mortar the cooled mixture from the plate, drop into it one egg, pound these well together, add then the veal and the remaining egg, and seasoning all with half of the salt and pepper, use again the pestle until all of these ingredients become smoothly blended.

Grease now a sauté or perfectly fresh frying-pan, prepare two dessert-spoons by dipping them into boiling water, and taking one in the right hand and the other in the left, dip into the mortar the right hand spoon, filling it with the paste, and with the left hand spoon scoop the mixture from the one to the other, forming thus the quinelles, when they must be put into the sauté-pan carefully, that they may not lose their shape; and when the pan is so filled, pour in at the side as much boiling water as will cover the quinelles, when they should be placed over a slow fire, and allowed to poach for ten minutes.

Now melt in a small sauce-pan the remaining ounce of butter, stir into it the remaining ounce of flour, add by degrees a gill of stock, and let all boil up. When boiling, pour in the cream, season with pepper and salt, and taking it from the fire, add then the lemon-juice.

Arrange the quinelles when done, and taken from the water, in a circle upon a flat dish, and pour the sauce around them.

NOTE.—When a mortar and pestle are not available, the veal may be first cooked a little in boiling stock, and then chopped as finely as possible before being passed through the sieve.

Grenadines of Veal.—Two pounds of fillet of veal, one carrot, one turnip, one head of celery, one pint of white stock, six ounces of fat bacon, one tea-spoonful of whole white pepper, one half tea-spoonful of salt.

Removing the skin from the veal, cut it into shapely oval pieces about half an inch in thickness. Cut the bacon into thin strips two inches long and one-third of an inch wide, and threading a larding-needle with the bacon, lard the ovals of veal as thickly as possible with it.

Place in a sauce-pan the vegetables cut in small pieces, over which sprinkle the pepper and salt, and pouring in around the vegetables the stock, bring all to the boiling-point.

When the stock boils, place upon the vegetables the ovals of veal, taking care that they do not overlap one another; and covering the sauce-pan closely, draw it aside from the fire, and allow the contents to cook slowly for three quarters of an hour, basting occasionally meantime with the stock.

Take the grenadines now from the sauce-pan, place them upon a slightly-greased baking-tin, and brown them in a quick oven.

While the grenadines are browning, put the sauce-pan again over the fire uncovered, and let the stock reduce as fast as possible.

When all is done, arrange the grenadines tastefully in a flat vegetable-dish, and pour through a strainer over them as sauce the vegetable-flavoured stock.

Talleyrand Cutlets.—Two pounds of fillet of veal, three ounces of butter, one dessert-spoonful of chopped parsley, one half dozen of mushrooms, one eschalot, one half ounce of flour, yolks of two eggs, one table-spoonful of cream, one half tea-spoonful of salt, one half tea-spoonful of pepper, one half pint of white stock.

Cut the veal into small equal ovals, and place them in a sauté or very clean frying-pan, together with two ounces of butter. Over a slow fire cook the meat for five minutes, in order to whiten it, being careful to turn the pieces and not to let the butter brown.

Draw the pan then from the fire, and sprinkle over the meat the chopped parsley, the mushrooms, and eschalot, which must also have been chopped; and melting in a separate sauce-pan the remaining ounce of butter, stir into it the flour, add by degrees the stock, and bring all to the boil; and the instant this is accomplished, pour all over the veal in the sauté-pan, and leave all to cook for twenty minutes very slowly, turning the meat and the sauce-pan constantly while cooking, to prevent the meat discolouring.

Prepare now in a bowl the yolks of egg and cream, season this with the pepper and salt, when the veal should be taken from the sauce-pan and arranged upon a flat dish, and the cream and egg stirred into the sauce-pan with the sauce.

The contents of the sauce-pan must not be allowed to boil after the yolks of egg are added, but as soon as the sauce thickens with them by simmering slowly, it must be poured over the veal.

Timbales.—One quarter of a pound of macaroni, one half pound of cold roast beef, four ounces of bread crumbs, one ounce of butter, one ounce of flour, one half tea-spoonful of pepper, one half tea-spoonful of salt, one table-spoonful of catchup, one table-spoonful of Worcestershire sauce, two eggs, three gills of stock.

The macaroni must first be well washed in cold water, then put into a sauce-pan, covered with cold water, put on the fire, and boiled for fifteen minutes.

Now grease twelve deep cup-tins or ordinary tea-cups. When the macaroni is boiled, drain the water from it, and drying it lightly in a towel, cut it into inch lengths, and arrange these lengths upon end in the cup-tins.

Chop the cold meat very finely, and putting it into a bowl, mix with it the bread crumbs, and season this with the pepper and salt, adding also a little of the Worcestershire sauce and half of the catchup.

Drop in upon this the egg, together with a table-spoonful of the stock, and when the whole has been well mixed together, separate it into equal quantities; put a portion into each of the cups, and press it snugly down upon the macaroni with the blade of a knife.

Each tin or cup must be now covered with a small piece of kitchen-paper, and all placed in a shallow sauce-pan, in which there is boiling water sufficient to reach half way up their sides; when the sauce-pan should be covered, and the timbales allowed to cook very slowly for one hour, boiling water being added from time to time to keep the quantity the same.

Five minutes before the hour expires the butter and flour must be mixed together in a small sauce-pan, to which add the stock; and when this mixture boils, add the remainder of the catchup and the Worcestershire sauce, also the remainder of the pepper and salt, and allow all to cook for two minutes.

When the timbales are done, turn them carefully out in regular order upon a large deep platter, and pour the sauce around them, taking care not to spatter the tops.

NOTES.—In using catchup, caution should be exercised in the use of salt, as all catchups are highly salted in preparation.

Fresh beef-steak may also be used for this dish, with the difference that uncooked meat will require a little more time over the fire.

Fillet of Beef, with Sauce Hollandais.—One and one-half pound of fillet of beef, one pound of potatoes, yolks of two eggs, one table-spoonful of cold water, one table-spoonful of cream, one ounce of butter, one half table-spoonful of lemon-juice, one half tea-spoonful of pepper, one half tea-spoonful of salt.

The fillet must first be cut into slices nearly an inch in thickness, place them then upon a slightly-greased gridiron, and broil over a clear fire for seven minutes, turning them constantly meantime.

Take then a small tin sauce-pan, put into it the yolks of egg, pour over them the cold water, and whisk until well mixed with two forks or an egg-whisk. Add the cream, lemon-juice, and butter; season with a very little of the pepper and salt, and place the sauce-pan either in a larger sauce-pan of boiling water or over a very slow fire; and whisk the contents until the butter melts and it rises to a froth.

The slices of beef must now be arranged on a dish in a circle, the end of one piece being made to lap upon the other until the circle is complete, when the sauce should be poured over, and the whole garnished with a sprinkling of chopped parsley.

Around the meat there should be now placed a row of potato balls, which must be prepared in the following manner:—

Pare and wash the pound of potatoes, and cut from them with a French vegetable-cutter as many balls as the potatoes will furnish. Dry the balls well in a towel, and throw them into hot clarified fat or lard for four minutes. When fried, drain them for a moment upon a piece of kitchen-paper, and transfer them to the dish.

Cutlets à-la-Maréchal.—Five mutton cutlets, one dessert-spoonful of parsley, two ounces of veal, one salt-spoonful of nutmeg, one table-spoonful of cream, one half tea-spoonful of salt, one half tea-spoonful of pepper, one half dozen mushrooms, two table-spoonfuls of bread crumbs, one egg, two ounces of clarified fat.

Chop the veal very finely, and pound it in a mortar; rub it when pounded through a wire sieve, and add to it the

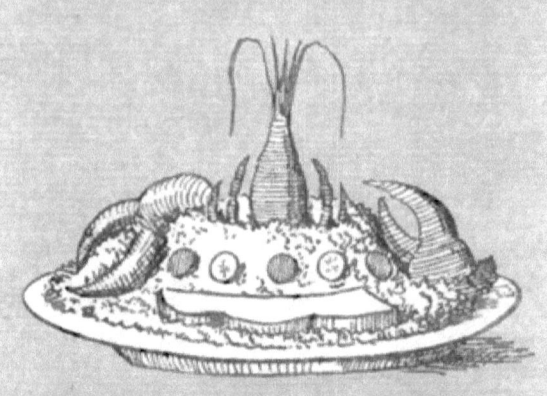

LOBSTER SALAD. P. 121.

FILLETS OF BEEF P. 94.

CHEESE FRITTERS. P. 132.

chopped parsley, season with a very little pepper and salt and flavour with the nutmeg, and stir all to a consistency with the cream.

Take the cutlets and trim them neatly, leaving on a part of the fat, and roll them in the egg, which must have been previously beaten.

Put the bread crumbs into a paper, and seasoning them with the remainder of the pepper and salt, roll the cutlets in this also; make hot in a frying-pan the clarified fat, and when the smoke arises, put into it the cutlets, and fry them for eight minutes, turning them once, and allowing four minutes.

When fried, take them from the fat, and spread over each one an equal quantity of the veal mixture from the mortar; chop the mushrooms, and sprinkle a little of this over each; and put them into a moderate oven, and let them bake for ten minutes.

Serve in a hot napkin, garnished with sprigs of parsley.

Browned Sweet-Breads.—One pair sweet-breads, one gill milk, three gills cream, one egg, two ounces of butter, one ounce flour, one pinch grated nutmeg, one salt-spoonful salt, one salt-spoonful pepper, six drops caramel.

First soak the sweet-breads for one hour in cold water; place them in a sauce-pan, and cover them with fresh cold water; place the pan on the fire, and allow the sweet-breads to boil for twenty minutes. Have in readiness a bowl of cold water; and when the sweet-breads are boiled, throw them into the water, and wash them well. Make an incision in the side of each, and squeeze into it a little lemon-juice.

Dip now the sweet-breads into the milk, and then roll them in the bread crumbs, placing the crumbs on a sheet of paper. Beat well the egg on a plate, and brush the sweet-breads over with it, and again roll them in the crumbs. Heat in a deep stew-pan as much clarified fat as will cover the sweet-breads. When the smoke rises from the fat, drop in the sweet-breads.

The instant the sweet-breads take a pale-brown colour, remove them and keep them hot. Melt then in a small stew-pan the butter, stir in the flour, and when well mixed add by degrees the cream, and drop in the caramel; season with the pepper, salt, and nutmeg; stir all till boiling, and pour at once over the sweet-breads, and serve immediately.

General Remarks.—Bermuda and Spanish are applied to onions to indicate size—Bermuda signifying a small onion or of the size of a Bermuda onion, and Spanish onion meaning a large onion or of the size of a Spanish onion, although if these especial growths of onions are to be conveniently procured, they will be found of superior quality to the ordinary.

Specified quantities of salt are given in the foregoing recipes in order to preserve proportions; but the use of this seasoning may be governed by the respective palates of those for whom the dishes are prepared, keeping in mind that while more may be required by those who are excessively fond of salt, less is always safer, as to salt a dish is easy, while to freshen one that is over-salted and acrid therefrom is generally impossible.

Harvey's and Worcestershire sauce being nearly the same, may be substituted for each other as convenience may require, but the result will be more satisfactory from using each as directed.

The recipes throughout this work have been kept as nearly as possible to quantities for serving four persons, using such surplusage as must necessarily occur in the proper cooking of joints in the cold meat preparations.

The etiquette of entrées making one service to a person sufficient, the proportion of quantity has still been in a measure preserved, as these are generally served in odd numbers, five, seven, nine, etc.

VEGETABLES.

Spinach with Eggs.—For this provide four quarts of spinach, one table-spoonful of cream, one ounce of butter, four eggs, one tea-spoonful of lemon-juice, one grain of cayenne, one dessert-spoonful of salt, one salt-spoonful of pepper.

The spinach must be thoroughly washed through three or four waters, and the stalks picked off. Put it when washed into a dry sauce-pan, sprinkle over it the salt, and covering the sauce-pan closely, place it over the fire. The salt and heat together will draw from the spinach enough of its own green liquor in which to boil; and when it reaches the boiling-point, allow it to boil for ten minutes.

At the end of this time remove the spinach to a colander that it may drain entirely of its liquor; and when drained, it must either be very finely chopped or passed through a coarse wire sieve.

Into a small sauce-pan put the butter and cream, and place all over the fire until the cream boils, then stir in the spinach, and let the mixture get very hot, but not boiling, as boiling will draw more liquor from the spinach and spoil the dish.

Season now with the cayenne and pepper, and draw the sauce-pan aside from the fire to keep hot until the eggs are prepared. Fill a small sauce-pan with boiling water, and into this put the lemon-juice. Break the egg into a cup, and drop it into the sauce-pan, the water in which must continue to boil; and as soon as the form of the first egg sets, break, and drop in the second in the same manner, which continue until the four eggs are in the sauce-pan, permitting each egg to remain about three minutes.

When the eggs are done, remove the spinach from its sauce-pan, and pile it high in the centre of a vegetable dish, smoothing the edges around and the top with a knife blade. Take the eggs from the water with a skimming spoon, and arrange them upon the flat top of the spinach.

This dish should be garnished for serving with corners of fried bread or toast.

NOTE.—If lemon-juice is not convenient, a few drops of vinegar may be used for poaching the eggs; but the flavour of it will always be detected, although it firms the egg quite as well as the lemon-juice, which leaves no taste of itself with the egg.

Cauliflower au Gratin.—Provide for this one cauliflower, one ounce of butter, one ounce of flour, one gill of cold water, two table-spoonfuls of cream, three ounces of grated Parmesan cheese, one grain of cayenne, one salt-spoonful of white pepper, one table-spoonful of salt.

A close firm head of cauliflower must be selected for this preparation, and this must be first thrown into a basin of strongly salted water, and left for twenty minutes, in order that sand, grit, or other foreign substances may be drawn out. Trim off the green leaves, and cut the stalk squarely across about two inches below the flower, after which prepare a large sauce-pan by putting it over the fire, filling it two-thirds full of boiling water with a table-spoonful of salt.

Into this sauce-pan put the cauliflower, the flower downwards, and cover it until the water boils up vigorously. Then removing the sauce-pan cover, all should be allowed to boil rapidly for fifteen minutes.

At the end of this time take the cauliflower from the water, and placing it upon a gratin plate with the flower uppermost, wrap over it thickly but lightly a clean towel, both to keep it hot and to absorb such moisture as may have remained in the top.

Melt in a small sauce-pan the butter, into which stir the flour, and add by degrees the cold water. When this boils, take it from the fire ; add to it the cream and two ounces of the grated cheese. Season all with the cayenne and pepper, and removing the towel from the cauliflower, pour this sauce over it. Sprinkle over the flower the remaining ounce of cheese, and place all into a quick oven, where the cheese upon the top must be allowed nicely to brown. Serve immediately.

NOTES.—If Parmesan cheese cannot be obtained, any strong old cheese that is dry enough to grate may be used instead.

In boiling all vegetables and cereals, the more rapidly the water boils, the more satisfactory will be the result.

If a gratin-plate is not available, the cauliflower must be put upon a plate that will stand the heat of the oven; and in serving, a napkin may be laid under, and prettily folded around to conceal the plate if unsightly.

Tomato Farci.—Provide for this one quart of fresh tomatoes, two Spanish onions, four table-spoonfuls of bread crumbs, three ounces of butter, one half tea-spoonful of salt, one tea-spoonful of pepper.

The onions must have been put into boiling water, and soaked over-night; and when required for the preparation, they should be dried in a towel, and then sliced, making the slices about a third of an inch thick.

Melt in a frying-pan an ounce of the butter, and when hot, brown on both sides in it the onion slices.

Slice the tomatoes, and arrange a layer of them in the bottom of a vegetable dish, and over this put a layer of the browned onion. Sprinkle over this a little of the bread crumbs, season with the pepper and salt, and with these alternating layers proceed to fill the vegetable dish, leaving a top covering of the bread crumbs.

When the dish is filled, distribute the butter in small pieces over the top, and place all in a moderate oven to bake for three quarters of an hour.

Note.—Canned tomatoes will answer for this farci, and when used, the half of a quart can will be sufficient.

Boiled Asparagus with White Sauce.—For this provide one bunch of asparagus, two ounces of butter, one ounce of flour, one gill of milk, two table-spoonfuls of cream, one salt-spoonful of salt, one salt-spoonful of pepper.

Trim the asparagus, and cut it into equal lengths; wash it in cold water, and putting it into a sauce-pan, cover with boiling water, and shut the lid of the sauce-pan for the first moment. When the water boils up vigorously, take off the cover, and let the asparagus boil for twenty minutes.

Five minutes before the asparagus is done, take a small sauce-pan, and mixing in it the butter and the flour, add to this by degrees a gill and a half of the liquor in which the asparagus is boiling. Stir this with the butter and flour until the mixture boils, when the milk should be added, and two minutes additional boiling allowed. Season with the salt and pepper, and drawing the sauce-pan aside from the fire, stir into it the cream.

Take the asparagus from the water at the expiration of the twenty minutes, and drain it upon a wire sieve; place it in a vegetable dish, and pour the sauce carefully around and across the tips, exercising caution not to spatter the ends of the stalks that are to be taken in the fingers.

NOTES.—Asparagus may be boiled in the above manner, and served upon toast instead of with the white sauce.

A very simple manner of boiling this vegetable is to stand the unbroken bundle of asparagus upon the stalk end upright in a sauce-pan containing boiling water enough to reach nearly to the tender green tips. It must be boiled rapidly until tender, and then, preparing a hot napkin upon a platter, take the asparagus from the water, and draining it for a moment, place it upon the napkin, cut the bands, and draw them away, and fold over all snugly the ends of the napkin. The white sauce which is used for this must be served in a gravy-boat.

A favourite way of serving boiled asparagus is to make it very cold by standing in the ice-box, and then serve with a sauce piquant, composed of vinegar, pepper, salt, and salad oil.

In this way asparagus may be used as a salad.

Green Pease.—One quart of shelled pease, one ounce of butter, one half tea-spoonful of powdered sugar, one tea-spoonful of salt, one half tea-spoonful of pepper, one sprig of mint.

Place the pease in a large sauce-pan of boiling water, in which should be thrown the sprig of mint, and covering, let them boil rapidly from ten to twenty minutes, as the age of the pease may require.

The moment the pease are done, they must be taken from the water and drained, as overcooking spoils them. While the pease are draining, melt the butter in the sauce-pan in which they have been cooked, and when this is melted, throw back into it the pease, sprinkle over them the pepper, salt, and sugar, and covering the sauce-pan, shake it over the fire until the pease are very hot, taking care that they neither brown nor break.

Turnips.—For this take six turnips, two table-spoonfuls of beef-dripping, one tea-spoonful of salt, one half tea-spoonful of pepper, one table-spoonful of cream.

First pare the turnips, taking care to cut off the white lining of the skin, which is bitter, and the thickness of which will be perceived by the clearly defined circle discovered in

cutting off the top. Wash the turnips thoroughly in cold water to whiten them and remove the finger-marks, and putting them into a sauce-pan, cover them with boiling water, and closing the lid of the sauce-pan, boil them rapidly until a fork will easily penetrate to their centres.

When done, drain the water well off them, add the beef-dripping, pepper, and salt, and with a potato-masher mash them finely, using a fork occasionally to break the lumps.

When mashed, stir in with them the cream, and pile them high in a vegetable dish, smoothing the edges around with a knife.

Boiled Cabbage.—For this provide one head of cabbage, three table-spoonfuls of beef-dripping, one tea-spoonful of salt, one half tea-spoonful of pepper, one lump of soda the size of a pea.

Select a large firm head of cabbage, wash it well, and cut away the coarse outer leaves. This done, cut off the stalk, and make cuts in the base of the cabbage, crossing each other in the centre, so that the water may penetrate to the heart and cook it equally.

Prepare a large sauce-pan of boiling water, into which throw the soda; put into this the cabbage, covering the pan until the water boils up. When removing the cover, it must be allowed to boil rapidly, until a skewer or fork will pierce readily through it.

Remove the cabbage now to a colander, and let the water drain from it, and chop it roughly with a knife when drained.

When chopped put it into a vegetable dish, pour over it the beef-dripping, sprinkle over the pepper and salt, when it must be tossed about with a fork very quickly in order that the cabbage may not cool. When the seasoning is thoroughly distributed, send it at once to the table.

NOTES.—This may be cooked exactly the same way, and served whole if preferred; in which case the dripping must be heated and poured over, and the pepper and salt sprinkled over afterwards.

Cabbage may also be boiled very palatably in the liquor in which either salt beef or salt pork is boiled.

Boiled Carrots with Brown Sauce.—For this prepare one bunch of young carrots, one ounce of butter, one half ounce of flour, one half pint of brown stock, one dessert-spoonful of catchup, one salt-spoonful of salt, one salt-spoonful of pepper.

Wash the carrots in cold water, and cut them squarely across at the tops. Throw them into boiling water, and boil them for twenty minutes. Ten minutes before this time expires, take the carrot-tops that have been cut off, dry them thoroughly, and melting the butter in a frying-pan, put in these top pieces, and brown them upon both sides.

When these are browned, stir in with them the flour, add by degrees the stock, and stir all together until the stock boils. Season with the pepper and salt, flavour with the catchup, and again let the sauce boil for two minutes.

When the carrots are boiled, take them from the water, and rolling them one by one in a towel, wring lightly to rub off the thin outer skin, stand them in regular order upright in a vegetable dish, and strain the sauce around them.

NOTE.—Old carrots may be used also in this way, but they must first be scraped and pared down to uniform sizes, and also will require a little longer boiling.

Boiled Potatoes.—For this provide ten potatoes, one half table-spoonful of salt.

Select the potatoes of nearly an equal size, and wash them well in cold water. Pare them very thinly, as the best part of the potato lies nearest the skin, and putting them into a sauce-pan, cover them with cold water, and bring the water quickly to the boiling-point. Throw in the salt, and covering the sauce-pan, let the whole boil rapidly until the surfaces of the potatoes begin to crack; then the water must be drained entirely off, leaving the potatoes dry in the sauce-pan, and re-covering them, put the sauce-pan at one side of the fire, turn it occasionally, that they may not catch on the bottom, and let them cook in their own steam until they can be easily pierced with a skewer.

When done, remove the cover, and set the sauce-pan for

a moment over the fire to aid the escape of the steam and dry off any moisture. They must be carefully transferred to a vegetable dish in order to preserve them unbroken.

Notes.—Instead of serving these potatoes whole, they may be passed through a colander or coarse wire sieve directly into a vegetable dish. The vegetable dish should be put into a very quick oven, and the potatoes browned over the top. Served in this way, the potatoes have a beautiful light appearance resembling well-boiled rice, besides being most delicious to the taste.

New potatoes should be boiled after the above method, with this difference: they must be scraped instead of pared, and thrown into boiling water to boil instead of into cold.

If the potatoes are desired plainly mashed, a little cream and butter should be added to them; and when mounded into the dish, a lump of butter may be let into the top, and some pepper dusted over all.

Colcannon.—Provide for this one pound of cold boiled potatoes, one pound of cold boiled turnip, one ounce of butter, one table-spoonful of bread crumbs, one salt-spoonful of salt, one salt-spoonful of pepper.

The bread crumbs must first be put upon a tin or plate, and into the oven and browned to a light brown. Grease slightly a plain mould holding about three pints, and sprinkle around the sides and over the bottom of this the browned bread crumbs. Put into a bowl the potato, and with it the turnip, which must first be pressed down and drained of any water that it may have gathered in standing to cool. Mix these thoroughly together, and season them with the pepper and salt, adding also the butter, and when all is stirred together, pack the mixture into the mould. Pressing it down with the blade of a knife, place the mould in a moderate oven, where it must remain until its contents be thoroughly heated; then turn the form carefully out into a vegetable dish, and serve steaming hot.

Boiled Haricot Beans.—Prepare one pint of dried haricot beans, four hard-boiled eggs, yolk of one raw egg, one table-spoonful of chopped parsley, two ounces of flour, two ounces of butter, one half pint of milk, one heaped tea-spoonful of salt.

VEGETABLES.

Soak the dried beans over night in an abundance of cold water. Two hours before they are required to serve, drain from them the water in which they have soaked, and putting them into a sauce-pan, cover them well with cold water, and let them boil briskly for two hours. The salt must meantime have been put into the water; and from time to time as the water in the sauce-pan reduces by boiling, cold water must be poured in to keep the quantity the same, taking care to do this with sufficient frequency to prevent cooling the boiling liquor too much by the quantity of cold water added.

Five minutes before the beans will be ready to dish up, melt in a small sauce-pan the butter, stir into it the flour, add by degrees the milk, and stir all until boiling. Let the mixture cook for two minutes, and season it with the salt.

When the beans are done, drain the water from them in the quickest and most convenient way, so that they be rendered perfectly dry, place them in a deep vegetable dish, take the sauce from the fire, drop into it the yolk of egg, and pour all immediately over the beans.

Take the shells from the hard-boiled eggs, cut them in two, and arrange them around the dish of beans with the rounded sides up. Sprinkle over each piece of egg a little of the chopped parsley, when the dish is ready for serving.

NOTES.—It is contended that the dried haricot beans cannot be properly cooked through without breaking their skins; but if the above directions are strictly followed in the particularities of adding *cold* water, and boiling *rapidly*, the result will be that the beans are not only thoroughly cooked to their centres, but have preserved their form unbroken.

The dried white bean in ordinary use may also be successfully boiled in this way.

Boiled Onions.—Take six Spanish onions, one half teaspoonful of salt, two ounces of butter, one ounce of flour, one half pint of milk, one gill of cream, one salt-spoonful of pepper, one lump of soda the size of a pea.

The onions must first be skinned and allowed to stand all night in water, which must have been poured over them boiling, and in which the soda has been dissolved.

An hour before required for use, the onions should be put into a sauce-pan, covered with cold water, put over the fire, and when boiling, boiled for fifteen minutes. At the end of this time the first water should be drained off, nearly all of the salt sprinkled over them, and re-covering them with boiling water, allow them to boil for half an hour longer.

While the onions are boiling, melt in a small sauce-pan the butter, stir into it the flour, and by degrees the milk; and when this mixture boils, add to it the cream, and let all cook together for two minutes, when it must be seasoned with the pepper and remaining salt.

Take the onions from the water, when boiled, one by one, with a draining spoon, pressing them against the side of the sauce-pan in lifting them, that the water may be entirely expressed. Place them in a vegetable dish, pour over them the white sauce, and they are ready to serve.

Baked Onions.—Take six Spanish onions, three ounces of butter, one half ounce of flour, one tea-cupful of brown stock, one half table-spoonful of salt, one half tea-spoonful of pepper, one lump of soda the size of a pea.

Soak the onions over night in a preparation of boiling water in which the soda has been dissolved, and an hour before they are required to serve, place them in a sauce-pan, cover them with cold water, place the sauce-pan upon the fire, and when boiling let them continue to cook briskly for fifteen minutes.

Take them when boiled from the water, and putting them into a vegetable dish, distribute over them two ounces of the butter, sprinkle over them the pepper and salt, and placing the vegetable dish into a moderate oven, let them bake for half an hour.

Ten minutes before the onions will be done, put into a bowl the flour, and make it smooth with the stock. Five minutes before taking the onions from the oven, pour the mixed flour and stock over them, distribute over all the remainder of the butter in small pieces, and when the remaining five minutes expire, take the onions from the oven and serve at once.

NOTES.—To fry onions, they should first be skinned, then boiling water poured over them. Dry them in a towel, cut them into thin slices, and fry in hot butter.

Onions are exceedingly indigestible, unless soaked for twelve hours before cooking. Fried onions cannot therefore be recommended for dyspeptics.

Lima Beans.—Take one pint of shelled lima beans, two ounces of butter, one tea-spoonful of salt, one half tea-spoonful of white pepper.

Put the shelled beans into a bowl, and pour over them some boiling water. Leaving them in this water five minutes, take them out and drain them; then placing them in a sauce-pan of boiling water in which the salt has been dissolved, allow them to boil for twenty minutes.

When done pour them into a colander, and when thoroughly drained pour them into a vegetable dish, sprinkle over them the pepper, and melting the butter, pour it also over them, and serve.

NOTE.—Succotash may be made from the boiled lima beans by adding to them an equal quantity of canned green corn, and an equal quantity of milk and water, seasoned with pepper, salt, and a lump of butter, being poured over the mixture while warming.

Cabbage à-la-Mode.—Provide one head of cabbage, one quarter pound of cold chicken, two ounces of cold pork, one quarter pound of rice, three ounces of butter, one half ounce of flour, one pint of brown stock, one tea-spoonful of salt, one tea-spoonful of pepper, one Bermuda onion.

A close firm head of cabbage should be selected, and this well washed in cold water, after which it must be placed in a large sauce-pan of boiling water, and boiled over a brisk fire for fifteen minutes.

At the end of this time, take the cabbage from the water, place it upon a platter to cool a little, and while this is cooling, put into a chopping bowl, and chop very finely the chicken and pork; chop the onion also, and mix it with the meat; season all with the pepper and salt; wash well the rice, and mix it with the pork, fowl, and onion; open the leaves of the cabbage gently, and inserting this mixture between them, bind the cabbage around with a piece of twine, and melting in a large sauce-pan the butter, fry the cabbage in it until thoroughly brown.

Mix the flour with a little of the stock in a bowl, and when the lumps are all beaten out, add the remainder of the stock. Pour this over the browned cabbage, and let all stew very slowly for three hours thereafter.

When done, serve in a vegetable dish with the sauce poured around.

NOTE.—Cold roast beef or lean roast mutton may be substituted when chicken is not convenient.

Boiled Parsnips.—Prepare ten medium-sized parsnips, three ounces of butter, three gills of milk, one table-spoonful of salt, one half tea-spoonful of pepper, one salt-spoonful of grated nutmeg.

Wash the parsnips as cleanly as possible in cold water, when they must be put into a sauce-pan of boiling water in which the salt has been dissolved. Boil them from half an hour to three quarters of an hour, as their age and size may demand; and when boiled until tender take them from the water, one by one, rubbing each in a clean towel to remove the skin, which will have become loosened by boiling.

Place them in a heated vegetable dish, and when the butter has been melted, the milk added thereto, together with the pepper and nutmeg, and all boiled, this should be poured over the parsnips, and all immediately served.

NOTE.—To fry parsnips, they must first be plainly boiled, then skinned, dried in a towel, and split into halves and fried in hot melted butter until browned.

Leeks au Gratin.—Provide eight leeks, one half table-spoonful of salt, one ounce of butter, one ounce of flour, one half pint of second stock, one salt-spoonful of grated nutmeg, three ounces of grated cheese.

Remove first the fibrous roots from the leeks, cut off the green stalks, leaving about an inch length of them on for use. Put them into a bowl, and covering them with boiling water, let the leek soak for ten minutes. At the expiration of this time, put them into a sauce-pan of boiling water, into which throw the salt, and let all boil for three quarters of an hour.

While the leeks are boiling, mix together in a sauce-pan placed over the fire the butter and flour, to which add the stock by degrees, and let all cook for two minutes, after which season with the pepper, throw in the nutmeg and one ounce of the cheese.

When the leeks are done take them from the boiling water, drain them, and place them upon a gratin-dish. Pour over them half of the sauce from the sauce-pan, sprinkle over with the remainder of the cheese, and placing the dish in a quick oven, let all become slightly browned.

When browned, remove the dish from the oven, pour around the leeks the remaining sauce, and serve.

NOTE.—When a silver gratin-dish is not available, an ordinary flat dish may be used, with the consideration that it must be something that will not be injured by the heat, and also that the preparation must be served in the same dish in which it is baked.

French or String Beans.—Provide: one quart of beans, two ounces of butter, one salt-spoonful of pepper, one dessert-spoonful of salt, one grain of cayenne.

First string the beans, observing always to begin at the stem end of the pod when the strings will strip easily downward. Lay them flat upon a board, and with a sharp knife cut them through the centres lengthwise, when they must be gathered into small bunches of equal size and secured with a piece of twine.

Place the bunches now in a sauce-pan two-thirds full of boiling water, in which the salt has been dissolved, and boil them for twenty minutes if the beans are very young, but if older they will require quite half an hour to become tender.

When done drain off the water, and transferring each little bunch to a vegetable dish and cutting the strings, arrange them neatly therein.

Melt the butter, season it with the cayenne and pepper, and pour it over all just before serving.

NOTE.—String beans are sometimes served cut in small squares and with a sauce of melted butter and milk, seasoned with salt and pepper.

Stewed Tomatoes.—Provide: two quarts of fresh tomatoes, two ounces of butter, two milk biscuits, one half tea-spoonful of pepper, one half tea-spoonful of salt.

Put the tomatoes into a sauce-pan two-thirds filled with boiling water, and let them boil until the skins begin to crack and curl. Take them from the water, drain them in a colander, and when thoroughly drained, dry the bottom of the colander and rub the tomatoes through it.

Return them to the sauce-pan, and let them stew slowly for one hour, when the butter, pepper, and salt must be added; and just before serving stir in the biscuit, which must have been crushed fine with a rolling-pin preparatory to using.

NOTE.—Canned tomatoes may be prepared also in this way, except that, having already been cooked in the process of canning, they require only to be drained, made fine, and thoroughly heated.

Stewed Celery.—Prepare: one head of celery, two ounces of butter, one ounce of flour, three gills of milk, one half tea-spoonful of pepper, one tea-spoonful of salt.

Wash the celery thoroughly, cut it into inch lengths, when it should be put into a sauce-pan, covered with boiling water, and cooked until tender, the length of time for which depends entirely upon the age and quality of the celery.

When tender the water must be poured off, the milk and flour mixed together in a bowl, which season with the pepper and salt, and pouring it over the celery, return the sauce-pan to the fire, stirring all until the milk boils, when the butter must be added and the stew served hot.

Boiled Beets.—Provide: six medium-sized beets, one half pint of vinegar, one blade of mace, one half tea-spoonful of white pepper-corns, one half tea-spoonful of black pepper-corns, one ounce of butter, one tea-spoonful of salt.

The beets must be carefully washed in cold water, taking care not to break off the fine fibrous roots, in order that they may not bleed in boiling and so lose their colour. Put them when washed into a large sauce-pan with plenty of boiling water, and boil them until a skewer or fork will pierce easily to their centres. When tender drain off the boiling water, and taking each beet separately, rub off their skins in a clean dry towel.

Take four of the beets and cut them into slices about a quarter of an inch in thickness. Place these slices into a vegetable dish, melt the butter and pour it over them, and sprinkling over also the pepper and salt, they are ready to serve.

Meantime, while the beets have been boiling, the vinegar, mace, and pepper-corns must have been put together in a sauce-pan and boiled five minutes. When the remaining two beets have been also sliced and arranged in a vegetable dish, the prepared vinegar should be thrown over them, and the whole put away to become cold before serving.

NOTES.—Beets prepared as above with the vinegar will keep for a week if desired.

Beets as well as potatoes may be baked in the oven, and will be found very sweet; but a long time is required to have them become thoroughly baked, the length of which must be determined by testing with a skewer.

Macaroni and Cheese.—Three ounces of macaroni, three ounces of grated Parmesan cheese, one half pint of milk, two ounces of butter, one gill of cream, one egg, one tea-spoonful of dry mustard, one salt-spoonful of grated nutmeg, one salt-spoonful of salt, one salt-spoonful of pepper.

Wash the macaroni in cold water, and removing it from the water, place it in a sauce-pan, cover it with cold water, and let it boil in this for fifteen minutes.

At the end of this time drain off the water, cover the macaroni with the milk, and allow all to boil for three quarters of an hour longer.

When this is done put the cream into a bowl, beat it until very light, add the egg, and beat both together until thoroughly blended. Season this mixture with the pepper, salt, cayenne, and mustard, pour into it the boiled macaroni, add to this two ounces of the cheese and one ounce of the butter, and when all has been well mixed, pour it out upon a platter, sprinkle over the remainder of the cheese, and distribute over also the remaining ounce of butter in small pieces. Place the platter in a moderate oven, and bake its contents for ten minutes, and serve at once upon the dish upon which it is prepared.

Dressed Cauliflower.—One large cauliflower, two ounces of butter, one egg, four table-spoonfuls of bread crumbs, one tea-spoonful of salt, one half tea-spoonful of pepper.

Lay the cauliflower in a basin, pour over it sufficient water to cover it, and sprinkle in a good table-spoonful of salt. Allow the cauliflower to lie in the water for twenty minutes.

Bring to the boiling-point a large sauce-pan of boiling water, drain well the cauliflower from the salted water, put it into the boiling water, and let it boil for twenty minutes.

When cooked, take the cauliflower from the water and chop it up finely, add to it an ounce and a half of the butter, also the bread crumbs, pepper, and salt; then stir in the egg, which must first be lightly beaten. Mix all well together, and place in a flat dish, and put over the top in small pieces the remaining butter. Bake this now in the oven until it has a pale brown colour, or merely brown it before the fire.

NOTE.—This dish is generally made from cauliflower which has sprung a little; cold boiled cauliflower may also be made up in this way.

Turnips in White Sauce.—Ten young turnips, one half pint of white stock, one ounce of butter, one half ounce of flour, one gill of milk or cream, one salt-spoonful of salt, one half salt-spoonful of white pepper.

Wash well the turnips; pare them thickly in order to remove the bitter part, which lies near the outside.

Place in a sauce-pan the stock and allow it to boil; throw into it the turnips, and boil them for half an hour.

When tender place in a small bowl the flour, make it smooth with a table-spoonful of the cream or milk, add the pepper and salt, then the remainder of the cream. Draw the sauce-pan from the fire, stir into it the contents of the bowl, add then the butter, stir all well together until the butter is melted; but do not let it boil. Serve at once.

Maître d'Hôtel Potatoes.—Six boiled potatoes, one table-spoonful of chopped parsley, two ounces of butter, one half ounce of flour, one half pint of boiling water, one half table-spoonful of lemon-juice.

Pare six potatoes that have been boiled in their skins, cut them into slices about half an inch in thickness.

Melt in a sauce-pan the butter, and stir into it the flour. When well mixed pour over the boiling water, and squeeze in the lemon-juice.

Place carefully in this mixture the potatoes, also the parsley, toss all gently over the fire until the potatoes are quite hot; but take care not to break them. Season to taste with pepper and salt, and serve on a very hot dish.

Turnip Radishes.—One dozen of radishes, one half table-spoonful of salt, two ounces of butter.

Dissolve in a large sauce-pan of water the salt; when boiling throw into it the radishes, which ought first to be carefully trimmed, leaving on them a few of the green top leaves.

When the radishes have boiled thirty minutes, remove them to a very hot dish, melt the butter in a small sauce-pan, and pour it over.

Vegetable Marrow Stuffed.—One vegetable marrow, two ounces veal, two ounces ham, one ounce bread crumb, one ounce butter, the yolk of one egg, one tea-spoonful salt, one quarter tea-spoonful pepper.

Chop very finely the veal and ham, place them in a basin; add the pepper, salt, bread crumb, and butter, stir all well together; add the yolk of egg, stir well again. Pare the marrow, cut it in half, and scoop out the seeds; place in the stuffing, and put the sides of the marrow together again. Grease well a sheet of kitchen-paper, and roll it round the marrow. Place the marrow on a baking-tin, and bake it for from half an hour to three quarters, according to size of marrow. Take it out of the paper, place it on a very hot dish, and pour round a brown sauce. (See page 176.)

Stewed Celery.—Two heads of celery, one half pint white stock, one ounce butter, one half pound flour, one gill cream, one half tea-spoonful salt, one salt-spoonful pepper, one salt-spoonful grated nutmeg.

Wash well the celery, strip off the outer stalks. Cut the centre stalks into pieces about four inches in length. Place the celery in a stew-pan, pour over the stock, and allow it to simmer by the side of the fire for half an hour. Place now on a plate the butter, and with the point of a knife work into it the flour.

When the celery has cooked half an hour, add to it the butter, flour, and cream, also the salt, pepper, and nutmeg. Stir all till again boiling, simmer five minutes, and then serve.

SALADS.

Chicken Salad.—One cold chicken, one tea-spoonful of salt, one tea-spoonful of white pepper, **one half head of** celery, one grain of cayenne, yolks of two eggs, one table-spoonful of vinegar, one table-spoonful of capers, one head of lettuce, one gill of salad oil.

Cut the chicken into small square pieces and remove the skin. The celery should be well washed, and also cut into pieces of a similar size. Put into a bowl the yolks of eggs, drop into this, drop by drop, the oil, and beat them together with the back of a wooden spoon.

When this is done the mixture should resemble a thick

cream, to which the vinegar should be added; and putting the chicken and celery together in a salad-bowl, pour over them this compound, sprinkle on also the pepper, salt, and cayenne, and mix all thoroughly together with a fork.

Take then the fresh green leaves of the lettuce, and, washing well first, arrange them around the edge of the salad-bowl, sprinkle the capers over the top, and garnish the centre with tips of celery to give the salad an attractive appearance.

NOTE.—Cold turkey may be substituted for chicken in making a salad.

Potato Salad.—Eight large potatoes, two table-spoonfuls of vinegar, one half of a Bermuda onion, one table-spoonful of chopped parsley, yolks of two eggs, one gill of salad oil, one tea-spoonful of white pepper, one tea-spoonful of salt, one head of lettuce.

Wash and pare the potatoes, and put them to boil in a sauce-pan containing as much cold water as will nicely cover them. Boil them until tender, but not broken on the surfaces, when the water must be drained off, and the potatoes allowed to get quite cold. Cut them first into quarters, and then these quarters into slices, place the slices into a salad-bowl, sprinkle over them the chopped parsley, and also the onion, which must have been chopped exceedingly fine, when the vinegar, pepper, and salt must be added, and all tossed with a fork until thoroughly mixed. Put now into a small bowl the yolks of eggs, and drop in thereafter the salad oil, drop by drop, stirring all until it comes to a cream, when the mixture must be poured over the salad in the salad-bowl, and the dish garnished with the fresh green leaves of the lettuce.

Shrimp Salad.—One can of shrimps, two heads of lettuce, one gill of salad oil, one table-spoonful of vinegar, one tea-spoonful of salt, one half tea-spoonful of white pepper, yolks of two eggs.

The heads of lettuce should be carefully trimmed, well

washed, and thoroughly dried in a towel, avoiding as much as possible the crushing of the leaves, which causes them to wilt.

They should next be picked apart, and the outer leaves torn into medium-sized pieces, reserving the tender inner leaves for garnishing.

Place the torn lettuce in the bottom of a salad-bowl, and removing the shrimps carefully from the bag in which they are, put into the can, take from them any bits of shell or specks of black that may mar them, taking care not to break their form, and pile these high upon the lettuce in the centre of the bowl.

Put the yolks of eggs into a small bowl, drop in upon them, drop by drop, the salad oil, and beat these to a thick cream, when the vinegar must be added, also the pepper and salt, and all stirred together until thoroughly blended.

Pour this dressing over the shrimps, garnish around the sides and in the centre of the top with the pale, delicate inner leaves of lettuce, and serve.

This salad must not be mixed at all until it is served at table, as to stir it destroys the fine appearance of the shrimps, which are so delicate as to be easily broken.

NOTES.—Mayonnaise dressing should invariably be stirred one way, as to reverse the current of the liquid causes it to curdle. If by accident curdling occurs, its smoothness may be recovered by dropping in the yolk of another egg, and paying strict attention to the rule for stirring.

When fresh shrimps instead of the canned ones are used, a large sauce-pan of boiling water, in which have been placed salt, a little lemon-thyme, mint, and bay-leaf, should be prepared, and the shrimps plunged into this, confined in a wire-basket, and boiled until they change their colour, the length of time for which depends upon the size of the shrimps.

Lobster Salad.—One quart of brown stock, one half ounce of gelatine, one table-spoonful of vinegar, one sprig of parsley, one tea-spoonful of pepper, two gills of cold water, whites of two eggs, one bay-leaf, one lobster, one ounce of butter, one table-spoonful of cream, one half tea-spoonful of lemon-juice, two tea-spoonfuls of salt, one grain of cayenne, one head of lettuce, two table-spoonfuls of salad oil, yolks of two eggs, one tea-spoonful of tarragon vinegar.

The aspic jelly required for the preparation of this salad must be made the day before it is designed for use, in order that it may have time to become quite firm. It is to be prepared as follows :—

Put the stock into a copper or porcelain-lined sauce-pan, and make it hot over a quick fire. While this is heating, soak the gelatine in half a gill of cold water. When the stock has come to a tepid degree of heat, put into it the table-spoonful of vinegar, parsley, bay-leaf, and soaked gelatine. Whip up the whites of egg in a bowl, and mix with it half a gill of cold water and a little pepper and salt.

Pour this egg mixture into the stock, and stir all together rapidly with an egg-whisk or two forks until the stock boils. Cover the sauce-pan closely, and draw it aside from the fire, allowing its contents to simmer for ten minutes. Strain all through a clean towel into a bowl, and stand the jelly in a cool dry place to become firm.

When the lobster has been boiled and becomes cold, twist off the head, which will be used in garnishing, and remove the coral, if possible, without breaking it. Place the coral upon a plate, and stand it where it may be exposed to heat sufficient to dry it rapidly, but neither bake nor brown it. Remove also the meat from the tail and claws of the lobster, and cut it into convenient pieces.

Melt the butter in a sauce-pan, stir into it the flour, and add to it by degrees a gill of cold water. When this is boiling let it cook for two minutes thereafter rapidly, and take it from the fire, add to it the cream, the lemon-juice, cayenne, and a little pepper and salt, also the pieces of meat from the lobster.

When this is well mixed together it must be turned out upon a plate, and put in a cool place, and allowed to become quite cold.

When cold, divide it into five portions, and form each one into a cutlet about three inches long.

Wash the lettuce, dry the leaves carefully with a towel, and tearing it into irregular pieces, arrange them in the bottom of a salad-bowl.

Mix in a separate bowl the yolks of egg and salad oil, which must be dropped upon the egg drop by drop, and when these are beaten to a cream, add thereto the tarragon vinegar. Pour this over the lettuce in the salad-bowl, sprinkle over all the remainder of the pepper and salt, and toss all lightly with a fork to distribute the dressing through the lettuce.

Chop the aspic jelly now coarsely, and arrange a wall of it around the sides of the salad-bowl, taking care to keep the centre clear, and within this wall place the lobster cutlets in a circle.

Into each of the cutlets stick one of the feelers from the lobster, rub the head with a little oil to brighten and bring out the colour, and place it in the centre of the dish.

Take the dried coral, and either pound it lightly in a mortar or roll it fine upon a board with a rolling-pin, and sprinkle a little of this over each cutlet, and the remainder over the wall of jelly.

NOTES.—To boil lobsters, plunge them into boiling water in which a little salt has been dissolved, and boil them for twenty minutes rapidly.

A plain lobster salad may be made by following the directions for shrimp salad, by substituting the meat of the lobster cut in coarse pieces for the shrimps.

Cucumber Salad.—Three medium-sized green cucumbers, two table-spoonfuls of salad oil, one table-spoonful of vinegar, one tea-spoonful of salt, one half tea-spoonful of black pepper.

The cucumbers should be kept upon the ice until thoroughly chilled, which renders them pleasantly brittle, after which they should be pared lengthwise, taking care to cut deep enough to remove all of the green inner skin, which is exceedingly bitter, and when pared slice them into round, thin slices. Arrange these slices in a mound in a shallow salad-bowl, and mixing together the pepper, salt, oil, and vinegar, pour this dressing over the cucumbers, and stir all together until the dressing is well distributed when serving.

Note.—A tomato salad may be prepared in the same manner, with this difference : a little sugar must be added to the ingredients for the dressing.

Beef Salad.—One pound of rare roast beef, one quarter of a boiled beet, one table-spoonful of vinegar, three table-spoonfuls of salad oil, one tea-spoonful of salt, one half tea-spoonful of black pepper, one head of lettuce.

Wash the lettuce, each leaf separately, dry them thoroughly with a towel, taking care not to crush or wilt them, and reserving the few delicate inner leaves for garnishing, tear the rest into irregular pieces, and arrange them in the bottom of a salad-bowl.

Cut the beef into small square pieces, slice the beet and cut it also into pieces ; mixing both lightly together, put them in a pyramidal shape upon the lettuce in the bowl, and sprinkle over all the pepper and salt. Mix together in a separate bowl the vinegar and oil, and when thoroughly blended, pour this dressing over the salad, and garnish at the top with the small lettuce leaves.

Note.—A salad may be made of sliced cold tongue by following the above directions, and substituting the tongue for the cold roast beef.

Lettuce Salad.—Two heads of lettuce, one dessert-spoonful of salt, one half tea-spoonful of pepper, one table-spoonful of salad oil, three table-spoonfuls of vinegar, two hard-boiled eggs.

Separate the leaves of the heads of lettuce, wash them carefully, and dry each leaf thoroughly with a towel, handling them gently that they may be neither crushed nor wilted. Tear the leaves into pieces, and arrange them lightly in a salad-bowl. Sprinkle over them the pepper and salt, and mixing the vinegar and oil together in a separate bowl, pour it, when well blended, over the salad, and stir all together at table when serving. Cut the hard-boiled eggs into quarters and garnish the dish with them.

Notes.—Endive, eschalot, chiccory, water-cress, celery, and all green salads may be prepared as the lettuce salad is prepared. All green salads should have the material of which they are composed made very cold and crisp before dressing.

If French dressing is preferred to the vinegar dressing, the proportions of vinegar and oil may be simply changed from the above given quantities to three table-spoonfuls of salad oil, one table-spoonful of vinegar.

Green salads should be stirred as little as possible before being sent to the table, in order that their freshness may be preserved until the moment of serving.

Salad à-la-Russe.—One boiled carrot, one boiled turnip, two boiled potatoes, one-third of a head of fresh celery, one boiled beet, four olives, four anchovies, yolks of two eggs, one table-spoonful of vinegar, one tea-spoonful of tarragon vinegar, one tea-spoonful of salt, one half tea-spoonful of pepper.

First put into a small bowl the yolks of eggs, and drop upon them the salad oil, drop by drop, beating this to a cream as the oil is dropped in. Stir in both the vinegar and tarragon vinegar, and season with a little of the pepper and salt. Cut the carrot, turnip, potato, and celery into small dice, arrange these dice in pyramidal form upon a flat platter, and pour over them the mayonnaise dressing.

Cut the boiled beet into regular round slices, and place them around the dish, lapping one upon the other. At each corner place one of the four olives, around each of which must be twisted one of the anchovies; sprinkle over all the remainder of the pepper and salt, and serve.

Notes.—Hard-boiled eggs may be used for garnishing salads as the fancy or taste may dictate.

Olives are frequently used in chicken, turkey, and lobster salad, and for those who have a fondness for this relish they may be used at discretion.

Potato salad may be made, if desired, with a simple vinegar dressing instead of the mayonnaise.

CROQUETTES AND FRITTERS.

CROQUETTES.

Potato Croquettes.—One pound of mashed potatoes, one ounce of butter, two table-spoonfuls of milk, one half tea-spoonful of pepper, two eggs, four table-spoonfuls of bread crumbs, one grain of cayenne, one half tea-spoonful of salt.

First melt the butter in a sauce-pan, add to it the milk, and bring them together to the boiling-point. Pass the mashed potatoes through a sieve, and add them to the boiling milk and butter. Beat all well together until the potatoes are very hot, when the sauce-pan must be taken from the fire, the pepper, salt, and cayenne thrown in; then drop in the yolks of eggs, and stir until the heat of the potato dries the egg.

Roll this mixture into small balls, using a little flour to prevent it sticking to the hands, beat up the whites of the eggs and roll each ball therein.

Place the bread crumbs upon a sheet of kitchen-paper, and putting the balls one by one into this, roll them from side to side until covered with the crumbs, when they must be put into hot clarified fat or lard and fried for two minutes.

NOTE.—The yolks of egg are mixed with the potato in order to bind it together, and to give the croquette a rich yellow colour. If the whites were put in also, difficulty would be experienced in forming the croquettes, and the colour would not be so fine.

Chicken Croquettes. — One half of a chicken, three ounces of butter, two ounces of cold tongue, seven ounces of flour, one salt-spoonful of grated nutmeg, one tea-spoonful of salt, one half salt-spoonful of pepper, the rind of one lemon, one half tea-spoonful of lemon-juice, one egg, six table-spoonfuls of bread crumbs, one half gill of cold water.

First bone the chicken, remove the skin, and chop the meat very finely. Chop the tongue finely also, and mix it with the chicken. Flavour this with the rind of lemon grated and the nutmeg; season with the pepper and nearly all of the salt.

Place the flour into a bowl and rub into it the butter. When mixed, make a well in the centre of it, put into it the water, lemon-juice, and the remainder of the salt, kneading all firmly together. Roll this paste out as firmly as possible, and cut it into rounds with a biscuit-cutter.

Beat the egg until very light, and brush the edges of the rounds with it. Put into the centre of each round of paste as much of the mixed chicken and tongue as it will hold, when the edges must be gathered up and pinched firmly together. When filled, roll each of the croquettes first into the egg and then into the bread crumbs, and throwing them into hot clarified fat or lard, let them cook for five minutes.

When done, take them from the fat, place them for a moment upon a piece of kitchen-paper to drain, arrange them neatly in a napkin folded in cup shape, and garnish with parsley.

Rice Croquettes.—One quart of milk, three quarters of a pound of rice, three ounces of sugar, one tea-spoonful of lemon-juice, two eggs, four table-spoonfuls of bread crumbs, one half salt-spoonful of salt.

Wash the rice thoroughly, put it into a sauce-pan, and pour over it the milk. Cover the sauce-pan closely, and putting it over the fire without having stirred the contents, let all simmer slowly for twenty minutes. At the end of this time remove the sauce-pan from the fire, stir in the yolks of eggs, lemon-juice, salt, and half of the sugar, beat all thoroughly together, and turn out, when mixed, the compound into a bowl, and let it stand until it becomes thoroughly cool. When this mixture is quite cold, mould it into small equal-sized balls, beat the whites of egg until quite light, and dip the balls therein.

Roll them in the bread crumbs, which must have been placed upon a sheet of kitchen-paper for this purpose, and throwing the croquettes from this into hot clarified fat or lard, let them fry for two minutes.

When done, take them from the fat, place them upon a sheet of kitchen-paper to drain for a moment, and serve them in a folded napkin, with the remainder of the sugar sprinkled over them.

NOTES.—If it is preferred, these croquettes can be made without the sugar; and if so done, a little more salt may be used.

It must be observed that the rice is not to be stirred when boiled for this preparation, otherwise the grains will be broken and the danger be incurred of its sticking fast to the bottom of the sauce-pan, and so scorching.

Crab Croquettes.—Two crabs, three ounces of butter, three ounces of flour, one half pint of milk, one tea-spoonful of anchovy sauce, four table-spoonfuls of bread crumbs, one egg, one half tea-spoonful of pepper, one tea-spoonful of salt, one grain of cayenne.

Throw the crabs into boiling water, and let them boil for fifteen minutes. Remove the meat from the shells and chop it coarsely.

Melt the butter in a sauce-pan, stir into it the flour, and add to this by degrees the milk. When this is brought to the boiling-point, let it boil for two minutes thereafter, and take it from the fire.

Throw into the sauce-pan the meat from the crabs, add to the mixture thus formed the cayenne, salt, pepper, and anchovy sauce, and when thoroughly mixed, turn it out upon a plate and allow it to cool.

When quite cold, form the compound into small equal rolls three inches in length, beat the egg, and dip each roll therein, after which they must be placed upon the bread crumbs, which must be prepared upon a sheet of kitchen-paper for the purpose, and rolled therein from side to side until each croquette is blanketed with the crumbs.

Drop them into hot clarified fat or lard, and fry them for two minutes; taking them from the fat, drain for a moment upon a sheet of kitchen-paper, and serve them in a folded napkin, garnished with sprigs of parsley.

Croquettes of Shad-Roe.—Four medium-sized shad-roes, two boiled potatoes, one ounce of butter, one ounce of flour, one gill of cold water, one table-spoonful of chopped parsley, one tea-spoonful of salt, one half tea-spoonful of pepper, one tea-spoonful of lemon-juice, two hard-boiled eggs, one raw egg, four table-spoonfuls of bread crumbs.

Throw the roes into boiling water and boil them for twenty minutes. Take them from the water, drain them, and placing them in a bowl, separate them with a wooden spoon. Add to the roes the pepper, salt, and chopped parsley. Place a sieve over the bowl, and rub through it the yolks of the hard-boiled eggs. Rub through upon this the potatoes; remove the sieve, add the whites of the hard-boiled eggs, finely chopped, and the lemon-juice.

Melt in a sauce-pan the butter, stir it into the flour, and the gill of water by degrees, and when this boils, pour it over the materials in the bowl, and stir all thoroughly together.

Fashion this mixture into small equal shapes resembling the shad-roes in miniature, beat the raw egg, and dip the croquettes into it, place the bread crumbs upon a sheet of kitchen-paper, and roll them in turn in it, and putting them into hot clarified fat or lard, fry them for two minutes, after which they must be drained of any superfluous grease upon a sheet of kitchen-paper, and served in a folded napkin.

Croquettes of Salmon.—Three quarters of a pound of cold boiled salmon, five table-spoonfuls of bread crumbs, one and one-half ounce of butter, two eggs, one-half of a lemon, one tea-spoonful of anchovy sauce, one half tea-spoonful of salt, one half tea-spoonful of pepper, one salt-spoonful of grated nutmeg, one salt-spoonful of powdered mace.

Shred the salmon with two forks, and remove from it the bones and skin. Place it when prepared into a bowl, and mix it with the bread crumbs. Melt the butter and pour it over this mixture, add thereto the pepper, salt, mace, and nutmeg, and beating all thoroughly together, squeeze over it the lemon-juice.

Add to the compound the anchovy sauce and the two eggs, stir all again together, and form this into croquettes of equal size, about three inches in length, using a little flour upon the hands to prevent the mixture from sticking.

Drop the croquettes one by one into hot clarified fat or lard, fry them for two minutes, then removing them from the frying-pan, drain them a moment upon a piece of kitchen-paper. Serve in a napkin folded in the form of a basket.

Croquettes of Macaroni.—One quarter pound macaroni, one half pint milk, one ounce butter. one half ounce flour, one gill cream, two ounces cheese, two eggs, one half tea-spoonful salt, one salt-spoonful pepper, one grain cayenne, three table-spoonfuls bread crumbs.

Wash well the macaroni, place it in a sauce-pan, cover it with the milk, and boil it slowly for three-quarters of an hour. Drain the macaroni well on a sieve, and cut it in half-inch lengths. Melt in a sauce-pan the butter, add the flour, then by degrees the cream, stir all till boiling, boil two minutes, take the pan at once from the fire, add the cut macaroni, the pepper, salt, and cayenne. Grate the cheese, add it also, then drop in the yolks of the two eggs, stir it well together and place it on one side till quite cold. Roll then the mixture into small balls, beat well the whites of egg on a plate, roll the balls in the whites, then place the bread crumbs on a paper, and roll the balls also in it. Heat some clarified fat in a stew-pan; when the smoke rises drop in the balls and brown them for two minutes. Drain on a sheet of kitchen paper, and serve very hot.

Anchovy and Egg Croquettes.—Two tea-spoonfuls anchovy paste, two hard-boiled eggs, one ounce cold boiled tongue, quarter tea-spoonful pepper, one raw egg, four table-spoonfuls bread crumbs.

Dip the hard-boiled eggs into cold water, and then remove the shells; chop the eggs up very finely, place them in a basin, and add to them the anchovy paste. Beat this mixture well together with the back of a wooden spoon. Chop now almost to a powder the tongue, add it to the mixture in the basin, and season all with the pepper. Take a tea-spoonful of the mixture and roll it into a small ball. When all is used up, beat well on a plate the raw egg, and dip each ball into it. Place now on a sheet of paper the bread crumbs, and roll each ball in them. Heat some clarified fat until the steam rises, and just before dropping in the balls make a small hole in each with the point of the finger. When the balls have taken a pale brown colour place them for a second on a sheet of paper; then arrange them on a hot napkin, place in the centre of each a tea-spoonful of maître d'hôtel butter, and send to table at once. (Directions for maître d'hôtel butter will be found on page 118).

CROQUETTES AND FRITTERS.
FRITTERS.

Potato Fritters.—Six boiled potatoes, three ounces of flour, one table-spoonful of salad oil, one gill of tepid water, one half tea-spoonful of white pepper, one tea-spoonful of salt, white of one egg.

Put the flour into a bowl, mix with it the salt and pepper, pour into the centre the salad oil, and over this the tepid water, beating all well together. Whip the white of egg to a stiff froth, and add this to the mixture in the bowl, stirring very carefully in order not to break the froth. Quarter the potatoes, and dip each piece separately into the batter. Throw them into hot clarified fat, and let them fry three minutes. Remove them from the frying-pan, drain them of grease upon a sheet of kitchen-paper, and serve piled high in a vegetable dish.

NOTES.—All batters should be made an hour or two before using, adding the white of egg just at the moment of use, as the grains of flour soak and swell out by standing after being moistened, and so the batter becomes lighter.

Parsnip fritters may be prepared with the same kind of batter used for the potato, but when parsnips are used they must be thoroughly dried before being dipped into the batter.

Oyster Fritters.—One dozen large oysters, four ounces of flour, one gill of milk, one half tea-spoonful of lemon-juice, two eggs, one dessert-spoonful of salad oil, one half tea-spoonful of salt, one half tea-spoonful of pepper.

Drain the liquor from the oysters, and dry them each thoroughly with a towel. Spread them out upon a plate, keeping them as separate as possible, that they may develop no moisture from contact, while the batter is being prepared.

Put the flour into a bowl, mix with it the pepper and salt, and making a little hole in the centre of this, drop into it the yolks of the eggs and the salad oil. Pour over the yolks of the eggs and the salad oil the milk by degrees, and mix the flour into it from the sides, taking care that it does not lump, then beat all smoothly together, and whipping the whites of the eggs to a stiff froth, mix this lightly into the batter.

Pierce the oysters through the ear with a skewer, and lifting them in this way, dip them one by one into the batter, and throwing them into hot clarified fat or lard fry them, allowing each oyster to remain in four minutes.

Drain off such superfluous grease as may cling to them upon a sheet of kitchen-paper, and arranging the fritters in a hot napkin, spray over them the lemon-juice.

Cheese Fritters.—Three ounces of flour, one egg, one gill of tepid water, one salt-spoonful of salt, one half tea-spoonful of pepper, three ounces of Parmesan cheese, one half tea-spoonful of dry mustard, one half ounce of butter.

Put the flour into a bowl, and melting the butter, pour this into the centre of it. Add to this by degrees the water, beating all together meantime. Drop in the yolk of the egg, season with the pepper, salt, and mustard. Stir in also the grated cheese, and last of all the white of the egg, which must first be whipped to a froth. Dip from this mixture table-spoonfuls, and drop them one by one into hot clarified fat or lard. As the fritters become firm and arise to the top, turn them over with a skewer that they may brown evenly all around.

As soon as they become brown, remove them from the fat, and place them upon a sheet of kitchen-paper to drain for a moment, when they must be piled tastefully upon a hot napkin, and served garnished with sprigs of parsley.

NOTE.—Any strong old cheese that is dry enough to grate may be used instead of the Parmesan cheese for these fritters.

Apple Fritters.—Three large apples, three ounces of flour, one dessert-spoonful of salad oil, one ounce of sugar, one gill of tepid water, white of one egg.

The apples must be very thinly pared and cored, leaving them whole. They must be cut around into slices about a third of an inch in thickness.

Put the flour into a bowl, and pour into the centre thereof the salad oil. Over this pour the tepid water, and beat all well together. Beat the white of egg to a stiff froth, and stir this into the batter very lightly, and when all is smoothly mixed, lift the slices of apple with a skewer, and dipping them into the batter, throw them one by one into hot clarified fat or lard, and fry them therein until the skewer will easily pierce them through, the time required for which depends upon the quality and kind of apple used.

When done, drain them for a moment upon a sheet of kitchen-paper, and arranging them in a circle upon a flat dish, sprinkle the sugar thickly over them, and serve.

NOTE.—Sugar should never be put into any kind of batter, as it tends to render it heavy. It is better to use it, as with these fritters, by sprinkling over when the dish is ready for serving.

Corn Fritters.—Four ears of boiled maize, four ounces of flour, one gill of milk, two eggs, one half tea-spoonful of pepper, one tea-spoonful of salt.

First put the flour into a bowl, and dropping in the yolks of eggs, pour over them the milk, and mix in the flour from the sides while pouring on the milk.

When all is smooth, season with the pepper and salt, whip the whites of egg to a stiff froth, and mix this with the batter very lightly.

Cut the corn from the cob and stir it into the batter; dipping the mixture from the bowl in large spoonfuls, drop them into hot clarified fat or lard, and fry until thoroughly brown, turning them constantly meantime, that they may brown evenly. Serve in a flat vegetable dish upon a hot napkin, having drained them for a moment upon a sheet of kitchen-paper after removing them from the frying-pan.

NOTE.—Instead of using the corn freshly cut from the cob, half of a quart of canned corn may be used, after being put on a sieve or in a strainer and all liquor well drained from it.

Banana Fritters.—Four bananas, three ounces of flour, one dessert-spoonful of salad oil, one gill of tepid water, white of one egg.

Put the flour into a bowl, pour into the centre of it the salad oil, and add by degrees the water, mixing the flour in from the sides as the water is poured over.

Whip the white of egg to a stiff froth, and stir it together with the mixture in the bowl very lightly. Take the skin from the bananas and split them into halves.

Melt in a frying-pan three ounces of butter, and when the blue smoke arises therefrom dip the slices of banana into the batter, and placing them with the flat side downward into the frying-pan, baste them with the hot butter over the rounded sides until done to a nice light brown.

When done, they must be removed from the frying-pan with a cooking shovel, in order that they may not be broken in lifting, as they become deliciously tender in process of frying.

Serve upon a flat china fruit plate with fine sugar, if desired.

ALBERT PUDDING. P. 142.

AMBER PUDDING. P. 150.

APPLE FRITTERS. P. 133.

CHRISTMAS PLUM PUDDING. P. 149.

SOUFFLÉS.

Potato Soufflé.—Four large potatoes, one ounce of butter, one half gill of milk, one half tea-spoonful of white pepper, one half tea-spoonful of salt, yolks of three eggs, whites of four eggs.

First scrub the potatoes well in cold water, and then put them to bake in a moderate oven for half or three quarters of an hour, which may be determined by testing the potatoes with a skewer, removing them from the oven when it will readily pierce through them.

Cut off the tops of the potatoes when baked, and scoop the flour from them, taking care not to break the skins. Rub the potato flour through a sieve to make it perfectly smooth, and putting the butter into a sauce-pan, add to it the milk, pepper, and salt, and placing the sauce-pan over the fire, allow the milk to boil.

When this boils, throw into it the potato flour, and stir all well together until the potato becomes hot.

Take the sauce-pan from the fire and drop in the yolks of the eggs, stirring each one thoroughly together with the potato mixture before putting in the next, to prevent curdling.

Put the whites of the eggs upon a plate, and whip them with a knife to a very stiff froth. Mix this into the compound in the sauce-pan, being careful not to break the froth, and when this is done, fill each of the potato skins two-thirds full of this mixture, place them upright in a baking-tin, and bake them in a quick oven from seven to ten minutes.

The length of time required for the baking is determined by the heat of the oven, which should be quick; and the soufflé may be pronounced done when the finger may be pressed upon the top of the stuffing of the potato skins and removed again without any of the mixture adhering.

Serve on a small platter.

NOTE.—Sometimes in preparing these soufflés there will be a

little of the potato-flour mixture left after the skins are sufficiently filled, and when this occurs, the remnant may be utilized by baking it in a greased cup.

Lemon Soufflé.—Two lemons, one pint of milk, two ounces of butter, two ounces of flour, one ounce of arrowroot, two ounces of sugar, yolks of four eggs, whites of five eggs.

Grease a broad band of paper, and secure it with a piece of twine around the top of a quart soufflé tin, in order that it may project and deepen the tin, and so prevent the soufflé running over the sides as it rises. Grease the sides and bottom of the soufflé tin.

Cut from the lemon its thin yellow rind, and put it into a sauce-pan with a gill of the milk. Allow this to come to the boiling-point, and, drawing the sauce-pan aside from the fire, let its contents simmer slowly for five minutes.

Put into a copper or porcelain-lined sauce-pan the butter, and stir into it, as it melts, the flour. Add the arrowroot and sugar, and by degrees the remainder of the milk.

Stir this until it boils, and when boiling strain the lemon rind from the milk, and add the flavouring liquid to the mixture in the sauce-pan.

Draw the sauce-pan aside from the fire, let it cool slightly, and drop into it, one by one, the yolks of eggs. Stir this well together, when the whites of the eggs must be put upon a plate and whipped to a stiff froth, and this also added to the contents of the sauce-pan, stirring lightly in order not to beat down the froth.

Put this mixture quickly into the soufflé tin, that the froth of egg may not fall; place the tin into a deep sauce-pan containing sufficient boiling water to reach half-way up the sides of the tin; cover the sauce-pan closely; draw it to one side of the fire, and let the water simmer for three-quarters of an hour, taking care to keep the sauce-pan closely covered all the time, and so keep confined all the steam generated in which the soufflé is being cooked.

At the end of this time remove the soufflé from the sauce-pan, cut from it the band of paper, transfer it to a silver soufflé dish, or fold a napkin around the tin in which it is prepared, and serve immediately.

If the dining-room be distant from the kitchen, the soufflé should be carried in upon a hot shovel, otherwise it may be chilled, and so fall from its perfect state.

NOTE.—Should it be desired, the soufflé prepared as above may be divided and put into pint soufflé tins, baking one and steaming the other.

Vanilla Soufflé.—One ounce of flour, one and one-quarter ounce of butter, one dessert-spoonful of sugar, one gill of milk, one half tea-spoonful of the essence of vanilla, yolks of three eggs, whites of four eggs, one table-spoonful of raspberry jam, one half tea-spoonful of lemon-juice, one glass of sherry, six drops of cochineal.

Grease a band of paper, and secure it around the top of a pint and a half soufflé tin, in order to deepen the tin and keep the souffle in form as it rises. Grease the sides and bottom of the tin inside.

Melt the butter in a sauce-pan, stir into it the flour, add to this the gill of milk, and stir all together until boiling. Draw the sauce-pan aside from the fire, throw into it the sugar and essence of vanilla, and drop in also one by one the yolks of eggs, stirring all thoroughly together.

Whip the whites of the eggs to a stiff froth, and stir this in also, taking care not to break the froth.

Pour the mixture now into the soufflé tin, which it should about two-thirds fill; place the tin into a deep sauce-pan containing sufficient water to reach half-way up the sides of the mould, and, covering the sauce-pan closely, draw it aside from the fire and let the water therein simmer slowly for thirty minutes, keeping it always covered.

Five minutes before this time expires, rub through a horse-hair sieve the jam, add to it the sherry and lemon-juice, also the cochineal, put all into a small sauce-pan; place over the fire, and stir until the mixture boils.

Draw it then from the fire. Remove also the soufflé from

the sauce-pan, cut the paper from it, and turn the soufflé out upon a hot, flat dish. Pour the sauce around it, and serve immediately.

NOTE.—The lemon soufflé may also if desired be served upon a hot platter, with the above sauce poured round it.

Chocolate Soufflés.—Three ounces of grated chocolate, one ounce of sugar, one ounce of butter, one ounce of flour, one gill of milk, yolks of three eggs, whites of four eggs.

Grease and bind around a pint and a half soufflé tin a band of paper to form a wall above the tin and confine the soufflé as it rises. Grease also the interior of the tin.

Melt the butter in a small sauce-pan, stir into it the flour, and adding the milk stir all until boiling. When boiling, take the sauce-pan from the fire, throw into it the chocolate and the sugar, and drop in the yolks of the eggs one by one, stirring all meantime.

Whip the whites of the eggs to a stiff froth and stir this in this also, very lightly.

Pour the mixture into the soufflé tin, which should make it about two-thirds full, and place the tin into a deep sauce-pan containing sufficient water to reach half-way up the sides of the form. Cover the sauce-pan, and, drawing it aside from the fire, allow the water to simmer therein for thirty minutes, keeping it all the time covered.

When steamed, take the soufflé from the sauce-pan, transfer it quickly to a silver soufflé dish, or fold around the tin in which it is prepared a napkin, and serve at once, carrying the dish upon a hot shovel if the dining-room be distant from the kitchen.

Omelette Soufflé.—Yolks of two eggs, whites of three eggs, one tea-spoonful of powdered sugar, one tea-spoonful of essence of vanilla, one half ounce of butter, one grain of salt.

First put into a small bowl the yolks of the eggs, together with the sugar and vanilla, and with a wooden spoon stir these until they come to a thick cream, which will take three or four minutes.

Put the whites of the eggs upon a perfectly dry plate, sprinkle over them the grain of salt, and with a dry knife whip them to a very stiff froth.

Melt the butter in an omelette pan, taking care that it does not get hot.

Mix together the whites and the yolks of the eggs, pour this into the omelette pan, and put the pan over the fire for one minute.

Transfer the pan to a quick oven, and allow it to remain there for five minutes.

Turn the soufflé out quickly upon a hot platter, fold it evenly together, and serve at once.

A table-spoonful of jelly or jam may be placed in the centre of the soufflé when served, if desired.

NOTES.—Salt is added to the whites of eggs for the purpose of cooling them, and if in the slightest degree stale, to aid in bringing them more quickly and lightly to a froth.

The whites of eggs must be whipped upon a dry plate and with a dry knife, as the slightest moisture will prevent their coming to a froth, and unless the froth of egg be very stiff the omelette soufflé will be made heavy by it and so spoiled.

Cheese Soufflé.—One ounce of butter, one ounce of flour, one gill of milk, one half tea-spoonful of white pepper, one half tea-spoonful of salt, one grain of cayenne, three ounces of grated cheese, yolks of three eggs, whites of four eggs.

Melt the butter in a small sauce-pan and stir into it the flour, adding also the milk, and stirring all until boiling. Throw into the boiling mixture the pepper, salt, and cayenne; when removing the sauce-pan from the fire, the yolks of egg must be added together with the grated cheese, and the whole very thoroughly beaten together.

Whip the whites of the eggs to a stiff froth, and stir this in also, using care not to beat down the froth.

Fill this mixture equally into small paper ramekins or cups, or into tin cups if more convenient, and bake them in a quick oven for ten minutes. Arrange the cups when the soufflés are done upon a hot plate, and serve immediately.

If the tin cups are used, a napkin may be folded in basket shape upon the plate, and the tins placed in it.

Chicken Soufflé.—The breast of one raw chicken, one gill of cream, one egg, one half ounce of butter, one half ounce of flour, one salt-spoonful of white pepper, one salt-spoonful of salt, two truffles.

Take the skin from the breast of chicken, chop it finely, and pound it when chopped in a mortar.

Melt the butter in a small sauce-pan, stir into it the flour and one table-spoonful of the cream. Let this boil, and, when boiling, take the sauce-pan from the fire and pour its contents over the chicken in the mortar, adding also one egg.

Pound all well together, and season with the pepper and salt. When pounded, pass the mixture through a sieve, and putting the remainder of the cream into a small bowl, beat it with a fork until it comes to a stiff froth; mix this very lightly with the strained mixture, grease a few cup tins, and, cutting the truffles into stars, place one of these in the bottom of each tin.

Fill the tins about half full with the mixture, and place them into a sauté can half filled with boiling water; cover them with a round of greased paper, and let them steam slowly for fifteen minutes.

When done, turn the soufflés out upon a hot platter, having the truffle stars uppermost, and serve at once.

NOTE.—Any shallow pan will answer if a sauté pan is not available, but care must be taken that the boiling water does not reach more than half-way up the sides of the cup tins.

Chestnut Soufflé.—One pint of fresh chestnuts, one and one-half gill of milk, yolks of three eggs, whites of four eggs, one ounce of powdered sugar, one ounce of butter, one ounce of flour.

Throw the chestnuts into boiling water, and boil them until the shells begin to crack open. Take them from the water, remove their shells and inner skins, pound them in a mortar, and make them perfectly smooth by passing them through a sieve.

Pour the milk over the chestnut flour, and stirring this together, put the mixture into a small sauce-pan and let it cook over a slow fire for ten minutes.

At the end of this time melt the butter in a separate sauce-pan, stir into it the flour, and, when these are mixed, pour in with them the milk and chestnuts.

The instant this boils take it from the fire, and adding the sugar and yolks of eggs, beat all well together. Whip the whites of eggs to a stiff froth, and stir this in lightly also, and, greasing a pint and a half soufflé tin, pour into it the mixture, and bake in a moderate oven for twenty minutes.

Serve in a silver soufflé dish or in a folded napkin, and without any delay.

PUDDINGS.

Welcome Guest Pudding. — Eight ounces of bread crumbs, one half pint of milk, four ounces of beef suet, three ounces of citron, four ounces of sugar, rind of one lemon, three ounces of almonds, four eggs, one grain of salt.

Place four ounces of the bread crumbs into a bowl, and, bringing the milk to the boiling-point, pour it over them. Cover the bowl with a plate, and allow the bread crumbs to soak in the milk for ten minutes.

While the bread crumbs are soaking, pour over the almonds some boiling water to blanch them and remove their skins.

Remove the skin from the suet and chop it very finely, and chop the almonds.

Stir into the bowl with the soaked bread crumbs the four remaining ounces of crumbs; add to this the chopped suet and almonds, also the grated rind of lemon together with the sugar and citron, which last must have been cut into very small pieces.

Separate the yolks from the whites of the eggs very carefully, drop the yolks one by one into the bowl, and stir all well together.

Whip the whites of the eggs to a very stiff froth, adding the grain of salt to cool and lighten it. Mix this lightly also with the other ingredients in the bowl, and, taking a quart mould, dry it thoroughly, and greasing the interior with butter, pour into it the mixture, and place securely over the top a greased sheet of kitchen-paper.

Place the mould when filled in a deep sauce-pan containing enough boiling water to reach half-way up the sides, and let the pudding boil therein for two hours.

When done, the mould should be removed from the boiling water; allow two minutes for it to cool, and then turn the pudding out upon a hot platter.

This pudding should be served either with a jam, wine, or lemon sauce, to prepare which see directions for sauces, pages 179 and 181.

Fig Pudding.—One half pound of figs, one half pound of bread crumbs, one half pound of sugar, one half pound of beef suet, three eggs.

Remove the skin from the suet, chop it very finely, put it into a bowl, and chopping the figs also very finely, mix both together. Stir into this the bread crumbs, beat in a separate bowl the eggs and sugar, mix this with the figs, suet, and bread crumbs, and, greasing the interior of a melon-mould, pour this mixture into it; put on the cover, and, plunging it into a large sauce-pan of boiling water, let it with its contents boil for two hours.

When done, the pudding should be turned out upon a hot platter and served with wine or brandy sauce poured around it, for the preparation of which sauces see pages 181 and 179.

Albert Pudding.—One quarter of a pound of butter, one quarter of a pound of flour, one quarter of a pound of sugar, three eggs, rind of one lemon, two ounces of raisins.

Grease well a pint and a half pudding-mould with butter,

and seeding the raisins, stick them against the walls of the mould at intervals, so that they may garnish the exterior of the pudding when done.

Put the butter into a bowl, rub into it the sugar with the back of a wooden spoon, and if the weather is cold the butter will require to be warmed a little, care being taken that it does not oil. Add to this cream of butter and sugar, a little of the flour, and the yolk of one of the eggs. Stir all well together, and repeat this process until the flour and eggs are all used.

Add to the mixture now the grated lemon rind, whip the whites of the eggs to a stiff froth, and stir this in also, very lightly.

By this time the butter with which the mould is greased will have cooled, and the pudding may be poured in, using a little care to avoid disarranging the raisins.

When the mould is filled, cover its mouth with a piece of greased paper, and, sinking it half its length into a saucepan of boiling water, boil the pudding therein for an hour and a half.

When the pudding is boiled, turn it out of the mould upon a hot platter, and pour around it a jam or lemon sauce, directions for making which will be found upon page 179.

Lowell Pudding.—Four tea-cupfuls of flour, one tea-cupful of beef suet, one and one-half tea-cupful of sweet milk, one and one-half tea-cupful of sugar, one tea-spoonful of salt, one tea-spoonful of bi-carbonate of soda.

Put the flour into a bowl, and removing the skin from the suet, chop it very finely, and mix it with flour. When these are well mixed, add the milk and sugar.

Put the bi-carbonate of soda upon a plate, and make it smooth with the back of a spoon, add this with the salt to the other ingredients, and stir all very thoroughly together.

Pour the pudding into a well-greased pudding-mould, and put on the cover, place the mould into a large sauce-pan, cover it with boiling water, and let it boil therein for three hours.

When done, remove the mould from the boiling water, let it cool for a moment, and turn the pudding out upon a hot platter, and serve with a hard or wine sauce; to prepare which, see pages 180 and 181.

Aunt Martha's Pudding.—Six ounces of bread crumbs, one gill of milk, yolks of three eggs, whites of two eggs, one tea-spoonful of essence of vanilla, three ounces of sugar, one half dozen of preserved cherries.

Grease a pint pudding-mould thoroughly inside with butter; stick into the bottom of it the preserved cherries, in order that they may garnish the top of the pudding.

Put the milk into a small sauce-pan, and bring it to the boiling-point, and putting the bread crumbs into a basin, throw over them the boiling milk.

Place in a separate bowl the yolks of eggs, and with them the sugar, and beat these well together. Whip the whites of the eggs into a stiff froth, and mix them lightly together with the yolks and sugar. Add to this the essence of vanilla, and mix this together with the soaked bread crumbs and milk, stirring all thoroughly.

Pour the pudding now into the mould, cover the mouth of it with a piece of greased kitchen-paper, place the mould into a sauce-pan containing sufficient water to reach halfway up its sides, and boil the pudding therein for one hour and twenty minutes.

When done, take the mould from the water, and letting it cool for a moment, turn the pudding out upon a hot platter, and serve with a jam sauce, the recipe for making which will be found upon page 179.

Cabinet Pudding.—One dozen lady fingers, one ounce of ratifias, four eggs, one ounce of sugar, three ounces of stale cake, one pint of milk, one tea-spoonful of essence of vanilla, one dozen preserved cherries.

Grease the sides and bottom of the interior of a pint and a half soufflé tin. Arrange in the bottom of this the cherries, so that when the pudding is turned out they may garnish its top. Line the mould with the lady fingers, placing them perpendicularly around with their flat sides against the sides of the mould. Break up what remains of the lady fingers and throw the pieces into the centre of the mould. Crush the ratifias in the hand, and throw them in also, and upon this the stale cake, broken into small irregular pieces.

Put the sugar into a bowl, and with it the eggs, beating these together until very light with a fork. When this is beaten, add to it the milk and vanilla; pour this mixture into the mould slowly, letting it have time to soak into the cake, and so making room enough for all of the liquid.

When filled, cover the mould with a piece of greased kitchen-paper, and standing it into a sauce-pan containing sufficient boiling water to reach half-way up the sides of the tin, allow the pudding to boil in this for one hour and twenty minutes.

When done, remove the mould from the sauce-pan, let it cool a moment, and then turning the pudding out upon a flat pudding-dish, serve it immediately with a lemon sauce poured around, the directions for making which will be found among the sweet sauces, page 179.

Lemon Pudding.—Six ounces of flour, three ounces of butter, one half gill of cold water, one grain of salt, three lemons, three ounces of bread crumbs, five ounces of powdered sugar, one gill of cream, yolks of six eggs, whites of two eggs.

Put the flour upon a mixing-board, and rub into it the butter with the hands. Add to this the grain of salt, and making a little well in the centre of the flour, pour into it the cold water, and knead all into a light dough.

When kneaded, flour a rolling-pin and roll the dough out very thinly. Wet the edges of a vegetable dish with cold water, cut some strips from the paste three inches in width, and line with this the edge of the dish all around. Cut also from the dough some small lozenges about the size of a thimble top, and arrange these around the dish upon the lining of dough, letting them slightly overlap each other in describing the circle.

Put the bread crumbs now into a bowl, and grate over them the rind of the lemons. Add to this the sugar, and then squeeze over all the juice of the lemons. Drop into the bowl one by one the yolks of the eggs, beating the mixture well while dropping them. Pour the cream over all, whip the whites of the eggs to a stiff froth, and stir this in also, very lightly, when the mixture should be poured into the vegetable dish, the dish be placed in a moderate oven, and the pudding baked for thirty minutes.

Sir Watkin Wynne's Pudding.—Three ounces of beef suet, six ounces of bread crumbs, four ounces of sugar, two eggs, one and one-half table-spoonful of orange marmalade.

Take the skin from the suet and chop it very finely. Put this when chopped into a bowl, and add to it the bread crumbs and marmalade.

In a separate bowl place the sugar and eggs, beating them very lightly together, when this should be poured into the bowl with the suet, bread crumbs, and marmalade, and mixed thoroughly together.

Grease the inside of a pudding-mould with butter, pour the preparation into it, put on the cover of the mould, and putting this into a sauce-pan containing enough boiling water to cover it, boil the pudding therein for one hour and a half.

When done, remove the mould from the sauce-pan and the pudding from the mould, and placing the latter upon a hot flat pudding-dish, pour around it, just before serving, a lemon sauce, to make which see directions on page 179.

Bread and Butter Pudding.—Four slices of bread, one half pint of milk, three eggs, one tea-spoonful of lemon-juice, two ounces of currants, two ounces of sugar, two ounces of butter.

Remove the crust from the bread, and spread each slice with the butter.

Grease with butter the inside of a deep pudding-dish, and place a slice of bread in the bottom thereof. Sprinkle over this a layer of currants, when a slice of bread should be placed upon the top of these, another layer of currants sprinkled over this, and repeating this process arrange all of the bread and currants into the dish.

Beat together in a bowl until very light the sugar and eggs, add to these the milk and lemon-juice, and pour this mixture over the preparation in the pudding-dish.

Let them stand for one hour, in order that the bread may absorb the liquid poured upon it, after which it must be baked in a quick oven twenty minutes.

This pudding may be eaten with milk or cream.

NOTES.—Currants should always be washed long enough before required for use, to enable them to become perfectly dry, otherwise they will cause a pudding, or whatever they may be used in, to be both sticky and heavy.

They must be dried by exposure to the sun and air, and not in an oven, as artificial heat hardens them.

Llanberries Pudding.—One quarter of a pound of butter, one quarter of a pound of powdered sugar, one quarter of a pound of flour, two eggs, three table-spoonfuls of orange marmalade, one tea-spoonful of baking-powder.

First put the butter into a bowl and beat it with the sugar to a cream. Stir into this a little of the flour and a little of the marmalade alternately, until the full quantity of each is stirred in. Drop into this mixture then the yolks of the eggs, sprinkle over these the baking-powder, and beat all thoroughly together.

Whip the whites of the eggs to a stiff froth, and stir this also into the bowl, taking care not to beat down the froth in the process.

Grease with butter the inside of a pint and a half soufflé tin, pour into it the pudding, and bake in a moderate oven for one hour.

Before placing the soufflé tin into the oven, a band of greased paper should be arranged around the top of the tin, in order to keep the pudding from bursting over the sides should the heat of the oven cause it to rise quickly.

When the pudding is done, it should be turned out upon a hot flat dish, and served with a custard sauce poured around it. The recipe for this sauce will be found on page 180.

Tapioca Pudding.—Three ounces of tapioca, three gills of milk, one table-spoonful of sugar, two eggs, one salt-spoonful of grated nutmeg.

Cover the tapioca with cold water twelve hours before the pudding is to be prepared, and let it soak in this until required.

When about to use, drain the tapioca as thoroughly as possible of the water, and when as dry as it can be made, put the tapioca into a sauce-pan, pour over it the milk, and placing it over the fire, stir slowly until the milk boils.

Take the sauce-pan from the fire, place the eggs and sugar into a bowl, and beating them to a cream, pour this into the sauce-pan with the tapioca and milk.

Grease with butter a deep pudding-dish, pour into it the pudding, sprinkle over the top the grated nutmeg, and put all to bake in a moderate oven for half an hour.

Overton Pudding.—Seven ounces of flour, three ounces of butter, one half tea-spoonful of baking-powder, one half gill of cold water, three table-spoonfuls of preserved strawberries, three ounces of dry cake crumbs, one gill of milk, one tea-spoonful of essence of vanilla, three ounces of powdered sugar, one salt-spoonful of salt.

First rub the cake crumbs through a coarse wire sieve into a bowl. Bring the milk to the boiling-point, and pour it over the crumbs, to which add also the essence of vanilla.

Place upon a mixing-board the flour, and into this rub the butter with the hands, sprinkle over this the salt, make a hole in the centre of the flour, pour into it the cold water, and kneading from the edges into this, mix all to a light paste.

Rub a little flour upon a rolling-pin, and with it roll out the paste to the thinness of a quarter of an inch, and cut from this ten lozenges about the size of a halfpenny.

Cut ten smaller lozenges of about half the circumference of the first, and, brushing a small platter over with cold water, roll the remaining crust out to the proper size, and line the platter therewith. Wet the edges of the lining paste with a little cold water, and arrange around them, at equal distances, the larger lozenges. Upon these place the small lozenges, pressing them down in the centre with the tip of the finger; spread over the centre surface of the crust-lined platter the preserved fruit, over this spread the soaked cake crumbs, and sprinkle over all the sugar.

Place the platter into a quick oven, and let the pudding bake therein for twenty-five minutes. Serve upon the platter on which the pudding is made.

Wakefield Pudding.—Four slices of bread, four table-spoonfuls of raspberry jam, one ounce of sugar, one ounce of corn starch, one half pint of milk, two eggs.

Cut the crust from the slices of bread, and place one of them in the bottom of a deep pudding-dish. Spread over this a table-spoonful of the jam, and so arrange alternate layers of bread and jam, one upon the other in the dish, until the given quantities of each are filled into it.

Put the corn starch and sugar into a bowl, and moistening them with a table-spoonful of the milk, mix these together. Drop into this mixture the eggs, and beat all with a fork until very light.

Put the remainder of the milk into a small sauce-pan over the fire, and when it boils pour it over the mixture in the bowl, stirring all the time while pouring. Pour the liquid preparation now over the bread and jam in the pudding-dish, and placing the pudding-dish into a quick oven, bake its contents for half an hour. Serve in the dish in which the pudding is prepared.

English Plum Pudding.—One half pound of bread

crumbs, one half pound of beef suet, one half pound of flour, one half pound of sugar, one half pound of raisins, one half pound of currants, one tea-spoonful of powdered cinnamon, one tea-spoonful of powdered ginger, one quarter pound of citron, rind of one lemon, one gill of milk, four eggs, one half tea-spoonful of baking-powder, one quarter of a nutmeg.

Chop the suet, after taking off the skin very finely, and put it together with the flour and bread crumbs into a large bowl. Seed the raisins, wash and dry the currants thoroughly, and mix these together, grate the lemon rind and the nutmeg over them, and adding the ginger and cinnamon, mix all thoroughly together.

Stir the fruit mixture into the bowl with the suet, add to this compound the sugar, baking-powder, and citron, which must be cut into small thin pieces; in a separate bowl beat the eggs until very light, add to them the milk, and when these are thoroughly blended, pour the liquid over the preparation in the large bowl, and stir all well together. Grease a quart pudding-mould with butter, put the pudding into it and shut the cover securely over it, then plunging the mould into a large sauce-pan filled with boiling water, let the pudding boil therein for four hours.

When done, the pudding should be turned out upon a hot platter, and served with brandy sauce; to prepare which directions will be found on page 179.

NOTE.—Plum puddings are prettier when boiled in a mould; but the traditional plum pudding is **boiled** in a double pudding-cloth greased with butter for the purpose, **and** served with plain brandy poured over and around it, which is **fired**, and the pudding so enveloped **in the historical blaze of glory.**

Amber Pudding.—Two pounds of apples, six ounces of flour, three ounces of butter, one gill of cold water, four eggs, rind of one lemon, three ounces of sugar, one half tea-spoonful of baking-powder, one grain of salt.

Pare, quarter, and core the apples. Put into a small sauce-pan two ounces of sugar and half of the cold water,

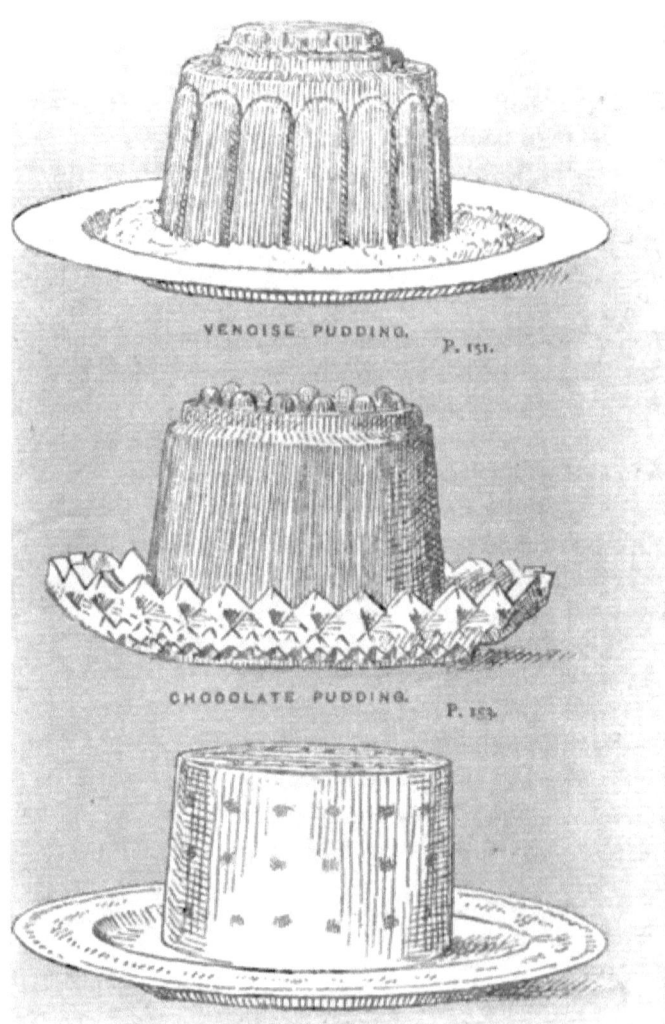

VENOISE PUDDING. P. 151.

CHOCOLATE PUDDING. P. 153.

COLD CABINET PUDDING. P. 164.

and place this over the fire; when it boils, put into it the apples and the lemon rind. Cover the sauce-pan, and let its contents simmer very slowly, until the apples are cooked; and while they are cooking, mix together upon a mixing-board the flour and butter, add to this the baking-powder and salt, and knead all to a light dough with the remaining cold water.

Roll this dough out very thinly, cut it into strips about three inches wide, and wetting the edges of a pudding-dish with cold water, line them with the strips of dough; also cut some small lozenges from the fragments of dough remaining, and place them ornamentally around on the rim of dough.

Take the apples from the sauce-pan, and pouring them into a sieve, rub them through it, in order to make them perfectly smooth.

Separate the yolks from the whites of the eggs, dropping the yolks into the apples, and putting the whites upon a dry plate. Stir the apples and yolks of eggs together, and pour these, when blended, into the pudding-dish. The pudding-dish must be placed in a quick oven, and allowed to remain ten minutes, to bake the paste and cook the eggs; and while this is being done whip the whites of eggs to a very stiff froth, and when the pudding is taken from the oven pile this froth upon the top of the apple very high, and smooth it over with a knife blade. Sprinkle over this the remainder of the powdered sugar, and return the dish to the oven for two minutes, that the froth of egg may set and brown slightly on the surface. Serve this pudding hot.

Venoise Pudding.—Five ounces of wheat bread, four ounces of sugar, three ounces of sultana raisins, two ounces of citron, one glass of sherry, one half pint of milk, yolks of four eggs, one tea-spoonful of essence of vanilla.

Cut the bread into dice and place it into a large bowl with three ounces of the sugar. Cut the citron in small thin pieces, and put these also into the bowl.

Place the raisins upon a towel, and folding the ends of it

over them rub them therein until the stems are all separated, and adhering to the cloth; then the raisins must be picked out and thrown into the bowl with the rest, and the sherry poured over all.

Put the remaining ounce of sugar into a small sauce-pan over the fire and let the sugar brown. Pour the milk over the sugar when brown, and drawing the sauce-pan aside from the fire, stir the milk until the sugar dissolves and colours it. Drop the yolks of eggs into a small bowl, and over these pour the coloured milk, stirring all together as the milk is poured in.

Over the dry preparation in the large bowl pour the liquid from the small bowl; grease a proper sized pudding-mould, and into this put the pudding; secure over the top a greased piece of kitchen-paper, place the mould into a sauce-pan containing sufficient boiling water to reach half-way up its sides, and allow the pudding to boil therein for one hour and a half.

When done, turn the pudding out upon a hot platter, and serve with a German sweet sauce poured around. (See page 179.)

Trifle.—Four small sponge-cakes, one quarter pound ratifias, one quarter pound macaroons, one half pint sherry, one pint cream, one quarter ounce pistachio nuts, four large table-spoonfuls strawberry jam.

Break up in rough pieces four stale penny sponge-cakes, place them in the trifle dish, add the macaroons, and pour over the sherry. Allow this to soak for two hours. Place then the pistachio nuts in a small sauce-pan, cover them with cold water, and boil them for two minutes; pour away the water, and skin the nuts, place them on a board and chop them very finely. Place the cream in a basin, and with an egg-whisk whip into a stiff froth. At the end of two hours place over the soaked cake and macaroons the jam, then pile very high the whipped cream over the top, arrange round the edges the ratifias, and sprinkle over all the pistachio nuts.

Railway Pudding.—One tea-cupful of powdered sugar, one tea-cupful of flour, one ounce of butter, one dessert-spoonful of baking-powder, three eggs, one half dozen drops of essence of almonds, one table-spoonful of milk.

Grease thoroughly with the butter the inside of a bread-tin. Mix together in a large bowl the flour and sugar, and add to these, when mixed, the baking-powder.

Break the eggs into a small bowl, and beat them until very light, pour in with them the milk, drop into this the essence of almonds; and when these are well stirred together pour all over the preparation in the large bowl.

Now stir all together, and when this is done pour the mixture into the bread-tin, and placing this in a very quick oven bake it for ten minutes.

When baked, take the pudding from the oven, cut it into six or eight equal pieces, and arranging these upon a flat dish, sprinkle over them a little powdered sugar. A wine sauce should be sent to the table with this, to be poured in ladlefuls over the pieces of pudding as they are served. (See "Sauces," page 181.)

Notes.—This pudding should be put into the oven immediately after it is mixed. The baking-powder begins to ferment the instant that it is moistened, and it is this process which must be taken advantage of in baking quickly, to raise the pudding and make it light.

This pudding may also be used as a tea-cake; and when so served the pieces should be split open and a spoonful of preserved fruit spread between the slices.

Chocolate Pudding.—One quarter of a pound of grated chocolate, one pint of milk, one half ounce of gelatine, two ounces of sugar, one tea-spoonful of essence of vanilla, yolks of four eggs, one half gill of cold water.

Cover the gelatine with the cold water, and allow it to soak therein for ten minutes. Place the gelatine, when dissolved, into a small sauce-pan, put it over the fire, and stir slowly until melted, taking care that it does not boil.

When melted, take the sauce-pan from the fire and allow the gelatine to cool a little.

Mix together the milk and grated chocolate until they come to a smooth paste, then, in a fresh sauce-pan, stir the mixture over the fire until boiling. Drop the yolks of eggs into a bowl, cover them with the sugar, and pour over all the hot chocolate mixture.

Return this compound to the ⸺ the fire and let its contents cook f⸺ stirring constantly to prevent boiling.

Remove the sauce-pan at t⸺ of this time from the fire, stir into the mixture it contains the melted gelatine, and drop in the essence of vanilla.

Dip a pint and a half mould into cold water, to wet it inside, and so prevent the pudding sticking; pour into it the pudding, an⸺ se⸺ way in a cool, dry place, until the gelatine congeals and the pudding has "set" in the mould; and when this has taken place turn the pudding out upon a crystal dish and serve.

Italian Pudding.—One half of a quart can of preserved peaches, four table-spoonfuls of bread crumbs, two eggs, one gill of milk, one tea-spoonful of lemon-juice, two ounces of sugar.

Arrange upon a flat dish a layer of the peaches, cover this with a blanket of the bread crumbs, and in this way arrange alternate layers of the fruit and bread crumbs until the specified quantity be used.

Put the yolks of the eggs into a bowl, and with them one ounce of sugar; bring the gill of milk to the boiling-point, and pouring this over the yolks of eggs and sugar, stir all together, and throw into the mixture the lemon-juice.

Pour this liquid over the fruit and bread crumbs by spoonfuls, in order that it may be absorbed thereby, and the preparation so become moistened but not juicy; when this is done place the pudding in a moderate oven and bake it for half an hour. At the end of this time take the pudding from the oven, beat the whites of the eggs to a light froth, and pile this roughly upon the top of it. Sprinkle over all the remaining ounce of sugar, place the dish once more in the oven for five minutes, to firm the froth of egg and brown it also slightly. Serve at once.

Note.—This pudding may also be made with preserved apples or pears, as taste or convenience may dictate.

Apple Dumplings.—Five apples, twelve ounces of flour, four ounces of butter, one ounce of sugar, one tea-spoonful of baking-powder, one and one-half gill of cold water, one salt-spoonful of salt.

Rub this flour and butter together in a bowl, add to them the baking-powder and the salt, and with the cold water mix all to a firm dough.

Place this dough upon a mixing-board, and cut it into five equal pieces.

Pare the apples now very thinly, and take from them their cores, leaving the form of the apple unbroken. Roll the dough into balls, and taking an apple, work it into the centre of a ball of the dough; and just before closing the ball so formed at the top, put into the place of the apple core a portion of the sugar.

When the apples are all prepared in this way with the dough and sugar, place them into a baking-tin, and the baking-tin into a quick oven for half an hour.

At the end of half an hour test the dumplings with a skewer, and if the apples be not soft to the centre they must remain in the oven until the skewer proves them entirely done.

When done take them from the oven, brush each over with a little milk, sprinkle them with a little sugar, and return all to the oven for one minute, and serve them with a hard sauce, directions for making which will be found on page 180.

Swiss Rissoles.—One half pound of pears, one quarter pound of raisins, two ounces of sugar, eight ounces of flour, four ounces of butter, one egg, one half gill of cold water, one half of a lemon.

First pare and core the pears, cut them into small pieces, squeeze into a sauce-pan the juice of the lemon, add to it half of the cold water and an ounce and a half of the sugar, and placing the sauce-pan over the fire, let its contents come to the boiling-point; when boiling, throw into it the pears, also the raisins, and let them cook therein very slowly for half an hour.

When done, turn the mixture out upon a plate. When quite cool, make up a crust by mixing upon a board the flour and butter; make a hole in the centre of this, into which drop the yolk of the egg, pour over the remaining cold water, and knead all lightly together.

Roll this out to about an inch in thickness, and cut it into pieces about four inches square. Beat the white of the egg lightly, and brush the edges of the crust with it; put into each of these squares an equal quantity of the cold mixture from the plate, fold the edges together, brush over each a little of the white of egg, sprinkle over each a little of the sugar, and placing the rissoles upon a slightly-floured baking-tin, bake them in a moderate oven for half an hour. Serve in a folded napkin.

Peach Sago.—One quart of peaches, one half pound of sago, three ounces of sugar, one pint of cold water.

Put the sago into a pudding-dish, cover it with the cold water, and allow it to soak therein for two hours; and when the sago is sufficiently soaked, skin and stone the peaches, place them regularly upright in the sago, sprinkle over all the sugar, and placing the pudding-dish into a moderate oven, let the pudding bake for one hour. Serve hot.

Corn Starch Pudding.—Four table-spoonfuls of corn-starch, one quart of milk, two ounces of sugar, one salt-spoonful of salt, two bay-leaves, two eggs.

Put the milk into a sauce-pan over the fire, and while it is heating moisten the corn-starch with a little cold milk, and beat it smooth. Just before the milk reaches the boiling-point, crush the bay-leaves in the hands, that the flavour may be more readily drawn out, and throw them into the milk, after which stir in the corn-starch; stir all constantly until boiling, and when boiling allow this to continue for five minutes, still stirring to prevent scorching, which the corn-starch and milk are both apt to do.

Draw the sauce-pan then aside from the fire to let its contents cool a little, and in the time allowed for this beat together the eggs and sugar, add to the sugar and eggs the salt, and removing the bay-leaves from the mixture in the sauce-pan, stir into it the sugar and eggs; after which all must be poured into a small pudding-dish, and this be placed in a moderate oven and permitted to bake for ten minutes. This pudding should be served hot.

NOTE.—Corn-starch blanc-mange may be prepared exactly as is the above pudding, except that the eggs must be left out; and instead of being baked, the preparation must be poured into moulds and allowed to stand in them until cooled into forms. This blanc-mange is served with jam or jelly and sweet cream.

Pancakes.—Three ounces of flour, two eggs, one half pint of milk, one ounce of sugar, one salt-spoonful of salt, one-half of a lemon, three ounces of butter.

Put the flour into a large bowl, in the centre of this make a little well, into which drop the yolks of the eggs, sprinkle over these the salt, and pouring in upon this little by little the milk, mix the flour into the centre from the sides until all the milk is added and the flour thoroughly mixed with the other ingredients, the yolks of eggs thus helping to prevent the flour lumping through the small percentage of oil which they contain.

Whip the whites of eggs now to a stiff froth, and stir this lightly into the batter; and when this is done melt one-fourth of the butter in a frying-pan, pour into this one-quarter of the batter from the bowl; and when this browns upon one side, turn it over with a pancake shovel or broad-bladed knife, taking care not to break the cake in the process.

When the second side is browned also, remove the cake to a plate, sprinkle it with a little of the sugar, squeeze over this a few drops of the lemon-juice, roll the pancake quickly into a round roll, sprinkle over the top a little more of the sugar and a little more of the lemon-juice, and place it upon a platter to keep hot while the others are being fried.

Divide the remaining batter into three equal parts, and in the manner above described pour into the frying-pan; fry and turn each portion until the three other pancakes are sugared, sprinkled with the lemon-juice, rolled and placed beside the first, when they may be arranged in the fashion of a cob-house, or as the fancy may direct, upon the hot platter. They should be served at once.

Note.—This batter may also be fried in smaller sized cakes, and served, well buttered and very hot, as a breakfast dish.

Rice Pudding.—One and one-half pint of milk, one half pound of rice, two ounces of sugar, one half tea-spoonful of salt, one egg, one ounce of butter.

Grease a deep pudding-dish thoroughly inside with the butter, and pour into this the milk, into which stir the dry rice.

Cover the dish with a plate, to confine the steam and prevent premature browning on the top should the oven be very hot, and placing all in a moderate oven let the pudding bake slowly for an hour and a half; by which time the kernels of rice will have soaked, and, swelling, absorbed nearly all of the milk, leaving the grains beautifully whole and the pudding devoid of the glutinous paste which by stirring processes is developed from the starch-flour of the broken rice. Ten minutes before removing the pudding from the oven beat the egg until very light, add to it the sugar and salt, and taking the plate off the pudding-dish stir this mixture into the pudding, and allow to bake for the remaining ten minutes uncovered, that it may brown on the surface. Serve with hard sauce, directions for making which may be found on page 180.

Note.—This pudding may be further enriched by the addition of a quarter of a pound of raisins; or, if desired more plain than as above, the egg may be omitted, and the sugar alone stirred in when the pudding is uncovered to permit its browning.

Snowden Pudding.—One breakfast-cupful of suet, one breakfast-cupful of bread crumbs, one breakfast-cupful of sugar, two eggs, one wine-glassful of sherry, one lemon.

When all skin and any discoloured part has been removed from the suet, chop it very finely. Measure one breakfast-cupful after it has been chopped, throw it into a bowl, also the sugar. Rub through a wire sieve the bread crumbs, add the other ingredients, and mix all well together. Wipe now well in a clean towel the lemon, and grate the thin yellow rind into the bowl; cut the lemon in two pieces, and squeeze all of the juice into the bowl also. Whip in a small bowl the eggs, and when very light moisten the mixture in the larger bowl with them. When well blended pour over the sherry. Grease well a mould, and garnish the bottom and sides with raisins or dried cherries, pour in the pudding mixture, tie over the mould a double pudding-cloth, or cover it with the tin cover, place the mould in a large pan of boiling water, and boil for five hours.

When the pudding is turned out, pour round it a white sauce. (See page 181.)

Marrow Pudding.—One pound beef marrow, one pint cream, one penny roll, four eggs, one wine-glassful of brandy, three ounces sugar, sixth part of a grated nutmeg.

Take a very stale roll and grate it into crumb, place it in a bowl, and pour over it the cream, which must first be placed in a sauce-pan and brought to boiling-point.

Cut the marrow into very thin pieces, add it to the cream and crumbs in the bowl, then mix in the sugar and nutmeg.

Beat in a separate bowl with a fork the eggs; when very light pour them over the other ingredients; when well mixed pour over the brandy.

Grease well a mould, pour in the mixture, and boil for three quarters of an hour.

French Pudding.—Eight ounces sugar, four ounces cornflour, one quart milk, four eggs, one pinch salt.

Place in a sauce-pan the milk and allow it to boil; when the milk is heating, place in a bowl the corn-flour, and drop into it, one by one, the yolks of egg.

Beat well together the yolks of egg and corn-flour, and the instant the milk boils pour it over, stirring well all the time; when well mixed add half of the sugar and salt, and return all to the pan in which the milk has been boiled. Place the pan again on the fire, and stir the contents until the eggs and corn-flour begin to thicken, but do not let the mixture boil. Pour now the mixture into a pie-dish and put it on one side.

Place on a dry plate the whites of egg, add a very little salt, and with a dry knife whip the whites to a very stiff froth, then add by degrees the remainder of the sugar.

Spread the whites of egg and sugar over the mixture in the pie-dish, and place the dish in a moderate oven from seven to ten minutes. This pudding may be eaten either hot or cold.

NOTE.—This pudding may be flavoured with fresh lemon-juice if desired.

Marmalade Pudding.—One quarter pound suet, one quarter pound bread crumbs, one quarter pound sugar, two ounces ground rice, two ounces orange marmalade, two eggs.

Place on a board the suet, remove all skin and discoloured parts; chop very finely and place it in a bowl with the ground rice and sugar.

Over a sheet of paper put a wire-sieve, and rub through with the hands the necessary quantity of bread crumb; add this crumb to ingredients in the bowl.

Whip now with a fork in a separate bowl the eggs, and then with them the marmalade, pour all the ingredients together, and when thoroughly blended, pour into a greased mould, and steam for four hours.

Follow the directions for greasing the mould and also for cooking given for Plain Suet Pudding, page 165.

Ginger Pudding.—Six ounces flour, one quarter pound

moist sugar, one quarter pound suet, one tea-spoonful ground ginger.

Mix well in a bowl the sugar and flour, and add to them the suet previously very finely chopped, add the ginger, and mix all thoroughly together.

Grease well a mould, and press firmly this mixture into it; put on the cover of the mould, or double a pudding-cloth, dip it in boiling water, and tie it firmly over. Put the mould into a large pan of boiling water, and boil for three hours.

Seven-Cup Pudding.—One cupful of suet, one cupful of flour, one cupful of bread crumbs, one cupful of currants, one cupful chopped apples, one cupful milk, one cupful sugar, two ounces chopped almonds, one tea-spoonful carbonate of soda, one half tea-spoonful of ground ginger, one half tea-spoonful ground cinnamon, one half tea-spoonful mixed spice.

Chop very finely the suet, and place it in a bowl with the flour, bread crumbs, chopped apples, and sugar.

Wash well and dry well in a towel the currants, and add them to the other ingredients, also the ginger, cinnamon, mixed spice, and chopped almonds.

Place the soda on a plate and smooth out the lumps with the point of a knife, add it then to the other ingredients, and moisten all well with the milk.

When all these quantities are well mixed, put the mixture in a well-greased mould, and boil for three hours.

Family Dumpling.—One pound flour, one half pound suet, one breakfast-cupful jam, one breakfast-cupful milk, one half tea-spoonful soda, one pinch salt.

When the skin and any discoloured part are removed from the suet place it on a board, and when it is finely chopped place it in a bowl with the flour, and sprinkle in the soda and salt.

Add now by degrees the jam and milk, stir thoroughly together, taking care that the flour does not lump.

Dip a pudding-cloth now in boiling water, sprinkle **over**

it a little dry flour, place it over a bowl, pour into the centre the pudding mixture, tie it into a ball with a piece of stout twine. Have in readiness a large pan filled with boiling water, add to it a table-spoonful of salt ; place in the bottom of the pan a small plate, put in the dumpling, cover the pan closely, and boil for two hours.

Note.—The pudding-cloth is placed over the bowl to give the mixture a round shape when placed in the cloth ; the plate is placed in the pan to prevent the pudding cloth getting burned.

Méringue Pudding.—One half quart canned peaches, two ounces butter, one quarter pound sugar, one and one-half ounce corn-flour, one quart milk, three eggs.

Place in a bowl the corn-flour, and pour over sufficient milk to moisten it; bring the remainder of the milk to the boiling-point, and pour into it the moistened corn-flour. Allow the milk and corn-flour to boil for five minutes, remove them from the fire, and stir in the butter.

When the butter is melted, drop in one by one the yolks of egg, sprinkle in half of the sugar, and beat all well together until quite smooth.

Place in a pie-dish the canned peaches, and pour the above mixture over, place the pie-dish in the oven, and bake twenty minutes.

Beat with a knife on a dry plate the whites of egg, and when very stiff and white sprinkle over them the remainder of the sugar. When the ingredients in the pie-dish have baked twenty minutes, pour over them the whites of egg and sugar, and allow the pudding three minutes longer in the oven. This pudding ought to be served cold.

Note.—Fresh fruit may be substituted for the canned peaches ; but when this is done a little more sugar must be used.

Cream Pudding.—One quarter pound butter, two table-spoonfuls arrowroot, one quart milk, four eggs, two ounces sugar, one salt-spoonful grated nutmeg.

Place in a bowl the arrowroot, and moisten it with a little

milk, stir till very smooth, add to it the nutmeg, and break into it the butter in small pieces.

Place now the remainder of the milk in a pan, and allow it to come quickly to the boiling-point; pour it at once over the moistened arrowroot and butter, and mix well together until the butter is melted.

Break now into a separate bowl the eggs, add the sugar, and beat them with a fork until the eggs are very light.

Mix all the ingredients well together and pour them into a pie-dish, place the dish in a moderate oven for twenty minutes.

Rice Méringue.—One half tea-cupful rice, one quart milk, three ounces sugar, four eggs.

Place the rice in a strainer, and placing the strainer under the water-tap, allow the water to run through it for two or three minutes; this will remove from the rice all dust and also any flour from the grains. Put the rice in a stew-pan, pour over the milk, and placing the pan over a very slow fire, allow the milk to simmer very slowly for three hours. During this time do not stir the contents of the pan, but shake the pan occasionally to prevent the rice settling to the bottom.

At the end of three hours pour the rice and milk into a bowl, and when half cold add half of the sugar and the yolks of eggs, which must first be well beaten.

Stir all these ingredients well together, and pour them into a pie-dish, place in a moderate oven, and bake twenty minutes. While this is baking whip the whites of egg on a dry plate to a stiff froth, add to them what remains of the sugar, and pour them over the baked rice.

After the whites of egg are poured over, allow the méringue to remain in the oven till the eggs have a pale brown colour.

Glacé Pudding.—One ounce gelatine, one half pound sugar, one quart cream, one half gill milk, one cupful rum, one cupful strawberry jam, three eggs.

Soak the gelatine in the milk for ten minutes, pour them into a small sauce-pan, and stir over a slow fire until the gelatine melts.

Place now in a jug the cream, add the sugar and eggs; the latter must first be well beaten.

Put the jug into a large pan of boiling water, and stir well the eggs, cream, and sugar together until the eggs thicken. Take the jug from the water, and when the custard in it is quite cold, pour into it the rum, stirring well meanwhile.

Add now the melted gelatine, also the jam, mix all well together, and pour into a mould to firm.

The mould must first be dipped into cold water before the mixture is poured in.

NOTE.—Brandy or sherry may be used instead of rum, but the rum is preferable.

Cold Cabinet Pudding.—Six stale sponge-cakes, one gill sherry, one tea-spoonful essence of vanilla, two ounces gelatine, one quart milk, yolks of four eggs, whites of two eggs, four ounces of sugar.

Soak the sponge-cakes for twenty minutes in the sherry, soak also the gelatine for the same time in as much of the milk as will cover it.

Beat well in a bowl the yolks and whites of egg, and bringing the milk to the boiling-point, pour it over, stirring well meanwhile; when well blended pour back into the pan in which the milk was boiled, and returning the pan to the fire, stir well until the eggs thicken, but do not let the mixture boil or the eggs will curdle. When the eggs thicken and a custard is thus formed, add the sugar, and melt in a sauce-pan the soaked gelatine; pour all together while hot, and flavour with the vanilla.

Dip now a large mould in cold water, place in it the sponge-cakes, pour over them the custard and gelatine. Set the mould in a cool place until the pudding is firm enough to turn out. When turned out the sponge-cakes will be found in the bottom.

Plain Suet Pudding.—One cupful suet, one cupful raisins, one cupful treacle, one cupful sweet milk, three cupfuls flour, one tea-spoonful carbonate of soda, one tea-spoonful salt.

Remove from one quarter pound beef suet all skin and any discoloured part; chop it very finely, and place one tea-cupful of it in a bowl.

Remove all seeds from the raisins, and place them in the bowl with the suet; add then the flour, treacle, and salt.

Place on a plate the soda, and smooth out all lumps with the point of a knife, add it to other ingredients in the bowl, and moisten all with the milk.

Take a perfectly dry mould or bowl, place in either a piece of butter, dip into a pan of boiling water, and when the butter melts turn the mould or bowl from side to side, so as to insure the butter greasing the entire surface.

Pour into the mould the mixture, tie over the top a pudding-cloth, which must first be dipped into hot water. Place the mould in a pan half filled with boiling water, and boil it for three hours.

NOTE.—This pudding will be much lighter if the water in which it is cooked is only allowed to come half-way up the sides of the mould.

Alexandra Pudding.—One tea-cupful of milk, one tea-cupful of sugar, one table-spoonful flour, three eggs, the rind of one lemon, four table-spoonfuls powdered sugar.

Line a pie-dish with pastry, following the directions for lemon pudding in page 145. Place the flour and sugar in a basin, grate over them the lemon-rind, then drop in one by one the yolks of egg. Stir well together, then add by degrees the milk. Still continue stirring until the mixture is quite smooth.

Pour this mixture into the pie-dish, place the dish in rather a quick oven, and bake twenty-five minutes. Place on a dry plate the whites of egg, and with a dry knife whip them to a stiff froth. Sprinkle over them four table-spoonfuls of powdered sugar. Take the pie-dish from the oven and place the whites of egg and sugar very roughly over the top. Return the pie-dish to the oven until the whites of egg have a pale-brown colour.

Strawberry Jam Pudding.—One pound flour, one half pound suet, one breakfast-cupful of strawberry jam, one half pint of milk, one half tea-spoonful of carbonate of soda, one pinch of salt.

Remove all skin from the suet, place it on a board, and with a sharp knife mince it very finely. Place the chopped suet in a basin, add the flour and salt, stir all well together. Place now on a plate the soda, and with the blade of a knife make it very smooth, then add it to the mixture in the basin.

Add now the jam and milk, stir all well together. Dip the centre of a pudding-cloth in boiling water, sprinkle over it a little dry flour, place it in a dry basin, then pour the mixture into the centre. With a piece of strong twine tie the mixture into the centre of the towel. Place in a large sauce-pan of boiling water a small plate, add half a table-spoonful of salt, put in the pudding, and allow it to boil two hours.

Vermicelli Pudding.—Four ounces of vermicelli, two ounces suet, one gill and a half of milk, one quarter of a pound of sugar, one table-spoonful of marmalade, six eggs, six drops ratifia.

Take a dry mould, place in it a small piece of butter, dip the mould in boiling water, and when the butter melts, take the mould from the sauce-pan, and turn the mould from side to side to allow the butter to run into all the corners.

Remove now from the suet all skin, and placing the suet on a board chop it very finely.

Place the suet in a sauce-pan, and add to it the milk and vermicelli. Place the pan over the fire and stir all together till boiling. Place this mixture now in a large basin to cool. When quite cold, beat until very light the eggs; add them, also the sugar, marmalade, and ratifia. Stir this mixture well with a wooden spoon, and pour it into the buttered mould. Twist over the top a piece of kitchen-paper, place the mould in a pan half filled with boiling water, and allow the water to boil two hours. Turn it out and pour round a wine sauce. (See page 181.)

NOTE.—The appearance of this pudding is much improved by arranging in the mould a few dried cherries before pouring in the mixture.

Devonshire Junket.—One quart milk, one table-spoonful brandy, one table-spoonful essence of rennet, one half pint thick cream.

Place in a sauce-pan the milk and heat it over the fire till tepid. Pour the milk into a shallow dish, and add the rennet and brandy. Stir well together, then let it stand till quite cold. Pour over the top the cream, and send it at once to table.

NOTE.—This may be garnished with dried fruit.

Turban.—One pint of red currants, one pint of raspberries, six ounces of sugar, twelve slices of very thinly-cut bread, one half pint double cream.

Place in a preserving-pan the fruit and sugar, stir all well over the fire till boiling, draw the pan then on one side, and let the contents simmer very slowly for half an hour. Take the pan from the fire and allow the fruit to become quite cold. Place now in a deep crystal dish alternate layers of the cooked fruit and the slices of bread. Place now in a basin the cream, and with an egg-whisk whip it to a solid froth, and pile it high over the fruit and bread.

Lothian Pudding.—One half pound of suet, one half pound of bread, one half pound apples, one half pound currants, one half pound sugar, four eggs, two ounces almonds, one ounce candied peel, one half of a nutmeg.

Remove from the suet all skin, place it on a board and chop it finely. Remove from the bread all crust, and rub the crumb through a wire sieve. Pare the apples, remove the cores, and chop them up rather roughly. Place the almonds in a basin, pour over a little boiling water, then remove the skins and chop them up very finely. Cut the candied peel into very thin strips and place the strips in a basin; add to them the bread crumb, suet, currants, almonds, sugar, and apples. Stir all well together, and grate over the nutmeg. Beat now till very light in a separate basin the eggs, then mix well together the contents of both basins. Prepare a mould in the same way as for the vermicelli pudding, pour in the mixture, cover the mould with a tin cover, place it in a pan of boiling water, and boil two hours and a half.

Swiss Apple Pudding.—One and a half pound of apples, one quarter pound brown sugar, the rind of one lemon, one gill cold water, two ounces of butter, three ounces bread crumb.

Pare and core the apples, cut them in small pieces. Place then in a sauce-pan the water, and when it boils add the sugar and lemon-rind, and stir till again boiling. Put now in the sauce-pan the pieces of apple and allow them to cook slowly till soft. Grease well with the butter the bottom and sides of a pie-dish, sprinkle over a layer of bread crumb, place in the cooked apples, sprinkle over what remains of the bread crumbs. Place now over the top the remainder of the butter in small pieces. Place the pie-dish in a quick oven, and bake for twenty minutes.

Bakewell Pudding.—One quarter of a pound of puff paste, two ounces of candied peel, one **table-spoonful** strawberry jam, one table-spoonful plum jam, one table-spoonful apricot jam, one half pound butter, one half-pound powdered sugar, the yolks of nine eggs, the whites of two eggs, two ounces of almonds.

Line two pie-dishes with puff paste. (See page 195.) Place in the bottom of each dish half of the preserve and half of the peel cut in small pieces. Place then in a basin the butter and sugar, and with the back of a wooden spoon beat them for ten minutes; add then one by one the yolks of egg, stirring constantly all the time. When all of the yolks are added, whip the whites of egg to a stiff froth and add them also. Pour half of this mixture into each of the pie-dishes, and place them in a moderate oven for forty minutes. While the puddings are baking pour over the almonds enough water to cover them. Remove the skins, and cut the almonds in long, thin strips. When the puddings are ready sprinkle over each a little white sugar, and stick over them thickly the almonds.

Derby Pudding.—One and a half pint new milk, three ounces of sugar, one and a half ounce of flour, three eggs, one wine-glassful of sherry, three small sponge-cakes.

Place in a small pie-dish the sponge-cakes, pour over them slowly the sherry, and let them soak for one hour.

Beat in a basin the eggs until very light, add to them the sugar and flour, beat well together again, and pour over the milk. When the sponge-cakes have soaked for an hour, pour over them the eggs, milk, and sugar; place the pie-dish in a *very, very* cool oven for an hour and a half.

Berlin Puddings.—Three eggs, the weight of three eggs in sugar, the weight of two eggs in flour, two large table-spoonfuls of apricot jam, one table-spoonful red currant jelly, one gill cream, one half ounce pistachio nuts, one wine-glassful of sherry.

Separate very carefully the yolks from the whites of the eggs, place the yolks in a basin, and add the sugar; beat with a wooden spoon the yolks and sugar well for ten minutes. Place on a dry plate the whites of egg, add a very small pinch of salt, and with a dry knife whip them to a stiff froth. Grease now with butter six cups or cup-tins; add very lightly the whipped whites of eggs, and then sprinkle in quickly the flour; stir all lightly together, and half fill each of the cup-tins with the mixture, and place the tins in a moderate oven for fifteen minutes.

When baked, turn the cakes out of the tins on to a wire

sieve, and let them get quite cold. Then with a tea-spoon scoop out the centre, making as large a hole as possible without breaking the edges. Rub over the outsides the red currant jelly, and in the cavity of each place an equal quantity of apricot jam; then pour over the sherry, and allow them to soak for a few minutes.

In the meantime, place in a small basin the cream, and with a couple of forks whip it to a froth, and then pile an equal quantity over the apricot jam in each cake. Place them carefully in a glass dish, and chop very finely the nuts, and sprinkle them over.

NOTE.—Prepare the pistachio nuts in the following manner before chopping them:—Place them in a small sauce-pan, cover them with cold water, and allow them to boil for two minutes; strain them from the water, place them in a basin of cold water, then remove the skins. The nuts when skinned ought to have a bright-green colour.

Fairy Butter.—Two ounces of butter, the rind of one lemon, one half tea-spoonful lemon-juice, ten macaroons, three ounces ratifia biscuit, one wine-glassful of sherry, two ounces of sugar.

Place the macaroons and ratifias in a crystal dish, pour over them in spoonfuls the sherry, and allow them to soak for an hour; sprinkle then over them the sugar. Place then in a basin the butter, grate over it the lemon-rind, add the juice, and with the back of a spoon beat all together till very smooth. Place a wire sieve over the crystal dish, and rub the butter through with the spoon, allowing it to fall over the macaroons.

Solid Custard.—One quarter pint cream, one quarter pint milk, one quarter ounce gelatine, the yolks of two eggs, two ounces of sugar, one small tea-spoonful essence of vanilla.

Soak the gelatine in a small basin with one gill of milk for ten minutes, then add the sugar and the remainder of the milk. Pour all into a sauce-pan, and stir over the fire until boiling. Take the pan from the fire, and when the mixture is almost cold add the cream and vanilla. Break now in a basin the eggs when beaten till very light, pour over them the mixture in the sauce-pan; pour all back into the pan, return the pan to the fire, and stir the contents until very hot, but do not let it boil. Take the pan again from the fire, and allow the custard to become quite cold; stir it frequently while it is cooling, to prevent the gelatine settling to the bottom.

Dip a mould in cold water, and pour into it the custard, to allow it to set. When set, turn out into a glass dish, and arrange round a little red currant jelly.

Russian Pancakes.—One and one-half ounce of butter, two ounces of flour, two ounces of sugar, two eggs.

Grease well with butter four breakfast saucers. Place in a basin the butter, and beat it to a cream with the back of a spoon; add the sugar, then by degrees the flour. When the butter, sugar, and flour are thoroughly mixed, beat in a separate basin the eggs until very light. Add the eggs lightly and quickly to the other ingredients, and half fill the saucers with the mixture. Place the saucers in rather a quick oven, and bake for twenty minutes. When ready, turn them out of the saucers, fold them together, and, if desired, place a little jam in each. Very good only with sugar.

French Pudding.—One half pound bread crumbs, six ounces suet, two ounces of sago, five ounces of sugar, one large table-spoonful apricot jam, three eggs.

Place the sago in a basin, cover it with milk, and allow it to soak over night. Place on a board the suet, remove the skin, and chop it very finely; put it in a basin, and add to it the soaked sago and bread crumb. Mix all well together, and then add the sugar, yolks of egg, and jam. Place on a dry plate the whites of egg, and with a dry knife whip them to a stiff froth. Add to the other ingredients very lightly then the whites, pour the mixture into a well-greased mould, cover the mould with a sheet of kitchen-paper, place it in a sauce-pan half full of boiling water, and let it boil two hours.

German Pudding.—One half pound treacle, one half pound flour, one quarter pound suet, one gill of milk, one ounce of candied peel, one tea-spoonful carbonate of soda.

Remove the skin from the suet, place the suet on a board and chop it very finely. Place on a plate the soda, and with the blade of a knife smooth out the lumps. Place now in a large basin the flour, add the suet, then the soda, and stir all well together. Cut in small pieces the peel and add it also. In a separate basin mix well the treacle and milk. Now mix well the contents of both basins, and pour the mixture into a well-greased mould. Dip a pudding-cloth in boiling water, double it, sprinkle over a little flour, and tie it closely over the top of the mould. Place the mould in a large pan of boiling water, and boil the pudding three hours.

Tipsy Cake.—One stale mould of sponge-cake, one quarter pound of almonds, two table-spoonfuls of raspberry jam, two wine-glassfuls of sherry.

Cut the cake in half horizontally, pour over each half an equal quantity of sherry, then place on the top of the under half the jam; place on the top half. Lift the cake carefully into a glass dish. Cover the almonds with boiling water, let them soak five minutes, remove the skins, and cut them in strips. Stick the cake closely over with the strips of almond, and pour round as much of the following custard as the glass dish will hold.

Boiled Custard.—Three gills of milk, three eggs, two ounces of lump sugar, the rind of half a lemon.

Remove very carefully from the lemon the rind, place it in a sauce-pan, pour over the milk, and allow the sauce-pan to stand by the side of the fire for twenty minutes. Beat well in a basin the eggs, add the sugar. Take the pan from the fire, and when the milk has cooled a little, pour it through a strainer over the eggs. Stir this mixture well together and pour it into a jug. Place the jug in a pan of boiling water, and stir its contents until the eggs begin to thicken; but take care they do not curdle. When cold, pour the custard into the glasses, and grate over the top a little nutmeg.

NOTE.—To the above quantity one table-spoonful of brandy may be added if desired.

Apple Hedgehog.—Two pounds apples, one quarter pound sugar, two ounces almonds, four table-spoonfuls of marmalade, one gill cold water, the whites of two eggs.

Place in a shallow sauce-pan the water, add to it three ounces of the sugar, place the sauce-pan over the fire, and stir the water and sugar till boiling. Pare nine apples of equal size, remove the cores, but do not cut them up, place the apples in the sauce-pan, and allow them to cook very slowly until soft, but take care not to let them break. Lift them carefully from the sauce-pan, place them on a flat dish, and fill the centres with the marmalade. Pare, core, and slice the remainder of the apples, place them in the sauce-pan, and let them cook till a pulp. Pile this pulp as high as possible over the apples and marmalade, and smooth all with a knife. Place now on a dry plate the whites of egg, and with a dry knife whip them to a stiff froth; place an equal layer of this froth over the apples, spreading it smoothly with the knife. Put the almonds in a basin, cover them with boiling water, remove the skins, cut them in long strips, and stick very closely over the whites of egg. Place the dish now in a hot oven until the almonds are browned slightly, when the pudding is ready for use. To be eaten cold.

Chantilly.—One stale mould of sponge-cake, one half pound cherries, one glass of brandy, one half pint double cream, one ounce of sugar, six drops of essence of vanilla.

Cut the top from the sponge-cake, and with a spoon scoop out the centre, leaving a wall half an inch in thickness.

Place this on a glass dish, and place in the centre the cherries, pouring over them the brandy; then replace the top. Put now the cream in a large basin, add to it the sugar, and with an egg-whisk whip the cream to a stiff froth; add the vanilla, and pour all over the cake, when it is ready for use.

SWEET AND SAVOURY SAUCES.
SAVOURY SAUCES.

Oyster Sauce.—One pint of oysters, one half pint of milk, two ounces of butter, one ounce of flour, one half tea-spoonful of salt, one half tea-spoonful of pepper, one salt-spoonful of grated nutmeg.

Drain the liquor from the oysters. Melt the butter in a sauce-pan, stir into it the flour, and add to this by degrees the liquor from the oysters.

When this mixture boils, throw into it the oysters, and boil all together until the leaves of the fish begin to shrivel. Throw in the pepper, salt, and nutmeg, and having boiled the milk in a separate sauce-pan, stir it in also; then the sauce-pan must at once be removed from the fire, otherwise the milk will curdle and the sauce be ruined.

Egg Sauce.—One and one-half ounce of butter, three quarters of an ounce of flour, three gills of milk, one salt-spoonful of salt, one salt-spoonful of white pepper, two hard-boiled eggs.

Melt the butter in a small sauce-pan, stir into it the flour, and by degrees add to these the milk. When this mixture boils, throw into it the pepper and salt, and let all cook together for two minutes.

Remove the shells from the eggs, chop them into small, irregular pieces, and stir these in. When this is done, the sauce is ready for use.

Caper Sauce.—Two ounces of butter, one ounce of flour, one half pint of milk, one half pint of cold water, one half tea-spoonful of white pepper, one half tea-spoonful of salt, two table-spoonfuls of capers.

Put the butter into a small sauce-pan and let it melt. Stir into this the flour and the milk; when this comes to the boiling-point, by degrees pour in the water. Let the mixture again boil up, season with the pepper and salt, and let all boil together for two minutes.

At the end of this time throw in the capers and remove the sauce-pan from the fire, the sauce being now ready for use.

NOTE.—When this sauce is prepared to be used with a leg of mutton, a half pint of the liquor from the boiling meat may be substituted for the cold water with excellent flavouring effect.

Mint Sauce.—Two table-spoonfuls of chopped mint, six table-spoonfuls of vinegar, two table-spoonfuls of cold water, three table-spoonfuls of sugar.

The mint before being chopped should be thoroughly washed, and when washed and chopped it must be placed in a gravy-boat, the vinegar and water poured over it, and throwing the sugar into this, all should be stirred until the sugar melts.

This sauce is designed for roast spring lamb.

NOTE.—Two table-spoonfuls of white wine are sometimes substituted for the cold water in preparing this sauce.

Tartare Sauce.—Yolks of two eggs, one gill of salad oil, one salt-spoonful of salt, one half salt-spoonful of pepper, one table-spoonful of white wine vinegar, one half tea-spoonful of French mustard, one table-spoonful of gherkins.

The vinegar and yolks of eggs must first be slightly beaten together in a small bowl. Add to these drop by drop the salad oil, taking care to stir one way all the time. When this is done, season the mixture with the pepper, salt, and mustard; add also the gherkins, finely chopped, and serve in a gravy-boat with boiled salmon or cold meats.

NOTE.—Capers may be used for this sauce if preferred, or if the gherkins are not obtainable.

Onion Sauce.—Two Spanish onions, one ounce of butter, one half ounce of flour, three gills of milk, one salt-spoonful of salt, one half salt-spoonful of pepper.

Preparatory to making this sauce, soak the onions over night in water which must have been poured over them boiling.

When required, take the onions from the soak, put them into a sauce-pan, and covering them with boiling water, let them boil therein for half an hour.

When boiled, take them from the water, chop them finely, and placing them in a bowl, cover them at once with the milk in order to preserve their colour.

Melt the butter in a small sauce-pan, add the flour, and into this pour the onion and milk, when all must be allowed to come to the boiling-point, and the pepper and salt then being added, the sauce must be permitted to boil thereafter for two minutes, when it will be ready to serve.

Bread Sauce.—Two ounces of bread, one half pint of milk, one Bermuda onion, six pepper-corns, one salt-spoonful of salt, one half gill of white stock.

Put the bread, broken into convenient pieces, into a bowl and cover it with the milk. Throw into the bowl also the onion, pepper-corns, and salt, together with the stock. Stir all together, after which, pouring the mixture into a small sauce-pan, and placing this over the fire, allow all to cook slowly for half an hour.

Skim out at the end of this time the pepper-corns and onion, and serve the sauce in a gravy-boat with roast fowl.

Brown Sauce.—One carrot, one turnip, one half stock of celery, one table-spoonful of mushroom catchup, six drops of caramel, two ounces of butter, three quarter ounces of flour, three gills of second stock, one salt-spoonful of salt, one half salt-spoonful of pepper.

Melt the butter in a frying-pan, and washing and paring the turnip and carrot, slice these into the melted butter, also the celery.

Brown the vegetables well upon both sides, and when this is done stir in the flour. Add by degrees the stock, stirring all constantly; when the mixture boils, season it with the salt and pepper, and flavour with the catchup. Let all cook for two minutes, then drop in the caramel, and strain the sauce into a gravy-boat for serving.

This gravy is served with fried meats or fish, or broiled steak and cutlets.

Shrimp Sauce.—One pint shrimps, one ounce butter, one half ounce flour, one half pint water, one tea-spoonful essence of anchovies, one pinch pepper, one quarter tea-spoonful salt.

Prick the shrimps, melt in a small sauce-pan over the fire the butter, add the flour, stir well together, then add the water, stir till boiling, add the pepper and salt, and let all boil for two minutes; add then the essence of anchovy and the shrimps, and let all heat through, but do not let it boil after the shrimps are added.

Lobster Sauce.—One quarter tin lobster, one ounce butter, one half ounce flour, one half pint cold water, two table-spoonfuls cream, one quarter tea-spoonful salt, one salt-spoonful pepper, one dessert-spoonful essence of anchovy.

Melt in a small sauce-pan the butter, add the flour, stir well together, add the water, stir till boiling; cook for two minutes, then add the pepper and salt, the anchovy essence and the cream, stir well together, then take the pan from the fire. Remove carefully from the tin the lobster, and cut in small square pieces. Place them in the sauce-pan, and return the pan to the side of the fire till all is well heated through, but do not let it boil again.

Apple Sauce.—Four large apples, one ounce of butter, one ounce sugar, one gill cold water.

Pare and core the apples, cut them up in small pieces, place them in a sauce-pan, and pour over them the water. Place the pan over the fire, and let the apples cook slowly till soft.

Take the pan from the fire, add the sugar, and with a fork beat all till very smooth. Send to table in a tureen.

Tomato Sauce.—Six tomatoes, two ounces butter, one half ounce flour, one half pint stock, one tea-spoonful salt, one quarter tea-spoonful pepper, one stalk celery.

Place the tomatoes in a sauce-pan and pour over the stock, add the salt and pepper, cut off the celery stalk and add it. Place the pan over the fire and cook all slowly for half an hour. Place over a basin a wire sieve and rub through the tomatoes and stock, melt then in a sauce-pan the butter, add the flour, then stir well together, pour over the tomatoes and stock, and stir all over the fire till boiling, when the sauce is ready for use.

Dutch Sauce.—The yolks of two eggs, the juice of half a lemon, two table-spoonfuls of cream, one table-spoonful parsley, one half tea-spoonful salt, one quarter tea-spoonful pepper, one half table-spoonful water.

Wash well the parsley in cold water, pick the stalks from it, place it in the corner of a clean towel and wring out all the water. Place the parsley on a board and chop it very fine. Drop the yolks of eggs into a sauce-pan and whisk them well with an egg-whisk; add now the water, and whisk well again. Add now the lemon-juice, the chopped parsley, the cream, and the salt and pepper.

Place the sauce-pan over a very slow fire, and whisk all well together until the mixture gets quite frothy and thick, but do not let it boil. This sauce ought then to be poured at once round the fish or meat with which it is to be served. To it may be added, if desired, half an ounce of butter.

NOTE.—A good method of preparing this sauce is to place the mixture in a tin sauce-pan, and place the sauce-pan in a larger one containing boiling water. This prevents the sauce from boiling, but gives it the required consistency.

SWEET AND SAVOURY SAUCES.

SWEET SAUCES.

German Sweet Sauce.—Yolks of two eggs, one gill of sherry, one table-spoonful of sugar, one table-spoonful of cream.

Put the yolks of eggs into a small sauce-pan, pour over them the sherry, and whisk these slightly with an egg-whisk. Add the cream and sugar, and, placing the sauce-pan over a very slow fire, continue to use the egg-whisk until the froth arises, and from it the escaping steam.

Remove the sauce from the fire and serve.

Jam Sauce.—One heaped table-spoonful of jam, one half ounce of sugar, one gill of sherry, one table-spoonful of cold water, six drops of cochineal.

Place the jam in a small sauce-pan, pour over it the sherry and water, add to these the sugar, and stir all over a brisk fire until the mixture boils. When boiling drop in the cochineal, and the sauce is ready for serving.

Lemon Sauce.—One lemon, six pieces of cut loaf-sugar, one tea-cupful of cold water.

Pare the rind from the lemon and cut this into strips the thickness of a straw. Put these straws of lemon-rind into a small sauce-pan together with the lumps of sugar, and covering them with the cold water, squeeze into the mixture the juice of the lemon.

Put the sauce-pan over the fire, and stir the contents until boiling; when this takes place cover the sauce-pan, and drawing it to one side of the fire, let all simmer slowly for twenty minutes.

This sauce should be poured over the pudding with which it is served, in order that the straws of lemon-rind may garnish the top of the pudding.

Brandy Sauce.—One ounce of butter, one half ounce of

flour, one half pint of cold water, one wine-glassful of brandy, one ounce of sugar.

The butter must first be melted in a small sauce-pan, the flour stirred into it, and the water then added.

When this comes to the boiling-point, let it continue to boil for two minutes, add the brandy and sugar, and when all is well stirred together it is ready for serving.

Hard Sauce.—One quarter pound of sugar, one quarter pound of butter, one quarter of a nutmeg, white of one egg.

Put the sugar and butter together in a bowl and beat them to a cream, taking care that the butter does not oil, which may be prevented by keeping it cool.

Whip the white of egg to a stiff froth, and mix this lightly into the bowl. When this is done put the sauce into a crystal dish for serving, and grate over it the nutmeg.

Custard Sauce.—Two eggs, three gills of milk, one dessert-spoonful of sugar, one salt-spoonful of grated nutmeg.

Place the eggs in a bowl and beat them until very light. Pour them into a quart pitcher, place the pitcher into a sauce-pan of boiling water, and throwing in the milk, stir it together with the eggs until they begin to thicken.

Take the pitcher from the boiling water, stir the sugar and nutmeg into its contents, and pour the sauce around the pudding with which it is to be served.

Jelly Sauce.—Two heaped table-spoonfuls of currant jelly, one half of a lemon, one wine-glassful of sherry, one ounce of sugar, six drops of cochineal, one salt-spoonful of mace.

Put the jelly into a small sauce-pan, squeeze over it the juice of the lemon, add to this the sugar and wine, place the sauce-pan over the fire, and stir its contents until the jelly melts; then the cochineal and mace should be added, and the instant after this that the sauce boils it is ready for serving.

Wine Sauce.—Two ounces of butter, three ounces of sugar, one and one-half gill of boiling water, one gill of sherry, one half salt-spoonful of grated nutmeg.

Beat the sugar and butter to a cream in a bowl, pour over these the boiling water, stirring meantime; place the mixture into a sauce-pan and stir all over the fire until very hot, not, however, allowing it to boil.

Add the sherry and nutmeg, and the sauce may at once be poured around the pudding with which it is to be served.

White Sauce.—One gill of milk, one gill of cream, one tea-spoonful of arrowroot, one-third of a salt-spoonful pounded mace, one ounce of butter, one half tea-spoonful of lemon-juice, one half table-spoonful of sugar.

Melt first in a small sauce-pan the butter, and then stir in the arrowroot; when both are well blended, add by degrees the milk.

Continue stirring the mixture over the fire until the milk boils, then add the cream, mace, and sugar. Cook for two minutes longer, take the pan from the fire, and when it has stood for one minute, squeeze in the lemon-juice.

ICES, CREAMS, AND JELLIES.
ICES.

Iced Pudding.—Three gills of milk, three gills of cream, yolks of twelve eggs, ten ounces of sugar, six ounces of crystallized fruits, one small wine-glassful of brandy, one small wine-glassful of curacoa.

Mix very thoroughly together the yolks of eggs, cream, and milk. Place this mixture into a quart pitcher, and putting this into a sauce-pan of boiling water over the fire, stir the compound constantly until the egg yolks begin to thicken all.

Take the pitcher from the water, stir the sugar in with its contents, and allow this to stand until the custard is quite cold. Pour it into the freezer, and when it thickens by freezing to a thick batter and cleaves to the sides in lumps, take the fruit, pour over it a little boiling water, and draining this off at once, cut the fruit into small pieces, throw upon them the curacoa and brandy, and turning this mixture into the half-frozen custard, freeze all until stiff enough to mould.

Pour cold water into a quart mould, and having thoroughly wetted the inside thereof, stick some of the crystallized fruits around the sides and into the bottom of the mould, for the purpose of garnishing the pudding. Then work the frozen mixture smoothly into the mould, taking care that it is packed evenly into all of the crevices; pack the mould in ice, and let it remain for one hour, when it will be ready to turn out and serve.

NOTE.—Rock salt should be mixed with the ice used for freezing creams and puddings, as it increases the degree of cold, and prevents the ice from melting.

Frozen Pudding Glacé, or Tutti-frutti.—One quarter pound of raisins, one pint of milk, yolks of two eggs, one quarter pound of powdered sugar, two ounces of sweet almonds, two ounces of candied cherries, two ounces of citron, two limes, one pint of cream, one inch stick of cinnamon.

Stem and seed the raisins, put them into a sauce-pan with the milk and cinnamon, and placing this over the fire, let all simmer together for twenty minutes.

While this is simmering, place the yolks of eggs and the sugar into a bowl and beat them well. At the end of the twenty minutes strain the raisins and cinnamon from the milk, throw the cinnamon away, and put the raisins aside for further use.

Pour the strained milk over the yolks of eggs and sugar, and stirring them well together, return the mixture to the sauce-pan; place this over the fire, still stirring, and allow the yolks of eggs to thicken, taking care that the milk does not boil.

Take the sauce-pan from the fire, allow its contents to become quite cold, and while awaiting this, pour boiling water over the almonds to blanch them, remove their skins, and chop them very finely; cut the limes each into quarters, and the citron into very small thin pieces; add all these together with the cherries and raisins to the custard when it becomes cold, pour in upon them the cream, and stirring all well together, throw the pudding into the freezer and allow it to freeze until it is firm enough to mould; then it should be firmly worked into a quart mould, which must have been wet with cold water to keep the mixture from sticking, and the mould packed into ice for one hour, that the pudding may form and firm.

Lemon Water Ice.—Four lemons, one half pound of sugar, one and one-half pint of boiling water.

Grate the rind from the lemons into a bowl, squeeze upon this the juice, add to this the sugar, and pour over all the boiling water, stirring the mixture meantime until thoroughly blended.

Allow the preparation to stand until quite cold, after which strain it through a horse-hair sieve or a piece of muslin, and throwing it into a freezer, freeze until very hard; then the freezer must be packed in fresh ice to keep its contents from melting, and the water ice should be served from this as required.

NOTE.—Lemon water ices should be tasted always before frozen, in order that more sugar may be added to the preparation, if it be found not to have the desired sweetness.

Strawberry Water Ice.—One pint of fresh strawberries, one and one-half pint of cold water, one half of a lemon, three ounces of sugar, six drops of cochineal.

Put the fruit upon a horse-hair sieve, sprinkle over it a little of the sugar, and rub all through the sieve. Mix the cold water with this strawberry syrup, add the sugar, squeeze in the juice of the lemon, drop in also the cochineal, and stir them all well together; pour the mixture into a freezer, freeze it until hard, and pack the freezer in fresh ice to preserve its contents in a frozen condition until served.

Iced Soufflé.—Yolks of six eggs, whites of two eggs, one pint of milk, two ounces of sugar, one half tea-spoonful of grated nutmeg, one pint of double cream.

Beat the whites and yolks of eggs together, add to these the nutmeg and sugar, and heating the milk until almost at the boiling-point, pour this over the mixture, stirring all together while pouring in the milk. Pour this into the sauce-pan in which the milk was boiled, and stir it over the fire until the eggs begin to thicken, but exercising great care that the milk does not again boil.

Put the custard into a bowl, and allow it to stand until quite cold; then one half pint of the cream should be stirred in, and the whole poured into a freezer, and frozen until stiff enough to be conveniently moulded.

Work the frozen custard into a pint and a half soufflé tin. Tie around the soufflé tin a sheet of kitchen-paper in such a manner as to increase the depth of the tin five or six inches. Whip the remaining cream to a stiff froth, pile this upon the top of the frozen custard, and setting the tin with its contents into a freezer, pile around this sufficient ice and rock salt to freeze the soufflé.

This should be transferred carefully, when frozen, to a silver soufflé dish, or served in the tin in which it is prepared, with a napkin folded around the same.

ICES, CREAMS, AND JELLIES.

CREAMS.

Strawberry Ice-Cream.—One pint of milk, four eggs, one and one-half pint of fresh strawberries, one quart of cream, one half pound of sugar.

Beat the eggs until very light, make the milk hot, and pour it over them. Pour these together into a sauce-pan, and stir them over the fire until the egg begins to thicken.

Transfer the custard to a bowl and allow it to cool. In the meantime place the strawberries into a hair sieve, sprinkle over them a little sugar, and then rub them through the sieve with the back of a wooden spoon. When this is done, add the sugar to the syrup so formed, and when the custard has become quite cold, stir the fruit mixture into it. Add the cream, and stirring this well through the custard, pour all into a freezer, and freeze until quite solid, stirring the cream down from the sides from time to time, to keep it smooth while freezing, unless the freezer be arranged to do this while being turned.

NOTE.—In mixing rock salt with the ice to be used for freezing creams, etc., great care should be taken that not even a drop of salted water falls into the freezer itself, as the smallest quantity of salt inside will make the cream most difficult to freeze, and when frozen, cause it to melt quickly.

Vanilla Ice-Cream.—One quart of cream, three pints of milk, one pound of sugar, eight eggs, four tea-spoonfuls of essence of vanilla.

Beat the eggs until very light, and heating the milk, pour it over them, stirring both well together.

Place the eggs and milk in a bright sauce-pan, and stir them over the fire until the eggs begin to thicken, not, however, allowing the mixture to boil.

Pour the mixture into a large bowl, and when it becomes quite cool, add to it the cream, vanilla, and sugar. When these are thoroughly stirred together, pour the custard into the freezer, and freeze it moderately hard, remembering to stir the cream down from the sides occasionally while it is being frozen, if the freezer be not arranged so as to make this unnecessary.

NOTES.—All fruit creams may be made after the method here given for strawberry ice-cream, and all flavouring essences may be used as the vanilla is used in the above, which constitutes the only difference existing between the various creams made from extracts or essences.

A delicious cream called lalla rookh is made by the simple addition of a small quantity of fine rum to each service of vanilla ice-cream, which must be stirred in as the cream is eaten, and the amount of which may be regulated by the taste.

Orange Cream.—One half ounce of gelatine, one gill of cold water, one quarter pound of cut loaf sugar, one gill of milk, yolks of three eggs, one half pint of double cream, four oranges, two lemons.

First soak the gelatine in cold water for ten minutes, then taking the lumps of sugar, rub them over the rinds of the oranges and lemons in order that the sugar may become impregnated with the flavour. Squeeze over the flavoured lumps of sugar then the juice of the oranges and lemons, pour upon them the milk, and stir all over the fire until the sugar melts, exercising the greatest care that the milk does not boil during the time, as boiling will cause it to curdle and spoil the cream.

Place the yolks of eggs into a large bowl, pour over them the prepared milk, and stir all together, when the whole must be put into a sauce-pan, and placed over the fire for two minutes to remove the raw taste of the eggs; and this being done, the cream should be again turned into the bowl and left to cool.

Now whip the double cream to a stiff froth, mix it lightly into the bowl when its contents have cooled, melt the soaked gelatine over the fire, not allowing it to boil in the process; add it also to the preparation in the bowl, and stir all together; continue to stir the cream occasionally until the gelatine in it blends with the other ingredients and begins to firm, otherwise it will sink to the bottom directly, and reunite in one firm mass as it cools.

Prepare a mould by dipping it into cold water to prevent sticking, and pouring the cream into this, set it away in a dry cool place to harden and set into form.

Charlotte Russe.—One half pint of double cream, one half ounce of gelatine, one half gill of cold water, one ounce of sugar, one tea-spoonful of essence of vanilla, white of one egg, one quarter pound of lady-fingers, one dozen candied cherries.

Cover the gelatine with cold water, and soak it for ten minutes. Put the cream into a bowl, and with an egg-whisk bring it to a very stiff froth; add to this the sugar and

CHARLOTTE RUSSE. P. 180.

CALF'S-FOOT JELLY. P. 291.

PEACH PIE. P. 199.

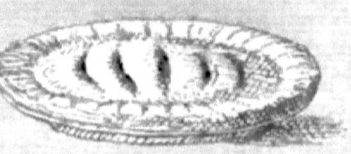
MINCE PIE. P. 199.

vanilla, then melt the gelatine over the fire, and pour it into the cream very carefully.

Now whip the white of egg to a stiff froth, and stir this also into the bowl, being careful not to beat down the froth while stirring; after which prepare the lady-fingers by splitting them apart, and cutting the sides of each so that they may fit squarely together, and line a pint soufflé tin, with these placed perpendicularly.

Pick the cherries up one by one with a skewer, and dipping them into cold water, arrange them in any fanciful form in the bottom of the tin. When the cream has commenced to firm a little in the bowl, pour it into the mould very carefully, in order that the wall of lady-fingers may not become disarranged, and set the whole away to harden.

When the charlotte russe has firmed sufficiently to be turned out of the mould, transfer it to a dessert-dish, using care not to break its shape or to disarrange the cherries which garnish the top.

Notes.—Charlotte russe may also be made by baking a sponge-cake in very thin sheets as for rolled jelly-cake, and cutting this into lengths about four inches wide and ten long, form these into small cups, sticking them together by brushing a little white of egg between the overlapping ends.

Arrange the cake cups upon a platter, placing a round of ornamental paper under each, fill them two-thirds full with the cream prepared as above; and when this hardens, whip sufficient white of egg to a stiff froth, and fill up the cups, placing upon the top of each a small lozenge cut for the purpose from the sponge-cake. When filled, they should be covered over with a sheet of paper, and placed in the oven for a moment to "set" the white of egg froth, when they are ready to serve. The lozenges upon the top of each may be garnished with a raisin or candied cherry if desired.

Rice Cream.—Two large table-spoonfuls of finely cracked rice, one pint of milk, one ounce of butter, two ounces of cut loaf sugar, rind of one lemon, one half ounce of gelatine, one half pint of double cream.

Prepare the gelatine by soaking it in the milk for one hour. Put into a fresh bright sauce-pan the butter, stir into it the rice, which must be as fine but not finer than granulated sugar; add to this by degrees the milk and gelatine, and rubbing the lumps of sugar upon the rind of the lemon to flavour them, throw these into the sauce-pan, place the sauce-pan over the fire, and stir its contents until the sugar melts and the mixture boils.

Allow the boiling to continue for five minutes; at the end of which time pour the compound into a bowl, and set it aside until it becomes nearly cold.

Beat the cream to a stiff froth, stir it lightly into the bowl, and pour all into a mould which must have previously been prepared by being dipped into cold water, after which the mould should be packed in ice until the cream becomes sufficiently firm to turn out and serve. Rice cream should be served with raspberry jam surrounding it.

Velvet Cream.—One ounce of gelatine, one half pint of white wine, one lemon, three ounces of cut loaf sugar, one pint of double cream, one half gill of cold water.

Cover the gelatine with cold water, and let it soak for ten minutes. Rub upon the rind of the lemon three or four of the lumps of sugar to flavour them, and placing these pieces of sugar in a copper or porcelain-lined sauce-pan, squeeze over them the juice of the lemon, add to these the wine and the remainder of the sugar, together with the soaked gelatine, and stir all over the fire until the gelatine melts. Pour the mixture from the sauce-pan through a strainer into a bowl and allow all to cool.

When cool, whip the cream to a stiff froth, mix it lightly with the strained preparation, and pouring the cream so completed into a mould, pack the mould in ice, and allow it to remain therein until its contents become firm enough to turn out in proper form and serve.

Italian Cream.—One pint cream, one half ounce gelatine, two ounces of sugar, one inch stick cinnamon, one half gill of milk, yolks of six eggs, grated rind of one lemon.

Soak in a small sauce-pan for ten minutes the gelatine and milk, then place the pan over a very slow fire, stir the gelatine and milk together until the former is quite dissolved, and then place the pan on one side. Place now in a larger pan the cream, which must be thick, and quite sweet; add to it the lemon rind, sugar, and cinnamon, allow the cream to boil, then take the pan from the fire. Beat now well in a bowl the yolks of eggs, and pour over them the hot milk and gelatine. Pour all now into the sauce-pan with the cream, return it to the fire, and stir well thereon for three minutes, taking great care not to allow it to boil. Remove the pan from the fire, lift out the cinnamon stick, and stir all until quite cold, but not set, then pour the mixture into a mould, which must first be dipped into cold water.

NOTE.—Unless the cream is very thick, a little more gelatine must be used in summer.

Snow Jelly.—One ounce of gelatine, one quarter pound of sugar, one half gill of brandy, the juice of two lemons, yolks of two eggs, whites of four eggs, the sixth part of a grated nutmeg, one half tea-spoonful of ground cinnamon, one quart of cold water.

Soak for one hour in one gill of water the gelatine. Place at the end of this time on the fire, in a bright, clear sauce-pan, the remainder of the water; when tepid remove the pan from the fire, and add the soaked gelatine, sugar, nutmeg, lemon-juice, cinnamon, and brandy. Whip now in a bowl the yolks and whites of two eggs, pour over them one table-spoonful of cold water, and pour this also into the sauce-pan; if the shells of eggs are quite clean throw them in. Return the sauce-pan to the fire, and with an egg-whisk stir the contents rapidly until boiling; the instant it boils remove the whisk, and allow the mixture to boil rapidly for two minutes.

Pour through a flannel bag a little tepid water. Have in readiness two dry basins, pour the jelly from the pan through the bag into one of them, draw the basin quickly from under the bag, and place under the remaining one. Pour the jelly which ran through first again into the bag, and continue doing so until the jelly runs through perfectly clear.

The egg-shells and sediment in the bag will serve as a filter; each time the jelly runs through it will become clearer. When the jelly is clear, place it on one side, until it begins to firm, then whip to a stiff froth the remaining whites of eggs, stir them very lightly into the jelly, taking great care not to mix them too much. The whites of egg ought to be in little white spots through the jelly. Place the mixture instantly into a wet mould, and allow it to firm. Turn the jelly out on a glass or silver dish, and serve with a boiled custard poured round.

NOTE.—In summer a little more gelatine must be added.

ICES, CREAMS, AND JELLIES.
JELLIES.

Lemon Jelly.—One and one-half ounce of gelatine, one pint of cold water, rind of two lemons, juice of three lemons, one inch of stick cinnamon, three ounces of lump sugar, one and one-half gill of sherry, whites of two eggs.

Cover the gelatine with cold water, and allow it to soak for ten minutes, after which pour all into a copper or porcelain-lined sauce-pan, adding the rind and juice of the lemons.

Throw into this the wine, stick of cinnamon, and sugar, and stir all over the fire until the gelatine melts. Put the whites of eggs into a bowl, whisk them slightly with an egg-whisk, pour them into the sauce-pan, and continue using the egg-whisk in this until the liquid boils.

Draw the sauce-pan to the side of the fire, cover it, and allow its contents to simmer slowly for ten minutes. Dip a flannel bag into tepid water, and pour the contents of the sauce-pan through it; then pouring the jelly into a mould, stand this upon ice, and when it has congealed and become firm, serve it turned out upon a crystal jelly-dish.

Orange Jelly.—Eight sweet oranges, two lemons, one

quarter pound of sugar, one gill of cold water, one ounce of gelatine.

Cover the gelatine with half of the cold water, and let it soak for ten minutes.

Put this into a sauce-pan, add to it the sugar with the remainder of the cold water, and stir all over the fire until the gelatine and sugar melt.

Take the sauce-pan from the fire, and having pressed out the juice of the oranges and lemons and strained it, add this to the contents of the sauce-pan, after which pour the mixture into a mould, and stand the mould upon ice; when it becomes jelly, turn it out upon a crystal or other jelly-plate, and serve.

Calf's-foot Jelly.—Two calf's feet, juice of two lemons, rinds of three lemons, one quarter pound of cut loaf sugar, ten cloves, one inch of cinnamon stick, whites of three eggs, one half gill of sherry wine, three pints of cold water.

Cut the feet into three pieces—across the first joint, and through the hoof. Place them in a large sauce-pan, cover them with cold water, and putting the sauce-pan over the fire, bring all quickly to the boiling-point.

When the water boils, take the feet from the sauce-pan, and throwing them into a basin of cold water, wash them thoroughly.

Put the feet when washed into a copper or porcelain-lined sauce-pan, pour over them the three pints of cold water, put the sauce-pan over the fire, and when the water boils draw it to one side, and let its contents simmer very slowly for five hours.

Strain the liquor through a horse-hair sieve, or if this be not convenient, through a coarse towel; let the stock so extracted stand over night, and then, removing the grease which will have gathered upon the top, dip a towel in boiling water and wash the surface of the stock, which will be found quite firm, having stood for twelve hours.

Now put the stock into a copper or porcelain-lined sauce-pan, and placing this over the fire, let it melt. Add to the melted stock the cinnamon stick, lemon rind and juice, sugar, and cloves.

Put the whites of eggs together with the shells, which must have been blanched with boiling water, into a bowl, beat them slightly, and pour them into the sauce-pan, continuing to use the egg-whisk until all is boiling.

When this point is reached, draw the sauce-pan immediately to the side of the fire, and allow its contents to simmer for ten minutes.

During this time prepare a flannel, or what is better, a felt bag, by pouring through it a little tepid water; and when the jelly has simmered ten minutes, pour it through this bag into a bowl, and repeat the process of straining until the jelly becomes perfectly clear. Pour it into a mould, and stirring into it the sherry, place the mould upon ice or in a very cool place until the jelly sets and becomes firm enough to turn out and serve.

NOTE.—Brandy may be substituted for the sherry in this preparation, if desired, and half brandy and half sherry is sometimes used to make up the quantity prescribed.

Lemon Sponge.—One ounce of gelatine, one pint of water, two lemons, one half pound of cut loaf sugar, whites of three eggs.

Put the gelatine into a bowl, cover it with the cold water, and let it soak for twenty minutes. At the end of this time add to it the rind of the lemons, squeeze over the lemon-juice, throw in the sugar, and pour all into a copper or porcelain-lined sauce-pan, place the sauce-pan over the fire, and stir its contents until boiling, after which it must be allowed to boil for two minutes.

At the end of this time pour the mixture through a sieve into a bowl, and let it remain therein until cold, but not long enough to set.

Beat the whites of eggs slightly, pour them into the mixture in the bowl, and stir all together, when all must be whisked with an egg-whisk until thick and white, which will take nearly or quite half an hour.

Pour the sponge into a mould, stand this in a cool dry place, and when "set," turn it out upon and serve in a crystal dessert-dish.

Apple Transparency.—Six large apples, one pint of water, one half pound of cut loaf sugar, rind of one lemon, six drops of cochineal, one half ounce of gelatine, white of one egg.

Put the gelatine into a bowl, and pour over it half a gill of the cold water, and allow it to soak in this for half an hour.

Pare the apples, and take the core from them, without breaking the form of the fruit.

Put the sugar into a shallow sauce-pan, and with it the lemon rind; pour over this the remainder of the cold water, and stir all until boiling. Into this syrup throw the apples, cover the sauce-pan, and placing it over the fire, let all cook very slowly until the apples become tender, and may easily be pierced through with a skewer or fork.

Remove the apples without breaking them, and place them in a crystal dish.

Throw the gelatine into the syrup that remains in the sauce-pan, stir all until the gelatine is melted, pour the mixture through a strainer into a bowl, add to it the cochineal, and stand the bowl in a cool dry place until the syrup congeals.

Cut the jelly so made into rough pieces, distribute it among the apples in the dessert-dish, and whipping the white of egg to a stiff froth, garnish the dish with this.

NOTE.—Double cream is cream that has been twenty-four hours in rising. Single cream rises in twelve hours, and cream for butter requires forty-eight.

Walnut Ice-Cream.—Six ounces of the kernels of walnuts, one gill and one half of milk, one-half table-spoonful of orange-flower water, six ounces of sifted sugar, one half pint of cream.

Place the walnut kernels in a mortar, add the orange-flower water and half a gill of the milk, pound all well together until the kernels are smooth. Place the mixture now on a wire sieve, and rub it through with a wooden spoon on to a plate. Add to this mixture then the sugar and the remainder of the milk, place it in the freezer and freeze for ten minutes, add then the cream and freeze all together.

Green Codling Ice-Cream.—Six large codlings, one half pint of water, one quarter pint cream, four ounces of sugar.

Rub the apples well in a clean towel, and slice them in thin round slices, place them in a sauce-pan, and add to them one gill and a half of the water; place the pan over a slow fire, and allow all to cook slowly for twenty minutes. Place then a hair sieve over a basin, and rub the apples while hot through the sieve; boil then in another sauce-pan the sugar and remainder of the water for ten minutes, add this to the apples, and mix all well together; add then the cream, and freeze in the usual manner.

Méringues.—One half pound sifted sugar, the whites of six eggs.

Place the whites of eggs in a basin and whip them to a very stiff froth. Stir in them with a spoon the sugar, as lightly and quickly as possible, to prevent the sugar having time to melt. Have in readiness a small board about one inch and a half in thickness, wet it well with cold water. Cut some stout foolscap paper in strips about two inches in width, place them on the table, take small spoonfuls of the mixture and place them about an inch apart on the paper. This must be done as quickly as possible; sprinkle over a little white sugar, and allow them to stand three minutes. Then place the strips of paper on the wetted board, and put the board in a moderate oven until the méringues take a very pale brown colour. Take the board from the oven, and lift the strips of paper; remove carefully each méringue, scoop out the centre, and lay them on baking sheets with the rounded sides down, and place them in a moderate oven till quite dry.

PIES AND PASTRIES.

PASTRIES.

Puff Paste.—One quarter pound of butter, one quarter pound of flour, yolk of one egg, one half gill of cold water, six drops of lemon-juice.

Sift the flour through a fine sieve upon a mixing-board. Put the yolk of egg into a small bowl, and add to it the lemon-juice and cold water, beating these together with a fork.

Make a well then in the centre of the flour, pour into it by degrees the mixture from the bowl, and mixing in the flour from the sides, knead all firmly together.

Flour a rolling-pin, and roll the paste out very thinly; place the butter in the corner of a towel, and covering it with the opposite corner, press out in this any moisture that the butter may contain; spread it upon half of the crust, fold the other half over it, and press the edges tightly together.

Roll this out again very thinly, taking care that the butter does not escape between the edges.

Fold the crust again in three layers, and again roll it out, but rolling across instead of lengthwise, in order that the butter may not run in streaks by being always rolled the same way, and repeat this process of folding and rolling seven times, remembering to let the crust cool between the rollings, otherwise the butter will oil.

The paste may now be used for vol-au-vent, or whatever purpose required.

NOTE.—If a larger quantity of this paste is required, it should be made in divisions, as a larger amount than is given above is not so successfully manipulated. When flour is in the least inferior, the quantity of water must be decreased, as there will not be sufficient gluten in it to absorb the quantity of moisture.

Flaky Crust.—One pound of flour, one half pound of butter, one tea-spoonful of baking-powder, one salt-spoonful of salt, one half gill of cold water, whites of two eggs.

Sift the flour through a sieve upon a mixing-board. Put the whites of eggs upon a plate, add to them the salt, and whip all to a light froth. Mix the flour to a firm dough with the froth of eggs and the cold water, roll it out very thinly, divide the butter into three pieces, and spread one of them upon the dough.

Fold the dough in three layers, and roll it out thinly again, reversing the order of rolling each time. Repeat this process until the butter is all rolled into the dough, when the crust is ready for use, and may be used for meat pies or fruit tarts.

Short Crust.—Six ounces of flour, four ounces of butter, one half gill of cold water, one half tea-spoonful of lemon-juice, yolk of one egg.

Place the flour when sifted upon a mixing-board, add to it the butter, and rub these gently together with the finger tips until all look like bread crumbs.

Make a little hole in the centre of the flour and butter, drop into it the yolk of egg, pour over it the lemon-juice, and adding the cold water by degrees, knead all lightly together.

This crust is used only for fruit tarts, and must be rolled out to about a quarter of an inch thickness when required.

Suet Crust.—One pound of flour, six ounces of beef suet, one tea-spoonful of baking-powder, one tea-spoonful of salt, one half pint of cold water.

First take the skin from the suet, and chop it very finely. Place it upon a mixing-board, and mix it together with the flour. Sprinkle over the mixture the salt and the baking-powder, make a hole in the centre, into which pour the water by degrees, mixing in the flour from the sides while pouring the water, when all must be kneaded lightly together, and rolled out, when required, to the thickness of half an inch.

This crust may be used for a boiled meat, or a boiled apple, pudding.

Rough Puff Paste.—Six ounces of butter, eight ounces of flour, one and one half table-spoonful of cold water, one half tea-spoonful of lemon-juice, yolk of one egg.

First sift the flour on to a mixing-board. Put with it the butter, and chop this up roughly with a knife, mixing at the same time with it the flour. Make a little well in the centre of the butter and flour, drop into it the yolk of egg, sprinkle over the lemon-juice and cold water, and knead all firmly together.

Roll the paste out thinly, fold it together, and roll again, reversing the order of rolling, and repeat this process four times, observing to change the direction of rolling each time.

The paste is then ready to be used, and is suitable for the covering of either fruit tarts or meat pies.

NOTE.—In preparing all crusts that require butter in the making, it will be found advantageous to put the butter upon ice until thoroughly hardened before using it.

PIES AND PASTRIES.

PIES.

Pie Crust.—Twelve ounces of flour, six ounces of butter, one tea-spoonful of baking-powder, one half tea-spoonful of salt, one gill of cold water.

Place the flour and butter together in a bowl, and mix them lightly with the fingers. When thoroughly blended, add the baking-powder and the salt, pour in upon this the cold water, and stir all well together, and flouring a mixing-board, turn this mixture out upon it, and knead all to a light dough. When required, roll this dough out very thinly, and line the pie tin with it.

NOTE.—When fresh sweet lard can be obtained, it may be substituted for butter in making pie crust, or mixed in equal parts with it.

Lemon Pie.—Two lemons, five table-spoonfuls of sugar, three eggs, one tea-cupful of milk, two table-spoonfuls of corn starch.

Grate the rind of the lemons into a bowl, chop the pulp of the lemon very finely, and mix it with the grated rind in the bowl. To this add the corn starch, and beat all smooth with the cold milk. Separate the yolks from the whites of the eggs, and placing the whites upon a plate, drop the yolks in with the mixture in the bowl, and beat all well together, adding two table-spoonfuls of the sugar.

Line a pie tin with pie crust (see p. 197), pour the mixture from the bowl into it, and placing the tin into a moderate oven, bake the pie for twenty minutes.

Whip to a stiff froth the whites of eggs, and to this add the remainder of the sugar; and when the pie is done, take it from the oven, and place over the top the sugared froth of egg, when it should be returned to the oven for five minutes, that the froth of egg may "set" and brown slightly upon the surface. Serve hot or cold, as the taste may dictate, although a lemon pie should never be allowed to stand long enough for the crust to become soaked with its moisture.

Apple Pie.—One and one-half pound of apples, three ounces of sugar, one table-spoonful of cold water, one half tea-spoonful of grated nutmeg.

Line a pie tin with pie crust (see p. 197), wet the edges of the crust with a little cold water, pare, core, and slice the apples, and arrange these in the tin. When this is done, sprinkle over the apples the sugar and nutmeg, and pour in the cold water; then cut a covering of the crust of the proper size, having rolled it to the thickness of one-third of an inch; cover the pie with this, pressing it firmly together with the lining crust at the edges, and cutting two or three slits in the top with a knife, to permit the steam to escape while the pie is baking.

This pie should be baked in a quick oven from twenty minutes to half an hour, according to the length of time the apples may require to be exposed to the heat before becoming soft.

Peach Pie.—One quart of peaches, three ounces of sugar, three table-spoonfuls of cream.

Line a pudding-dish with flaky crust (see p. 195), and cut also a round of the same, large enough to cover the top of the pudding-dish. Bake the crust lining and the covering upon flat baking-tins in a quick oven for fifteen minutes. While these are baking, pare and slice the peaches, which must be very ripe, mix together the sugar and cream, and pour over them; and when the crust is done, place the prepared peaches in the pie-dish, cover them over with the top crust, and place all in the oven for five minutes, in order that the fruit may steam through and the crust brown lightly upon the surface.

NOTE.—When small fruits are to be made into pies, such as strawberries, raspberries, etc., they should be treated in the manner above laid down, as baking them with the crust causes them to lose flavour and freshness.

Custard Pie.—Three eggs, three gills of milk, one ounce of sugar, one half tea-spoonful of grated nutmeg.

Line a pie tin with the pie crust (see p. 197), and putting the eggs and sugar into a bowl, beat them together until the eggs become very light. Add to this the milk, and pour all into the crust-lined pie tin. Place the whole in a moderate oven, and bake the pie for half an hour.

When done, grate over the surface the nutmeg, and serve cold or hot, as the taste may suggest, although custard pie should be cooled at once, if desired cold, as the crust soaks with standing and becomes unpalatable.

Mince Pie.—Fourteen pounds of brown sugar, eight pounds of suet, eight pounds of raisins, eight pounds of currants, one quarter pound of mixed spice, two pounds of citron, one half gallon of brandy, one table-spoonful of powdered ginger, one table-spoonful of powdered cinnamon, three ounces of apple, one half gill of cider, two ounces of lean boiled beef, two heaped table-spoonfuls of strawberry jam.

To prepare the mince meat, which should stand at least one month before being used, skin first the suet, and chop it very finely. Seed the raisins, and chop these also very finely. Wash the currants well, and drying them thoroughly, chop these finely with the citron, which must first be cut in very thin slices.

Place the chopped ingredients in a large bowl, mix them thoroughly together, and add to this the sugar, the mixed spice, cinnamon, and ginger, and stirring all well together, pour over the brandy, and stir all again until thoroughly saturated with the moisture.

This mince should be packed for keeping into a stone jar, and closely covered.

When a pie is desired, take out of the jar six heaped table-spoonfuls of the mince, put it into a bowl, and mix the cider and strawberry jam, also the beef, which must be minced exceedingly fine. Chop the apple also very finely, and stir this together with the mixture in the bowl; after which line a deep pie tin with puff paste (see p. 195), pour the mince, prepared as above, into it, cover all with a thin sheet of the paste cut to the proper size, and pinching the covering firmly to the lining paste at the edges, cut two or three gashes in the top, to let the steam escape while the pie is baking. Brush all over with a little white of egg or milk, and placing the tin in a quick oven, bake the pie for three-quarters of an hour.

NOTE.—There is a proverb that "mince meat becomes poison if minced too fine or kept too long," implying that it is impossible to do either. Mince prepared as above may be kept six months or a a year if desired.

BREAD AND CAKES.

BREAD.

Wheat Bread.—Three and one half pounds of flour, one ounce of compressed yeast, one dessert-spoonful of salt, one and three quarters pint of tepid water.

Place in a large mixing bowl or pan three pounds of the flour, and mix with it the salt.

Put the yeast cake into a bowl, and, covering it with the tepid water, let it dissolve.

Make a hole in the centre of the flour, and into this pour the yeast and water, pouring it through a strainer to remove any remaining lump. Stir into this from the side the dry flour until all becomes smooth, and, covering the bowl, place it in a warm, dry place, giving its contents two hours in which to rise.

At the end of this time sprinkle the remaining half pound of flour over the light dough, and knead all together until the dough cleaves cleanly from the sides of the bowl or pan.

Divide the dough into two equal parts, mould these into loaves, and, greasing slightly two bread-pans, place the loaves therein, and set them in a warm place for half an hour to rise. When this time expires place the bread-pans into a moderate oven, and bake the bread for one hour and a half.

When done, the bread should be placed upon a sieve or folded towel to cool before being put away, otherwise the steam which it generates, being put into a close place hot, will make it damp and heavy, and inclined to crumble when dry.

NOTES.—Rye bread may be made from wheaten potato sponge. The sponge must be set over night by taking three potatoes, boiling them, and mashing these in a half pint of the liquor in which they are boiled, stir in also wheat flour until a light batter is made, and, breaking into this half of a yeast cake, mix all thoroughly together and stand in a warm place to rise. With the addition of this yeast, the rye bread is prepared in the same manner as the wheat.

Flour should be sifted for bread as well as for pastries and cake.

Milk Rolls.—One pound of flour, one ounce of butter, one ounce of sugar, one tea-spoonful of baking-powder, one salt-spoonful of salt, one half pint of milk.

Put the flour into a bowl, and rub into this the butter with the hands. Add to this the salt, half an ounce of the sugar, and the baking-powder. Make a well in the centre of the mixture, pour into it the milk, stir into this the dry flour from the sides, and turning all out upon a mixing-board, knead all together as quickly and lightly as possible. Cut the dough into six pieces, and draw each piece quickly to the length of about four inches, with a sharp knife cut each roll twice across the top, place them side by side upon a slightly floured baking-tin, and bake them in a quick oven for twenty minutes.

At the end of this time withdraw the tin from the oven, brush the rolls over with a little milk, sprinkle over their tops the remainder of the sugar, and return them to the oven for one minute to dry the milk. Serve hot.

NOTE.—In using baking-powder for dough, the quicker the mixture containing it is baked, and the less handled, the more satisfactory the result.

French Rolls.—One ounce of butter, one salt-spoonful of salt, one half pint of milk, one egg, two table-spoonfuls of brewer's yeast, one and one half pound of flour.

First place the butter and milk together in a tin basin, and placing this over the fire, let them heat until the milk becomes tepid.

Put the yeast into a mixing-bowl, and pour over this the tepid mixture. Beat the egg thoroughly, and pour this also into the bowl, together with the salt, stir into the mixture the flour, cover the bowl with a cloth, and stand it in a warm place for two hours, to allow its contents to become light.

At the end of this time knead the light dough until it cleaves from the sides of the bowl, after which divide it into twelve rolls, form them upon a mixing-board, and place them on a slightly floured baking-tin, and allowing them to stand to rise for twenty minutes, bake in a quick oven for ten minutes. Serve hot.

Milk Biscuit.—One gill of milk, one ounce of butter, one tea-spoonful of baking-powder, one half pound of flour, one salt-spoonful of salt.

Put the milk into a small sauce-pan together with the butter, and place all over the fire.

When the milk becomes tepid, put the flour into a bowl, mix with it the salt and baking-powder, and pour into the centre of this the contents of the sauce-pan. Mix all to a stiff, smooth paste, turn this out upon a mixing-board, and roll it out as thinly as possible.

Take a small biscuit-cutter and cut the dough into rounds, pricking each several times on the top with a fork.

Arrange the biscuits upon a slightly greased baking-tin, and bake them in a moderate oven fifteen minutes.

Muffins.—One pint of milk, one pint of flour, one tea-spoonful of salt, two ounces of butter, three eggs.

Put the flour into a bowl, mix with it the salt, make a little hole in the centre of the flour, and separating the whites from the yolks of the eggs, drop the yolks into this hole, and place the whites upon a plate.

Melt the butter, taking care that it does not become hot, and pour this over the yolks of eggs, when the milk also must be poured in, and as it is poured the dry flour must be worked in from the sides.

When all the flour is mixed in, the mixture should be beaten until bubbles arise upon its surface.

Whip the whites of eggs to a stiff froth, and stir this lightly into the batter.

Slightly grease and heat twelve muffin rings, place them into a baking-pan, and pour into them equal parts of the batter, when they must be put into a very quick oven and baked for ten minutes. Serve hot.

NOTE.—A very delicious muffin may also be made after this recipe of equal parts of corn meal and wheat flour.

Tibbie Shiel's or Girdle Scones.—One pound of flour, one tea-spoonful of carbonate of soda, one half tea-spoonful of cream of tartar, one half tea-spoonful of salt, three gills of butter milk.

Put the flour into a bowl and mix through it the salt; place the soda and cream of tartar upon a plate, and make all smooth with the back of a tea-spoon. Mix this also with the flour, pour in the butter milk, and stir all thoroughly together.

Flour a mixing-board, pour the batter out upon this, and, adding a little flour from time to time to prevent sticking, knead the batter until it becomes a dough, stiff enough to roll out.

Cut the dough in two pieces, and roll each piece out round and to about half an inch in thickness. Divide each round into four pieces, place them on a heated girdle, and bake them fifteen minutes, turning them once meantime. Serve cold with butter.

Soda Scones.—One pound of flour, two ounces of butter, one ounce of sugar, one tea-spoonful of carbonate of soda, one half tea-spoonful of cream of tartar, three gills of butter milk, one half tea-spoonful of salt.

Put the flour into a bowl, mix through it the salt, and then rub into it the butter. Put the soda and cream of tartar together upon a plate, and rub them free of lumps with the back of a spoon, after which mix them in with the flour and butter.

Add to this mixture half of the sugar and all of the milk, and when these are stirred thoroughly in, pour the batter out upon a floured mixing-board. Knead it with a little dry flour until stiff enough to roll out, when, cutting the dough in two pieces, roll each of them to a round about half an inch in thickness, and marking each with a sharp knife from side to side at right angles, place them on a slightly floured baking-tin, and bake in a moderate oven for twenty minutes.

At the end of this time draw the tin from the oven long enough to brush the scones over with a little butter milk, sprinkle them with the remaining sugar, and return them to the oven for one minute. Cool the scones upon a sieve or folded towel before serving.

Note.—In using soda, care should be taken that the quantity given is not exceeded, and when a tea-spoonful is required, the spoon should be just level full, otherwise the preparation will be turned very yellow.

Folded Rolls.—One pint of milk, two ounces of butter, two medium sized potatoes, one half tea-cupful of brewer's yeast, one table-spoonful of sugar, one tea-spoonful of salt, two pounds of flour.

Bring the milk first to a tepid degree of heat, add to it the butter, and, when the butter has melted, pour all into a mixing-bowl, and add to these the potatoes, which must have been boiled and finely mashed. Mix in the salt and sugar, and thicken all with half of the flour.

Cover the bowl with a cloth, and set it in a warm place to rise through the night.

When light, knead the batter to a dough with the remainder of the flour, and let it rise the second time, the length of time required for this depending upon the quality of the yeast, heat, etc., but should not exceed an hour.

When light, place the dough upon a board, roll it out to about an inch in thickness, and cut this into rounds with a large-sized biscuit-cutter. Have ready now in a saucer a little melted butter, and brush over one half of the roll with this, folding the other half over upon it. When this is done, arrange the rolls upon a slightly floured baking-tin, set them to rise for the third time, and, when this is done, place the tin into a quick oven and let the rolls bake therein for ten minutes. Serve hot.

Note.—In preparing all yeasts and risen breads, care should be taken that the process of rising is not retarded by a chill, nor unduly accelerated by excessive heat, as the one will produce hard, heavy bread, and the other sour, hollow loaves.

Corn Lunn.—One tea-cupful of corn meal, two tea-cupfuls of wheat flour, one half tea-cupful of sugar, two ounces of butter, one half pint of sweet milk, three eggs, three teaspoonfuls of baking-powder.

The flour, corn meal, and sugar must first be well mixed together, and the baking-powder must be added to these. Melt the butter and pour it into the centre of the prepared flour, and mix all to a batter with the milk.

Break the eggs into a small bowl, and beat them until very light, pour this over the batter and stir it in.

Grease a bread-pan or pudding-dish, and pour the batter into it, filling it about half full. Place this in a quick oven, and bake for twenty minutes. Serve hot, covered with a napkin.

NOTE.—If corn bread is preferred not sweetened, the sugar may be left out of the above preparation.

Galettes.—One ounce of compressed yeast, one dessertspoonful of sugar, one and one half gill of milk, one gill of cold water, two pounds of flour, seven eggs.

Put the yeast and the sugar into a mixing-bowl. Bring the milk and water to a tepid degree of heat, and, pouring this over the powdered yeast and sugar, stir these together until both sugar and yeast dissolve.

Mix into this as much flour as will make a firm dough, covered with a towel, and place it in a warm place to rise, which will take about two hours.

Put into another bowl one pound of the flour, and into this drop one by one the eggs. To this add half a gill of milk, and beat all together with the hand for fifteen minutes.

When the dough has risen, mix into it the beaten flour, egg, and milk; beat all again with the hand until the different components are thoroughly blended.

Set this again for two hours in a warm place to rise, add the remainder of the flour, and knead the dough slightly. Cut from it pieces of dough, which should be moulded in the hands to the shape and size of a large egg. Gash them over the surface with a pair of scissors, place them upon a slightly floured baking-tin, let stand for a short time to resume their lightness, and bake in a quick oven for fifteen minutes, drawing them out, however, when about half done, long enough to sprinkle each galette with a little sugar. Serve either hot or cold according to taste.

BREAD AND CAKES.

CAKES.

Sultana Cake.—One half pound of flour, one quarter of a pound of butter, one quarter of a pound of powdered sugar, one quarter of a pound of sultana raisins, one tea-spoonful of baking-powder, rind of one lemon, one ounce of citron, one half gill of milk, two eggs.

First line a cake tin with a sheet of greased kitchen-paper, put the flour into a mixing-bowl, and rub into it the butter with the hands. Add to these the baking-powder and the grated rind of lemon, and, cutting the citron into thin small slices, stir this in also.

Put the eggs and sugar together in a small bowl; beat these until very light; stir into this the milk, after which the mixture should be poured into the mixing-bowl, and all thoroughly beaten together.

Place the raisins into a towel and rub them in this until the stems and all extraneous matter are rubbed off, pick them out and stir into the cake batter as quickly as possible, and, pouring all into the prepared baking-pan, bake the cake in a moderate oven for an hour and a quarter.

When done, remove the cake from the oven and place it upon a sieve to cool.

NOTES.—The cake tins should always be prepared before the cake, because when baking-powder is used there should be no delay in baking, as it effervesces but once, and the mixture to be raised should be firmed by the heat while the baking-powder is doing its work.

For this same reason the raisins should also be prepared prior to the stirring of the cake, and added last, because, being heavy, they naturally sink to the bottom of the mixture if allowed to stand. Raisins should never be washed, as it is extremely difficult to dry them thoroughly, and the moisture which they would gather in being washed must inevitably cause heaviness in whatever they are used.

Cakes should always be tested before being removed from the oven with a skewer or clean broom splint, for the reason that if exposed to a chill before thoroughly done they will always fall. If done, the skewer or broom splint will come out of the cake without any dough clinging thereto. The oven should always be kept closed until the cake dough firms, and opened thereafter as little as is consistent with the proper watching of the baking.

Cream Cake.—One tea-cupful of sugar, two tea-cupfuls of flour, one tea-spoonful of soda, two tea-spoonfuls of cream of tartar, four eggs, one half pint of milk, one table-spoonful of flour, two table-spoonfuls of sugar, one egg, one salt-spoonful of salt, six drops of essence of almond.

Put the flour and sugar into a mixing-bowl, and rub them together.

Place the soda and cream of tartar upon a plate, and rub the lumps out of them with the back of a spoon, and, mixing these with the sugar and flour, make a hole in the centre of the dry ingredients, and drop into it one by one the yolks of the four eggs.

Place the whites of eggs upon a dry plate, and with a dry knife whip them to a stiff froth, after which stir the froth lightly together with the contents of the mixing-bowl.

Grease well with butter four jelly cake tins, spread an equal portion of the cake batter upon each, and bake these in a quick oven for seven minutes.

While the cakes are baking, put the milk, into which throw the salt, into a sauce-pan over the fire, and bring it to the boiling-point.

While this is boiling, beat the one egg until very light, stir into this a table-spoonful of flour and two table-spoonfuls of sugar, and when the milk boils, remove it from the fire, let it cool for one minute, and add to it the egg mixture.

Return the sauce-pan to the fire, and let its contents boil for one minute, stirring it meanwhile to prevent scorching.

Take the sauce-pan again from the fire, and drop into it the essence of almond, and removing the cakes from the tins, place them one upon the other upon a flat dish, spreading between each layer of cake equal portions of the cream from the sauce-pan. Serve with a little powdered sugar sprinkled over the top.

Note.—Jelly cakes may be made also from this recipe, substituting jelly for the cream, and with this purpose the ingredients for the cake and cream have been given in separate quantities.

Orange Cake.—Two ounces of butter, six ounces of sugar, two tea-cupfuls of flour, one half tea-cupful of sweet milk, one tea-spoonful of cream of tartar, one half tea-spoonful of soda, three eggs, one orange.

Put the flour, butter, and three ounces of the sugar in a mixing-bowl. Rub them all lightly together, and making a well in the centre, drop into it the yolks of the eggs. Rub the cream of tartar and soda smooth of lumps, and stir them into the milk. Pour this over the yolks of eggs, and stir all well together. Whip the whites of two eggs to a stiff froth, mix this lightly in with the contents of the mixing-bowl, and greasing three jelly cake tins, spread the batter in equal portions over each. Bake these cakes in a quick oven for seven minutes.

While the cakes are baking, grate into a sieve the rind from the orange, place the sieve over a bowl, and squeeze through it the juice of the orange, passing the grated dust of the orange rind through at the same time.

Whip the remaining white of egg to a stiff froth, and add to this froth, by degrees, the remaining three ounces of sugar and the orange preparation.

Remove the cakes from the oven to a sieve, and when they become cool, arrange them one upon the other upon a flat plate, spreading between each layer of cake equal portions of the orange icing.

Snow Cake.—One pound of arrow-root, one half pound of powdered sugar, one half pound of butter, whites of six eggs, one tea-spoonful of essence of lemon.

Pass the arrow-root through a wire sieve to remove the

lumps. Beat the sugar and butter together to a cream, and add to these, by degrees, the arrow-root, beating the mixture constantly while sprinkling the arrow-root in.

Whip the whites of eggs to a stiff froth, and add these also to the mixture, after which beat all together for twenty minutes, until the mixture becomes a very smooth batter, and looks very white.

Add to the batter the lemon-juice, grease a cake tin with butter, and pour the batter into it, and placing this in a moderate oven, bake the cake for one hour and a half.

Pound Cake.—One pound of flour, one pound of butter, one pound of sugar, eight eggs, one wine-glassful of brandy, one salt-spoonful of salt, rind of two lemons.

Break the eggs into a bowl and beat them until very light.

Place the sugar in a large bowl, add to it the butter, and beat both to a cream. Stir into this cream the flour and the beaten eggs, pouring each in in alternate small portions, until all is well beaten together.

Add to the mixture the grated lemon rind, the salt and brandy, stir these until thoroughly blended, when, greasing a cake tin, pour into it the cake batter, and placing this in a moderate oven, bake the cake for one hour and three-quarters.

When done, place the cake immediately upon a sieve to cool.

Sponge Cake.—Three tea-cupfuls of sugar, three tea-cupfuls of flour, ten eggs, rind of one lemon, one table-spoonful of lemon-juice.

Put the sugar into a mixing-bowl, and separating the yolks from the whites of the eggs, place the whites upon a plate and drop the yolks one by one into the sugar, and beat these together for half an hour.

Whip the whites of eggs to a stiff froth, and stir this in with the contents of the mixing-bowl. Add to the mixture, by degrees, the flour, beating all constantly, and as the flour is being beaten in, sprinkle in from time to time the lemon-juice and the grated rind of lemon.

Pour the batter without any delay into a baking-tin that has been greased with butter, and placing the tin in a moderate oven, let the cake bake therein for an hour and a half.

Rock Cake.—One pound of flour, three ounces of butter, three ounces of sugar, three ounces of sultana raisins, two eggs, one tea-spoonful of powdered ginger, one half gill of milk, two tea-spoonfuls of baking-powder.

Put the flour into a mixing-bowl, add to it the butter, and rub these thoroughly together with the hands.

When this is done, add to the mixture the sugar, ginger, and baking-powder, and rub these also until well mixed.

Place the raisins in a towel, and rubbing from them the stems, pick them out and throw them into the mixture, stirring lightly while doing so.

Put the eggs into a small bowl, beat them until very light, add to them the milk, and stir this into the dry ingredients in the mixing-bowl, which should bring the mixture to a dough stiff enough to hold the spoon perpendicular in the centre.

Grease with butter a flat baking-tin, take two forks and lift with them rough pieces of the dough, and place them upon the tin.

Place the tin in a very hot oven, and bake the cake for fifteen minutes. Serve when cool.

Yorkshire Tea Cakes.—Three eggs, one pint of milk, one half tea-spoonful of salt, one piece of sal volatile, the size of a pea, one pound of flour.

Break the eggs into a bowl and beat them until very light. Add to them the milk, and dissolving the sal volatile and salt in sufficient water to cover them, add this to the milk and eggs, and add to the liquids the flour, by degrees, and beat all well together.

Grease some shallow tins the size of breakfast saucers, fill them half full with the batter, and placing them in a quick oven, bake them for fifteen minutes.

Notes.—If tins of the given size are not available, delf saucers may be used for baking these cakes.

These cakes make also a delicious breakfast dish.

Fruit Cake.—Two pounds of raisins, one pound of currants, one pound of citron, one pound of flour, four eggs, one half pint of milk, one pound of sugar, one quarter pound of butter.

Seed and pick the stems from the raisins, after which chop them roughly. Wash and dry the currants and put them together with the chopped raisins in a mixing-bowl. Rub together the butter and flour, and stir this in with the fruit, after which cut the citron into thin slices, and mix these in also, adding at the same time the sugar.

Break the eggs into a separate bowl and beat them until very light, add to them the milk, and pour this liquid over the fruit mixture, stirring all well together.

Put the cake mixture into a greased bread-pan, and bake in a slow oven for two hours.

Note.—Spices may be used in fruit cake if desired, also a wineglassful of brandy, and it will always be profitable, if convenient, to double or even treble the quantities here given for this cake, as the larger the bulk of fruit, the more delicious the cake, and also the longer fruit cake is kept the better it becomes.

Rusks (a hot Tea Cake).—Six ounces of flour, one half tea-cupful of sugar, two ounces of butter, one and one-half tea-cupful of sweet milk, one egg, one tea-spoonful of carbonate of soda, three tea-spoonfuls of cream of tartar.

Place in a bowl the flour, rub into it with the fingers the butter, then mix in the sugar.

Make the soda and cream of tartar quite smooth by placing them on a plate and with the point of a knife rubbing out the lumps, then add them to the flour.

Mix all well together, and drop into the centre the egg, which must first be lightly beaten, add by degrees the milk, and when a stiff batter is formed, pour the mixture into a well-greased Yorkshire pudding-tin, and bake in a quick oven for twenty minutes.

NOTE.—As the quantity of moisture required depends so much on the quality of the flour, judgment must be used in adding the milk: enough must only be used to form a very stiff batter.

Popovers (for Tea).—One cupful of milk, one cupful of flour, one egg, one pinch of salt.

Place on a baking-tin six or eight patty-tins, and two hours before the popovers are required place the baking-tin in the oven.

Place in a bowl the flour, add the salt, and drop into the centre the yolk of egg.

The milk must then be carefully added, the mixture being constantly stirred with the back of a spoon. The more this mixture is beaten the lighter the popovers will be.

Place on a dry plate the white of egg, and a very small pinch of salt, and with a dry knife whip the white to a stiff froth.

When the popovers are to be baked, mix into the batter very lightly the white of egg.

Draw the baking-tin from the oven and place into each patty-tin a piece of butter the size of a nutmeg, half fill each with batter, put the baking-tin quickly back into the oven, and bake twenty minutes.

NOTE.—A very hot oven is necessary for the popovers, and they ought to be sent to table the instant they are removed from the oven.

Tipsy Cake.—One pound sponge cake, three table-spoonfuls strawberry jam, one quarter pound almonds, one gill and one half sherry.

Cut the sponge through the middle (horizontally), place each half on a flat dish of any kind, and pour over each half, in spoonfuls, the sherry, and let them soak a little.

Place now the under half of the cake on a crystal dish, spread over it the jam, then place the top half over very carefully. The cake will then have its original shape. Pour now over the almonds a little boiling water, take off their skins, cut each almond in half (lengthwise), and stick them all over the surface of the cake. Pour round a custard sauce, directions for which will be found on page 180.

NOTE.—Stale cake is best for this receipt; great care must be taken not to break the cake after it is soaked.

Corn-Flour Cake.—One half pound corn-flour, six ounces butter, six ounces sugar, one half tea-cupful flour, one tea-spoonful cream of tartar, one half tea-spoonful soda, four eggs.

Make the soda and cream of tartar very smooth by rubbing out the lumps with the back of a spoon.

Place the flour and corn-flour in a bowl, and mix well the soda and cream of tartar with them.

Put now in a separate bowl the butter, heat the bowl very slightly, then with a wooden spoon beat it to a cream; but take the greatest care not to oil it, or the cake will be heavy.

Add now to the butter, by degrees, the sugar, corn-flour, and flour; as the mixture gets stiff drop in the yolk of an egg to moisten it.

When all these ingredients are added, including yolks of eggs, whip the whites to a very stiff froth, and mix them in also.

Line a cake-tin with a sheet of greased paper, pour in the mixture, and bake in rather a quick oven for forty minutes.

Seed Cake.—One pound flour, one half pound butter, one half pound sugar, one tea-spoonful caraway seeds, four eggs, one tea-spoonful baking-powder, one half gill milk.

Place in a basin the butter and sugar; with the back of a wooden spoon beat the mixture to a cream. Separate the yolks from the whites of the eggs. Place the whites on a dry plate, and drop into the basin one by one the yolks of egg, beat well this mixture, then add the milk. Whip to a very stiff froth the whites of egg, add them very gently, then add by degrees the flour. Dip a cake-tin in boiling water, dry it quickly, and line it with a sheet of greased paper. Just before pouring the mixture into the tin, add to it the caraway seeds. Place the tin in rather a quick oven for fifteen minutes, then place over the top a sheet of paper, change the tin to a cooler part of the oven, and allow the cake to bake slowly for an hour longer.

Snow Cake.—One pound potato flour, one half pound butter, one half pound powdered sugar, two eggs, one half tea-spoonful essence of vanilla.

Place in a basin the butter, and with the back of a wooden spoon beat it to a cream. The sugar must then be added and the mixture well beaten with the spoon for five minutes. Break into a small basin the eggs, beat them till very light, and add to them the vanilla. Add now the eggs and vanilla to the mixture in the large basin, and stir all well together. Mix in now quickly and lightly the flour. Line a Yorkshire pudding-tin with a sheet of greased paper; pour in the mixture and spread it smoothly with a knife; place the tin in a moderate oven and allow the cake to bake for three-quarters of an hour. Before taking the cake out of the tin allow it to cool a little, then cut it in small square pieces.

Soda Cake.—Two pounds flour, one half pound butter, one quarter pound lard, one pound sugar, one and one-half pound currants, one quarter pound lemon peel, one lemon, one table-spoonful of cinnamon, four eggs, one pint milk, two tea-spoonfuls carbonate of soda.

Prepare a large cake-tin by dipping it in boiling water, dry it quickly and line it with a sheet of greased paper. Place then on a plate the soda, and with the point of a knife make it very smooth. The butter, lard, and flour must then be placed in a large basin, and with the hands they must be well rubbed together until the mixture looks like bread crumb. Add then the currants, cinnamon, and soda; cut the peel in small pieces and add it also. Break now into a smaller basin the eggs, and with a fork beat them until very light; add to them the milk, stir well together and add the juice of the lemon. Pour now the contents of the smaller basin over the dry ingredients in the large basin, and mix all very quickly and lightly together. Pour all into the tin, and place the tin in rather a quick oven for the first twenty minutes, then change it to a cooler part of the oven for one hour longer. Run then into the centre of the cake a sharp knife; if when it is taken out it is quite dry, the cake is ready; if not, let the cake remain in the oven fifteen minutes longer.

NOTE.—Currants, before being cooked, ought always to be well washed, and dried at an open window, and kept for use in a closely-stoppered bottle or closely-covered jar.

Scones.—One pound flour, one egg, one tea-cupful milk, one tea-spoonful sugar, one tea-spoonful carbonate of soda, one half tea-spoonful cream of tartar, one pinch salt.

Place in a basin the flour; place on a plate the soda and cream of tartar; make them very smooth with the point of a knife. Beat well in a basin the egg, and add to it the milk; add now to the flour in the basin the sugar, salt, soda, and cream of tartar. Mix well with a spoon, and then moisten with the egg and milk. Turn out on a slightly floured board and knead very lightly together. Roll out an inch in thickness, cut in four, place on a floured baking-tin and bake twenty minutes in a hot oven. Cool on a sieve.

Sponge Sandwich.—Three eggs, one tea-cupful of sugar, one tea-cupful of flour, six drops essence of almond.

Separate carefully the yolks from the whites of the eggs. Place the yolks in a basin, add to them the sugar, and with a spoon beat both well together. Place the whites on a dry plate and whip them with a knife to a stiff froth. Stir very lightly the whites of egg to the sugar and yolks, add then the flour and essence of almond. Mix all well together, and pour the mixture into a well-greased Yorkshire pudding-tin. Place the tin in a quick oven and bake for twenty minutes.

Ginger Bread.—One pound flour, one pound treacle, one quarter pound moist sugar, one quarter pound butter, one ounce ground ginger, half an ounce caraway seeds, one gill milk, one tea-spoonful carbonate of soda, two eggs.

Beat in a large basin to a cream the butter, add the sugar, treacle, ginger, and caraway seeds, stir in by degrees the flour; when the mixture begins to get stiff, whip until very light in a separate basin the eggs, stir them into the mixture, and then add the last of the flour. Heat in a small sauce-pan till tepid the milk, dissolve in it the carbonate of soda, add this to the mixture in the large basin, stir all well together, and pour the mixture into a well-greased tin. Place the tin in a moderate oven and bake the ginger-bread for two hours.

Currant Cakes.—Six ounces of butter, one half pound powdered sugar, one pound flour, one half pound currants, one gill of milk, one tea-spoonful of volatile salts, four eggs.

Grease well some small round tins, place in a large basin the flour, add the butter, and with the hand thoroughly mix them together until the mixture looks like bread crumb. Add then the sugar and currants, place the volatile salts on a plate, and make it very smooth with the blade of a knife; add it to the other dry ingredients and stir all well together with a spoon. In a small basin beat till very light the eggs, add to them the milk, and stir well together. Mix now quickly together the contents of both basins, half fill the small tins with the mixture, and bake them in a quick oven ten minutes.

Plain Plum Cake.—One pound flour, one quarter pound butter, one quarter pound sugar, one quarter pound currants, three eggs, one half pint milk, one tea-spoonful carbonate of soda.

Place on a plate the soda, and make it smooth with the blade of a knife; add it to the flour, and pass both through a wire sieve. Beat in a basin the eggs until very light, stir to them the milk; beat now in a large basin to a cream the butter and sugar, either with the hand or with a wooden spoon. Add now by degrees the flour, and as the mixture stiffens add by degrees the milk and eggs. When all the ingredients are added, pour the mixture into a well-greased tin, and bake for an hour and a half in rather a quick oven.

NOTE.—This mixture may also be baked in small tins as in the former recipe.

Cream Cake.—Three tea-cupfuls of flour, three tea-cupfuls of sugar, two ounces of butter, three eggs, one tea-cupful of sour cream, one tea-spoonful essence of vanilla, half tea-spoonful of carbonate of soda, half a tea-spoonful cream of tartar.

Place on a plate the soda and cream of tartar, with the point of a knife make them very smooth; place then in a basin the flour, butter, and sugar, with the fingers rub all well together until thoroughly mixed; add then the soda and cream of tartar. Beat in a small basin the eggs, and when very light add the cream and vanilla; stir all well together. Grease now well with butter some small cup-tins. Mix then well and quickly together the contents of both basins, half fill the cup-tins with the mixture and bake in rather a quick oven ten minutes.

Queen Cakes.—One half pound flour, one half pound of butter, seven ounces of powdered sugar, six ounces currants, four eggs.

Grease well with butter some small queen-cake tins. Place in a basin the butter, and with the back of a wooden spoon beat it to a cream; add the sugar and beat well for five minutes. Place the eggs in a basin and beat them till very light. Add now to the butter and sugar a spoonful of the flour, then a little of the egg; continue adding alternately the flour and egg until both are used up. Stir all well together, and then add lastly the currants. Half fill the greased tins, and bake in rather a quick oven for fifteen minutes. When ready, turn the cakes out on a wire sieve to cool.

Lunch Cake.—Three tea-cupfuls of flour, one tea-cupful of sugar, one tea-cupful of butter milk, two tea-cupfuls of currants, three ounces of butter, two eggs, one ounce of orange peel, one half tea-spoonful carbonate of soda, one pinch salt.

Place in a large basin the flour, sugar, and butter; with the tips of the fingers mix all thoroughly together. Cut in very thin small pieces the peel, add it, also the currants. Place now on a plate the soda, and with the back of a spoon rub out all the lumps; add it and the salt also to the dry ingredients in the basin. In a small basin beat till very light the eggs, add the butter milk, and stir well together. Prepare now a cake-tin by dipping it in boiling water, drying it quickly, and lining it with a sheet of greased paper. Mix now quickly together the contents of both basins, pour the mixture into the tin, bake in a moderate oven for one hour and a quarter.

Plain Fruit Cake.—One and a half pound flour, one pound of sugar, one half pound currants, one half pound sultana raisins, one quarter pound candied peel, five ounces of lard, one pint milk, two eggs, one quarter ounce carbonate of soda, one quarter ounce tartaric acid.

Prepare the cake-mould as in foregoing recipe. Place in a large basin the flour, sugar, and lard. With the tips of the fingers mix all together till the mixture looks like bread crumb; add then the raisins and currants, also the candied peel cut in very small pieces. Place on a plate the soda and tartaric acid, rub out all lumps with the back of a spoon, and add them to the other dry ingredients. Beat now in a small basin the eggs, add to them the milk, and stir well together. Mix now quickly together the contents of both basins. Pour the mixture into the cake-mould, and bake it in rather a moderate oven for an hour and a half.

Syrup Cake.—One and one-half pound flour, one quarter pound sugar, one quarter pound lard, two ounces almonds, two pounds syrup, one half tea-spoonful baking-powder.

Place in a large basin the flour, add to it the sugar and

lard, with the tips of the fingers mix all well together. Pour over the almonds sufficient boiling water to cover them, take off the skins, cut them in half, and add them to the flour, lard, and sugar. Add now the baking-powder, and mix all well with a spoon. Pour in now the syrup, stir all well together again. Grease well with lard a cake-tin, pour in the mixture, place the tin in a moderate oven, and bake for an hour and three quarters.

Seed Cake.—One half pound sugar, one half pound butter, one half pound flour, one quarter pound almonds, one quarter pound orange peel, five eggs.

Place the almonds in a basin, cover them with boiling water, remove the skins and cut them in rough pieces, cut also in very small thin pieces the peel. Place the butter and sugar in a basin, and with the back of a wooden spoon beat them to the consistency of thick cream. Beat in a separate basin till very light the eggs. Add now to the butter and sugar, alternately by degrees, the eggs and flour, stirring well all the time. When all are added stir in the almonds and peel. Prepare a cake-tin in the same way as for lunch cake; pour in the mixture, and bake in a moderate oven one hour and a half.

Almond Gaufres.—One ounce flour, three ounces powdered sugar, four ounces almonds, two eggs, one half teaspoonful essence of vanilla.

Place in a basin the almonds, cover them with boiling water, and allow them to stand five minutes. Pour away the water, remove the skins from the almonds, place them on a board, and chop them very finely. Place in a basin the flour and sugar, add the chopped almonds and vanilla, then drop in the eggs. Beat all well together, then place a baking-tin in the oven to heat; when hot take it out and rub it over with white wax. Spread over very thinly the mixture from the basin. Place the baking-tin in a moderate oven for about four minutes, or until the mixture is set but not browned. Take the tin from the oven and stamp out the mixture in small rounds, return the tin to the oven until the rounds take a pale-brown colour. Place the tin before the fire, and as quickly as possible lift the rounds with a knife, then with the fingers twist them to the shape of a small horn. Return them on a plate to the oven for a couple of minutes. These make a very pretty dish when filled with whipped cream and sent to table in a crystal dish.

Sponge Cake.—One half pound flour, three quarters of a pound powdered sugar, the yokes of seven eggs, the whites of four eggs.

Grease well with butter a fluted cake-tin. Place then in a basin the sugar, and pour over it enough boiling water to moisten it, add then the yolks of egg, and with the back of a wooden spoon beat both well together until they become like cream. Place then on a dry plate the whites of egg, and with a dry knife whip them to a stiff froth. Add the whites of egg to the yolks and sugar, and beat all together until the mixture is very light. (This takes about quarter of an hour.) Mix then in as gently and quickly as possible the flour, and pour all into the tin immediately. Place the tin in rather a quick oven, and bake for one hour.

Sponge Cake.—Four eggs, the weight of four eggs in powdered sugar, the weight of two eggs in flour, the rind of one lemon.

Prepare a tin in the same way as for former recipe. Separate very carefully the yolks from the whites of egg. Place the yolks in a large basin and the whites on a dry plate. Add to the yolks of egg the sugar, and beat both well together for fifteen minutes. Stir in then as lightly as possible the whites of egg. Grate over the flour the lemon-rind, and mix both well together. Sift the flour as lightly and quickly as possible over the eggs and sugar; stir all lightly together, and pour quickly into the tin. Place the tin in a moderate oven for one hour and a quarter.

Note.—In baking sponge-cake the seldomer the oven door is opened the better.

Lemon Cake.—One quarter pound sugar, one quarter pound butter, six ounces flour, four eggs, one half tea-spoonful baking-powder, one half lemon.

Place the sugar and butter in a basin, and with the back of a wooden spoon beat the two together to a cream. Mix well together on a plate the baking-powder and flour. Beat well in a basin the eggs, and grate into them the rind of the lemon, then add the juice. Add by degrees the flour and beaten eggs to the butter and sugar, beating all meanwhile with a spoon. Line a cake-tin with a sheet of greased paper, pour in the mixture, and bake in rather a quick oven for an hour and a quarter.

Strawberry Short Cake.—One pound flour, four ounces butter, one ounce lard, one tea-spoonful soda, two tea-spoonfuls cream of tartar, one pinch of salt, one half pint milk.

Place the soda and cream of tartar on a plate, and rub out all the lumps with the point of a knife. Place the flour in a basin, and add the lard and butter. With the hand mix all together till the mixture looks like bread crumb, add the soda and cream of tartar, stir all with a spoon ; add then the milk, and make the mixture to a rather soft dough. Turn the dough out quickly on to a floured board, and knead lightly together, roll out about half an inch thick, and cut it in rounds about three and a half inches in diameter. Place a layer of the rounds on a floured tin, and then place a second round on each. Bake them for fifteen minutes. Separate the rounds, and place on the under rounds a layer of strawberries ; place on each the upper rounds, then place on another layer of strawberries, sprinkle thickly over with sugar, and serve with cream.

Soda Cake.—One pound flour, six ounces butter, six ounces moist sugar, twelve ounces currants, two eggs, one half pint milk, one tea-spoonful soda, one half tea-spoonful tartaric acid.

Place in a basin the flour, sugar, and butter, and mix all together with the fingers until the mixture looks like bread crumb, add then the currants. Place on a plate the soda and cream of tartar, and smooth out all the lumps with the point of a knife; add them to the flour and currants. Beat in a separate basin the eggs, add the milk, stir well together; then mix well together the contents of both basins. Line with greased paper a cake-tin, and pour in the mixture. Place the tin in a moderate oven, and bake the cake for an hour and a half.

Snow Cake.—One half pound corn-flour, three ounces butter, three ounces sugar, three eggs, one gill milk, one half tea-spoonful baking-powder, one tea-spoonful lemon-juice.

Place in a basin the butter and sugar, and beat them to a cream with the back of a wooden spoon. Mix well on a plate the corn-flour and baking-powder. Beat well in a basin the eggs. Then add alternately to the butter and sugar the corn-flour and eggs—a very little of each at a time. Add last of all the lemon-juice. Half fill some small greased tins, and bake ten minutes.

Pound Cake.—One pound flour, one pound sugar, one pound butter, two pounds currants, one quarter pound lemon-peel, eight eggs.

Heat very slightly a large basin, place in it the butter and sugar, and with the hand mix them together for fifteen minutes. Break into a separate basin the eggs, and beat them till very light; add them by degrees to the butter and sugar, stirring all meanwhile with a wooden spoon. Still continue stirring, and add the flour, a little at a time. Cut in small pieces the peel, and add it and the currants at the last. Pour the mixture into a well-greased cake-tin, and bake for an hour and three quarters in a moderate oven.

NOTE.—To this may be added, if desired, a wine-glassful of brandy.

Irish Seed Cake.—One half pound of butter, one pound of powdered sugar, three quarters of a pound of flour of rice, one quarter of a pound of almonds, one tea-spoonful of lemon-juice, one tea-spoonful of caraway seeds, one gill of rose-water, nine eggs.

Pass through a wire sieve the flour of rice. Break into a small basin the eggs, and beat them to a stiff froth with a fork. Place in a large basin the butter, and with the back of a wooden spoon beat it to a cream, then add by degrees the rose-water and sugar. Continue beating until all is thoroughly mixed. Add then the beaten eggs, stir all well together, and sprinkle in by degrees the flour of rice. Pour over the almonds enough boiling water to cover them, remove the skins, and chop the almonds finely. Add now to the mixture in the large basin the almonds, caraway seeds, and lemon-juice. Stir quickly together again. Pour all into a greased cake-tin, and bake in a quick oven for one hour and a half.

Short-Bread.—One pound flour, one half pound butter, one quarter pound sugar, the yolk of one small egg.

Place on a baking-board the flour, butter, and sugar, and mix them all well with the hands. Make then a little well in the centre, and drop in the yolk of egg. Knead all now well with the hands until the mixture becomes a soft dough. Fold in four a sheet of white paper, place on it the dough, and roll the dough out about half an inch in thickness. Dip the thumb and one finger of the right hand in flour, and pinch the dough all round the edge. With a fork prick the centre all over. Place the sheet of paper on a baking-tin, place the tin in a quick oven, and bake the short-bread twenty minutes.

Merveilles.—One half pound of flour, one quarter pound sugar, one ounce of butter, one ounce candied citron, one table-spoonful of brandy, two eggs.

Cut in very small pieces the citron. Place the eggs in a basin and beat them until very light; add to them by degrees the brandy, stirring all well together. Place then in a basin the flour, butter, and sugar. With the tips of the fingers mix all well together, then add the citron. Moisten the flour, butter, and sugar with the eggs and brandy. Flour well a baking-board, turn out the mixture on it, and knead lightly together. Roll it out then thinly, and cut it into small dice. Heat some clarified fat until the smoke arises from it, drop in one by one the dice, and allow them to take a pale-brown colour. This will take about three minutes. When ready they will float on the top of the fat. Drain them for one minute on a sheet of kitchen-paper. When cold pile them very high, and sprinkle over a little white sugar.

Ginger Bread.—One and one-half pound flour, one pound treacle, one quarter pound butter, three ounces orange-peel, one quarter pound almonds, two ounces sugar, one tea-spoonful soda, three tea-spoonfuls of ginger (ground), two tea-spoonfuls cinnamon, one quarter tea-spoonful grated nutmeg.

Place in a large basin the flour, add to it the butter, and with the tips of the fingers mix it well with the flour. When well mixed add the sugar, ginger, cinnamon, and nutmeg. Cut in small pieces the peel; add it also. Place the almonds in a small basin of boiling water, then remove the skins and chop them finely, and add them to other ingredients. Place on a plate the soda, and smooth out all the lumps with the point of a knife. Add the soda also, and mix all thoroughly with a spoon. Put the treacle in a sauce-pan, and stir it over the fire for five minutes. Pour the treacle now over the other ingredients, stir all well together, and pour the mixture into a well-greased Yorkshire pudding-tin. Place the tin in a moderate oven, and bake the ginger-bread for two hours.

Belvoir Castle.—Two pounds flour, five ounces dripping, six ounces sugar, six ounces currants, one pint milk, one ounce German yeast.

Place the flour in a basin, rub into it the dripping, add the sugar and currants. Place in a basin the yeast, heat in a sauce-pan over the fire the milk until tepid, pour it over the yeast and stir well together until the yeast is dissolved.

Make a hole in the centre of the flour, pour in the yeast and milk, stir all together, cover the basin with a towel, and place the basin in a warm place for two hours. Knead this well now, until the dough leaves the basin quite clean; turn the dough out on a board and cut it into eighteen pieces. Make each piece into a small ball, place the balls on a floured tin. Place the tin before the fire for half an hour, then bake the buns in a quick oven ten minutes.

Victoria Buns.—Ten ounces flour, three ounces sugar, three ounces butter, one tea-spoonful of baking-powder, two eggs, half a gill milk.

Place the flour, sugar, and butter in a basin, and rub them all together with the fingers till perfectly smooth; and then add the baking-powder.

Beat in a separate basin the eggs, add the milk, and then stir them quickly into the basin with the dry ingredients. Half fill some small greased tins with the mixture, and bake in a quick oven for fifteen minutes.

Plain Currant Cake.—One pound flour, one half pound powdered sugar, one half pound currants, one quarter pound butter, one gill milk, three eggs, one small tea-spoonful soda.

Place the flour in a basin, add the sugar and butter, mix all with the fingers till the mixture looks like bread crumbs. Wash well and dry the currants, add them to the flour; also the soda. Stir all well together. Beat well in a separate basin the eggs, add the milk. Prepare now a cake-tin by greasing it well with butter. Mix quickly together the milk and eggs with the dry ingredients, pour into the cake-tin, and bake the cake in a moderate oven one hour and a half.

Aberffrau Buns.—Four pounds flour, one quarter pound butter, three eggs, one pint milk, one pint water, six ounces sugar, two ounces German yeast.

Place in a large basin the flour, and add to it the sugar. Place in a small basin the eggs and beat them till very light. Place the milk in a jug, and boil the water and pour it over;

add now the butter, and stir all together till it is melted. Place in a basin the yeast, and pour over it the mixture in the jug, stir well together and add the beaten eggs.

Mix all now well together in the large basin, cover the basin with a towel, and place it in a warm place to rise for two hours. Knead it now well on a board and cut the dough into small pieces, draw them into a long shape, place them on a floured tin, and let them again rise for half an hour in a warm place. Then bake in a quick oven for fifteen minutes. This quantity makes two dozen and a half buns.

BREAKFAST DISHES.

Anchovy Eggs.—One tea-spoonful anchovy paste, two eggs, one ounce of butter, one salt-spoonful of salt, one-half table-spoonful of cream, one-half tea-spoonful lemon-juice.

Place the eggs in plenty of boiling water, and boil them for ten minutes; plunge them then into a basin of cold water, and remove the shells. Cut each egg in half, and cut a small piece as large as a threepenny piece from the end of each half; remove the yolks, and place them in a basin; add the butter and anchovy paste. Stir all well together, season with the pepper, and add last of all the cream and lemon-juice. Rub this mixture now through a wire sieve, then divide it into four parts; place a part in each half of egg. Dip a knife in cold water, and make the mixture as smooth as possible; then cut in four pieces the tops which were cut from the halves of eggs and arrange them neatly on the top. Garnish with a little parsley, and send to table on a neatly folded napkin.

Sheep's Trotters.—Six sheep feet, two table-spoonfuls of cream, one table-spoonful of chopped parsley, yolks of two eggs, one half tea-spoonful of pepper, one tea-spoonful of salt, one salt-spoonful of grated nutmeg, one dessert-spoonful of sherry.

When the feet have been scalded and scraped, put them

into a sauce-pan, cover them with cold water, and place the sauce-pan over the fire. When this water boils, drain it off, and cover them again with water that is boiling; allow them to simmer very slowly in this until the meat will separate from the bone. Take the feet from the sauce-pan, remove the bones, and cut the meat into small pieces. Put these pieces of meat into a fresh sauce-pan, and pour over them a pint and a half of the liquor in which the feet were boiled. Place this sauce-pan over the fire, and as the liquor boils up, skim it carefully. Add to the trotters the sherry, pepper, and salt, and let all simmer slowly together for twenty minutes.

Beat in a bowl the yolks of eggs, add to them the chopped parsley and nutmeg, and taking the sauce-pan from the fire, let its contents cool a little, and add thereto the egg mixture from the bowl.

Stir all well together, adding at the last moment the cream, and serve at once.

Calf's Liver.—One and one-half pound of calf's liver, one quarter pound of bacon, one tea-spoonful of mixed herbs, one tea-spoonful of salt, one half tea-spoonful of pepper, yolks of two eggs, one tea-cupful of cream.

Place the liver in a sauce-pan over the fire, and covering it with cold water, let it boil therein for three-quarters of an hour.

Take it from the water, allow it to become perfectly cool, and then grate it fine upon a carrot grater. Put the grated liver into a bowl, and chopping the bacon very fine, mix it therewith.

Add to this mixture the herbs, pepper, and salt; beat well together the yolks of the eggs and the cream, and mix these in also.

Put all into a sauce-pan, and placing this over a very slow fire, stir the preparation until very hot, not at any time allowing it to boil. Serve upon a hot dish.

Sheep-head Pie.—One sheep's head, one half pound of

bacon, one tea-spoonful of pepper, one dessert-spoonful of salt, two hard-boiled eggs.

When the sheep's head is cleaned, put it into a sauce-pan over the fire, and covering it with cold water, bring it quickly to the boiling-point; and when boiling, skim the surface very carefully. Draw the sauce-pan to one side of the fire, and let its contents simmer very slowly until the meat will separate from the bones.

Take the head from the boiling water, remove the meat from the bones, and cut this into small pieces. Skin the tongue and cut it into small pieces also. Mix the tongue and the meat together, put a layer of the mixture, about an inch in thickness, into the bottom of a pie-dish, cover this with a layer of bacon, and over this one of the hard-boiled eggs cut in slices. Sprinkle over all some pepper and salt, and repeat the alternating layers of chopped meat, bacon, and egg, until the materials are all filled into the dish.

Pour over the pie three gills of the liquor in which the head was boiled, cover all with a flaky crust (see page 195), and bake the pie in a quick oven for half an hour. This dish should be served cold.

Deviled Turkey.—One pair of turkey legs, one half tea-spoonful of salt, one half tea-spoonful of pepper, one grain of cayenne.

Cut the legs from a cold roast turkey, trim them neatly, sprinkle over them the pepper, salt, and cayenne; grease two sheets of letter paper, and wrap each leg in one of these, twisting the ends of the paper to secure it.

Place the legs thus prepared in a broiler, and broil them for seven minutes over a clear fire.

When broiled, remove the paper, and serve the legs very hot.

Kidney Omelette.—Eight eggs, four sheep kidneys, one gill of brown stock, one dessert-spoonful of mushroom catchup, one half tea-spoonful of pepper, one half tea-spoonful of salt, one half ounce of flour, three ounces of butter.

Put one ounce of the butter into a sauce-pan. Cut each kidney into eight pieces, put the flour upon a plate, and roll the pieces of kidney in it until they are completely blanketed with the flour. Throw the kidney into the hot butter, and brown each piece well upon both sides. Pour into the sauce-pan, over the browned kidney, the stock and catchup; season all with half of the pepper and salt; and covering the sauce-pan draw it to the side of the fire, and let its contents cook very slowly for one hour.

Beat in a bowl the eggs until the yolks and whites are mixed, sprinkle over them the remainder of the pepper and salt, melt an ounce of the butter in an omelette-pan, pour into this half of the well-beaten egg, and stir this with a spoon until it begins to firm around the edges; after which it should remain upon the fire until the egg becomes nearly all firm.

Put upon the omelette half of the stewed kidney; fold the omelette over so that the outer edges meet. Let it remain a minute longer in the pan, and turn it quickly out upon a hot platter.

Repeat this process with the remaining egg and kidney, and when the second omelette is ready, place it beside the first upon the platter, and serve as speedily as possible.

Ham Omelette.—Eight eggs, one tea-spoonful of pepper, one tea-spoonful of salt, two ounces of butter, three table-spoonfuls of cold boiled ham, chopped.

Break the eggs into a bowl, and beat them with a wooden spoon until the yolks and whites blend.

Melt one ounce of the butter in an omelette-pan, stir into the beaten egg the chopped ham, pepper, and salt, and pour half of the mixture into the pan with the hot butter.

Stir all until the omelette begins to set at the edges; draw all down to one side of the pan, and when it becomes firm on the under side, turn the omelette quickly over to the other side of the pan, without breaking its form, and remove the omelette to a hot platter.

Repeat this process for the second omelette, the cooking

of which should only take about two minutes, and serve both as quickly as possible.

Dried Herb Omelettes.—One dessert-spoonful of chopped parsley, two tea-spoonfuls of dried mixed herbs, a piece of eschalot the size of a bean, eight eggs, one half tea-spoonful of pepper, one tea-spoonful of salt, two ounces of butter.

Put the eggs into a bowl, and with them the chopped parsley, dried herbs, pepper, and salt. Chop the eschalot finely, and throw it in also.

Beat all together until the eggs are thoroughly blended, the yolks with the whites. Melt in an omelette-pan one ounce of the butter, and when the blue smoke arises pour into it half of the mixture from the bowl, and stir this until the omelette begins to firm at the edges.

Draw all down to one side of the pan, and when the omelette becomes firm on the under side, turn it over to the other side of the pan, and transfer it from this at once to a hot platter.

Repeat this process of cooking with the remaining omelette mixture, and with as much despatch as is possible; place the second omelette beside the first, and serve immediately.

NOTE.—Omelettes should always be cooked over a very quick fire, and should never consume more than two minutes in the doing.

Eggs au Plat.—Eight eggs, eight table-spoonfuls of bread crumbs, four ounces of butter, one tea-spoonful of pepper, one tea-spoonful of salt.

Spread half of the bread crumbs upon a platter, sprinkle over them half of the pepper and salt, and distribute over this, in small pieces, two ounces of the butter.

Break over this, one by one, the eggs, arranging them in a circle upon the bread crumbs; sprinkle over them the remaining bread crumbs, pepper, and salt; also distribute over this the remainder of the butter, in small pieces, and place the platter in a hot oven for ten minutes.

When done, the bread crumbs should show a surface of

pale brown, and the eggs be cooked rare. Serve upon the same platter on which the dish is prepared.

Scrambled Eggs.—Eight eggs, one and one-half gill of cream, four ounces of butter, one tea-spoonful of salt, one half tea-spoonful of pepper.

Put the cream and butter together in a small sauce-pan over the fire, and stir them until the butter melts. Take the sauce-pan from the fire and break into it the eggs. Sprinkle over these the pepper and salt, and returning the sauce-pan to the fire, stir its contents with a fork briskly until the eggs begin to firm. When this takes place, turn all quickly out upon a hot dish and serve at once.

Eggs on Toast.—Eight eggs, two slices of buttered toast, one half tea-spoonful of salt, one dessert-spoonful of lemon-juice.

Place a shallow sauce-pan over the fire, fill it nearly full of boiling water, and into this throw the salt and lemon-juice.

Break the eggs one by one into a tea-cup, and pour them gently from this into the water, letting each egg form before another is put in.

Allow two minutes and a half to each egg, and removing them from the water with a skimmer, place them, so drained, upon the slices of buttered toast.

Curried Eggs.—Eight eggs, three ounces of butter, one and one-half ounce of flour, three gills of white stock, one table-spoonful of curry-powder, one half tea-spoonful of salt, one half tea-spoonful of sugar, one tea-spoonful of vinegar.

Drop the eggs into a sauce-pan of boiling water, and let them boil therein for ten minutes.

Throw them, when boiled, into a basin of cold water to cool, and while they are cooling melt the butter in a small sauce-pan, stir into it the dry flour and curry-powder, add the stock by degrees; and when this mixture reaches the boiling-point, let it continue to boil for two minutes thereafter.

Throw in the salt, sugar, and vinegar, and draw the sauce-pan aside from the fire.

Take the shells from the eggs and cut them into halves, put them into the sauce-pan with the prepared curry, and allow all to remain over the fire until the eggs are heated through, taking care, however, that the mixture does not boil, as this will cause the eggs to break up and so injure the appearance of the dish.

When done pour all carefully into a hot deep dish, and serve with boiled rice.

Mushrooms.—One and one-half dozen of large, fresh mushrooms, four table-spoonfuls of bread crumbs, one eschalot, one half tea-spoonful of pepper, one half tea-spoonful of salt, two ounces of butter.

Take eight of the largest mushrooms, skin them, and cut off the stalks.

Chop the eschalot as finely as possible, and chop also finely the remainder of the mushrooms.

Put the butter into a frying-pan, and place this over the fire, letting the butter melt and become hot. Brown in this the eschalot and chopped mushrooms, sprinkle over them the pepper and salt, and stuff the centre of the eight skinned mushrooms with this mixture.

Sprinkle over each of these equal portions of the bread crumbs, place the mushrooms into a baking-tin, and placing this in a brisk oven, let them bake therein until a skewer will easily penetrate to the centres of the mushrooms.

Take the mushrooms, when done, carefully from the tin, to avoid breaking them or disarranging the stuffing in their centres, and serve them in a hot dish.

Potato Sauté.—One quart of potatoes, one and one half ounce of butter, one tea-spoonful of salt, one salt-spoonful of white pepper.

Young potatoes should be used for this preparation, and should be first scraped, then thrown into boiling water, and allowed to boil rapidly for ten minutes. Drain the water carefully from them, cover the sauce-pan, and let the potatoes cook in their own steam until a fork will pierce easily to their centres.

When done, sprinkle over the potatoes the pepper and salt, throw in with these the butter, and shake the sauce-pan over the fire until the potatoes become a pale brown upon their surfaces. Serve very hot.

> NOTE.—Old potatoes may be used for a sauté if young ones are out of season; and when the old potatoes are so used, they should be cut into balls or other fanciful small shapes.

Stuffed Potatoes.—Eight large potatoes, one pound of beef-steak, one dessert-spoonful of mushroom catchup, one tea-spoonful of salt, one half tea-spoonful of pepper, one grain of cayenne, two ounces of butter, one egg.

Wash and pare the potatoes thinly, and cut off about an inch of the smaller end. With a strong tea-spoon scrape out the centre of the potato, leaving a shell of potato unbroken about a third of an inch in thickness; and throw these shells and their tops into cold water, to keep them white until used.

Chop the steak very finely, add to this the pepper, salt, catchup, and cayenne, and stir all together.

Take the potatoes from the water, and, drying them thoroughly with a towel, pack the meat mixture firmly into them.

Beat the egg until very light, and roll in this both the stuffed potatoes and the tops, and cover the meat stuffing with the top cut from each potato, pressed firmly on.

Melt the butter in a shallow sauce-pan, and when the blue smoke arises place the potatoes carefully in the hot butter, that the tops may not be disarranged; and, covering the sauce-pan, let the potatoes cook slowly therein for one hour, turning them occasionally in order that they may brown evenly on all sides.

Serve in a hot vegetable dish.

Dresden Patties.—Two slices of white bread, three

table-spoonfuls of cream, four table-spoonfuls of bread crumbs, one half pound of cold boiled salmon, one tea-spoonful of salt, one half tea-spoonful of pepper, one ounce of butter, one half ounce of flour, one gill of milk, one egg.

Shred the salmon in small pieces, removing from it all the skin and bone.

Melt the butter in a small sauce-pan, stir into this the flour, add the milk, and stir all together until boiling.

Throw into this mixture the shredded salmon, and season all with half of the pepper and salt. Cover the sauce-pan, and, drawing it to one side of the fire, let its contents simmer, but not boil, until the fish is heated through.

The slices of bread should be cut at least an inch and a half thick, and cut a large round from each with a biscuit-cutter. With a smaller cutter cut these rounds half-way through in the centre.

Put the cream upon a plate, and dip the rounds in this quickly, in order that they may not soak soft; beat the egg thoroughly, and roll the rounds in this; after which, season the bread crumbs with the remaining pepper and salt, and roll the rounds in these also.

Throw the prepared rounds into hot clarified fat or lard, and fry them for three minutes. Take them from the fat, drain them upon kitchen-paper, and splitting carefully off with a sharp knife the inner round to the depths at which it is cut, scrape out from the centre of the large round all of the bread remaining soft.

Into this bread cup fill in equal portions the fish mixture, and place over this the small rounds of bread. Serve the patties garnished with sprigs of parsley.

NOTE.—These patties may also be made with oysters, lobsters, truffles, mushrooms, or any kind of boiled fish.

Chickens' Livers.—One and one-half dozen of chickens' livers, one quarter of a pound of fat bacon, one salt-spoonful of pepper, one salt-spoonful of salt.

Place the livers into a sauce-pan, cover them with cold

water, throw in the salt, and, bringing the water quickly to the boiling-point, let the livers boil for five minutes.

When done, remove the livers from the water, slice them lengthwise carefully, in order not to break them, and, cutting the bacon into very thin slices, and of a size similar to the slices of liver, thread alternate slices of liver and bacon upon a spit, and broil all over a bright fire five minutes, turning them constantly in order that they may brown evenly.

When broiled, sprinkle over all the pepper, and send them to the table on the spit.

NOTE.—Livers of chicken or turkey boiled in the manner above described may also be served with a hot, thick brown sauce poured over them, with the addition, if desired, of a little chopped onion, browned in butter.

Pig's Feet.—Four pig's feet, one and one-half pint of milk, one tea-spoonful of salt, one half tea-spoonful of pepper, one ounce of flour.

When the feet are cleaned and scraped, cut them each across the knuckle, deep enough to let the water penetrate to the joint.

Place them in a large sauce-pan, cover them with cold water, and, putting all over the fire, let the water boil up. When this occurs, drain the first water off.

Cover the feet with boiling water, and allow them to boil in this very slowly until the meat becomes tender.

Pour the water off again, cover the feet with the milk, and let them simmer in this very slowly for half an hour longer.

Mix the flour in a bowl with a little cold water, and beat it smooth. Stir this into the milk in the sauce-pan, sprinkle in also the pepper and salt, and let all cook together for five minutes, when the feet should be removed to a hot, deep platter, and served with the sauce poured over them.

NOTE.—Pig's feet are also very delicious broiled, and are prepared by first boiling until tender, as directed above. When cool, they should be rubbed over with butter, placed in a broiler, and broiled for ten minutes over a clear fire.

Boiled Oatmeal.—One quart of cold water, eight table-spoonfuls of oatmeal, one half dessert-spoonful of salt.

Put the water into a sauce-pan, sprinkle in the oatmeal, stirring constantly, and when all has been made smooth, place the sauce-pan over a quick fire, and stir its contents until boiling.

When boiling, throw into the porridge the salt, and draw the sauce-pan to one side of the fire; let all simmer slowly for half an hour, stirring it occasionally meantime.

NOTE.—Oatmeal should always be thrown into *cold* water when desired to boil, as cold water swells the grain of the meal better, and makes it less heating to the blood.

Boiled Rice.—One half pound of rice, three quarts of boiling water, one dessert-spoonful of salt.

Wash the rice thoroughly in cold water, and drain it in a strainer. Place it into a sauce-pan, pour over it the three quarts of boiling water, throw into it the salt, and allow all to boil rapidly for fifteen minutes. If at the end of this time a grain of the rice may be readily floured by rubbing it between the finger and thumb, it is sufficiently boiled; but if it be still hard, continue to boil until the rice comes to this state, keeping in mind that the quicker this cereal is boiled, the drier it will remain, and the more free from starchy matter.

Pour the rice, when done, from the sauce-pan into a sieve, shaking the sieve as the water drains off, to release any fugitive drops that may be held in the cereal; and when dry serve at once, heaped lightly in a hot vegetable dish.

NOTES.—When rice is desired to fry, it must be boiled slowly and without stirring, in milk; and when boiled, cut into slices an inch thick, and fried in hot clarified fat or lard, until it becomes a delicate brown on both sides.

Corn meal mush, which is made by stirring sifted corn meal into boiling water, until a batter as thick as can be stirred with a spoon is formed, is also delicious fried in this way or in hot butter, as the taste may decide.

Casserole of Chicken.—Four ounces of cold breast of chicken, four ounces of butter, four ounces of bread crumbs, two eggs, one half tea-cupful of milk, one tea-spoonful of salt, one half tea-spoonful of white pepper.

Chop first the breast of chicken very finely, and rub it through a wire sieve.

Put the meat into a bowl, add to it the yolks of the eggs and the butter, and beat all together for ten minutes.

Add the bread crumbs and the milk, season all with the pepper and salt. Whip the whites of eggs to a stiff froth, and mix this lightly in.

Pour the compound, when thoroughly mixed, into a well-greased pint and a half mould, cover the top of this with a piece of paper, and place the mould in a sauce-pan containing sufficient water to reach half-way up the sides of the mould, and allow its contents to cook in this while the water boils for one hour.

Turn the casserole, when done, out into a deep, hot dish, and serve with egg sauce poured over and around it; for which sauce see recipe on page 174.

This dish may be garnished with red and green chillise, if desired.

Boiled Tripe.—Eight pounds of tripe, one half tablespoonful of salt.

Cover the tripe with cold water, and let it stand in this over night.

Removing it from the bath, place it in a sauce-pan, cover it with cold water, put the sauce-pan over a quick fire, and, when boiling, drain the water off, and cover it with additional cold water.

Continue to drain off and re-cover the tripe with successive quantities of cold water, until the water at last boils up quite clear, and ceases to give off a disagreeable odour. Draw the sauce-pan to one side of the fire, and allow its contents to simmer very slowly for five hours, keeping the pan covered that the water may not boil away.

When done, add the salt, and the tripe is ready to

dress in any manner desired, or may be served simply as it is.

Tripe with Onion Sauce.—Two pounds of boiled tripe, three gills of milk, one half tea-spoonful of white pepper, one Spanish onion.

Cut the tripe into small irregular pieces. Put these into a sauce-pan, cover them with the milk, and allow all to stew over a slow fire for half an hour.

Throw the onion into boiling water, and boil it also for half an hour. Take the onion, when done, from the water, drain it thoroughly, and chop it very finely.

When the tripe has cooked in the milk the appointed length of time, draw the sauce-pan aside from the fire, and stir into it the chopped onion. Season all with the pepper, and serve at once.

Baked Tripe.—Two pounds of boiled tripe, four ounces of bread crumbs, two eggs, one half pint of the liquor in which the tripe is boiled, one tea-spoonful of salt, one half tea-spoonful of pepper.

Cut the tripe into small irregular pieces, and put a layer, a half inch deep, of it into the bottom of a deep dish. Sprinkle over this a layer of the bread crumbs and a little of the pepper and salt, and continue these alternating layers of tripe, seasoning, and bread crumbs until the material is all filled into the dish, leaving a last layer of bread crumbs upon the top.

Put the eggs into a bowl and beat them until very light. Add to them the tripe liquor, stir these together, and pour the mixture over the tripe and bread crumbs in the dish.

Place the dish in a moderate oven, and let its contents bake half an hour, when it must be served in the dish in which it is prepared.

NOTES.—When the liquor in which the tripe is boiled is not available, milk or water may be substituted for it.

In boiling tripe, the salt should never be used until the tripe is done, otherwise it will be discoloured thereby.

Brain Cakes.—Brain of two calves' heads, two eggs, one ounce of butter, one table-spoonful of chopped parsley, one tea-spoonful of salt, one half tea-spoonful of pepper, one salt-spoonful of powdered mace, four table-spoonfuls of bread crumbs.

Throw the brains into a strong mixture of salt and water, and let them remain in this for an hour.

Put them into a sauce-pan over the fire, cover them with cold water, and allow them to boil therein for twenty minutes.

At the end of this time take them from the water, chop them into rough pieces, place these in a bowl, and rub into them the butter. Add to the brains two table-spoonfuls of the bread crumbs, and season all with the pepper, salt, and mace.

When these are mixed, sprinkle over the preparation the chopped parsley, and drop in upon it the yolks of the eggs.

Beat all well together, and flouring the hands slightly to prevent sticking, form the mixture into small, flat, round cakes.

Whip the whites of the eggs, dip the cakes into this, roll them in the remainder of the bread crumbs, throw them into hot clarified fat or lard for two minutes. When done drain them for a moment upon a piece of kitchen-paper, and serve them in a folded napkin garnished with sprigs of parsley.

Stewed Kidneys.—One ox kidney, one quarter pound flour, two ounces butter, two ounces fat bacon, one large onion, eight cloves, one half tea-spoonful salt, one quarter tea-spoonful pepper.

The day before this dish is required bring a large sauce-panful of water to boiling-point.

Throw into the water the kidney, which has been previously washed; stick into the onion the cloves, and put it in also. Make now three ounces of the flour to a very stiff dough with a very little cold water, and roll out this dough round and the size of the top of the sauce-pan.

Throw into the water the bacon, and cover all closely with the flour paste or dough.

Cover the sauce-pan also closely, and allow the water to simmer slowly four hours.

Remove the kidney from the water, and let it stand on one side over night.

Half an hour before this dish is to be sent to table melt in a pan the butter, and stir into it the remainder of the flour; when mixed well, add by degrees three gills of the water in which the kidney was boiled, and stir all till boiling.

Slice now in very thin slices the kidney, add the pieces to ingredients in sauce-pan, and when all has cooked slowly for ten minutes, sprinkle in the seasoning, and the dish is now ready for the table.

Jellied Tongue.—One ox tongue, one quart beef stock, one ounce gelatine, one tea-spoonful whole white pepper, one tea-spoonful whole black pepper, one half gill cold water.

Place the tongue in a large sauce-pan, pour over it sufficient water to cover it, place the pan on the fire, and when the water boils remove all the scum which rises with a spoon.

Draw the pan then on one side, and allow the tongue to cook slowly till tender, allowing quarter of an hour to each pound.

When the tongue is ready take it from the water, skin it and curl it up, and place it in a mould. Soak the gelatine for ten minutes in half a gill cold water; place it in a sauce-pan with the stock and pepper-corns, stir all over the fire till boiling, and then pour the liquid through a flannel bag. Pour now the strained stock over the tongue in the mould, and when quite cold and firm turn out on a flat dish.

TEAS, COFFEES, AND CHOCOLATE.

Breakfast Coffee.—One table-spoonful of coffee for each person, three gills of boiling water to each table-spoonful of coffee.

The coffee should be finely ground, then measured, put into the coffee-pot, and the boiling water poured over it.

Put the pot over the fire, and let the coffee boil up, when it should be drawn quickly aside from the blaze, and when the gas arising from the grains of coffee has escaped, return the pot again to the fire, and let it again boil up. Draw it aside from the fire, and let it stand for five minutes to settle, when it is ready for the cups.

NOTES.—In making black or after-dinner coffee, the quantity of coffee allowed for each person should be the same, and the amount of water added to each table-spoonful of coffee should be decreased one-half.

Sugar and cream are used in breakfast coffee, but sugar only in black coffee.

Teas.—One tea-spoonful of tea for each person, and a tea-spoonful additional, three gills of boiling water to each tea-spoonful of tea.

Pour first in and out of the tea-pot a little boiling water. Put into it the required amount of tea, and pouring over this the boiling water, cover the tea-pot so that no steam may escape, and allow the tea to stand and infuse for seven minutes, when it should be poured at once into the cups.

NOTES.—Tea should never be boiled, and should not be allowed to infuse longer than seven minutes, as the strength of the leaf will all draw out in that length of time, and if allowed to stand longer, will develop the tannin in it which gives it the acrid, bitter taste of which there is general complaint, and which, besides being unpleasant to the palate, is destructive to the coating of the stomach, being a powerful astringent.

Teas when properly infused should have a pale, greenish amber colour; when boiled or let stand until the tannin develops, it will turn to a dark red.

Cream and sugar are used in English breakfast and black teas. Green teas are usually preferred clear, and sometimes with a small piece of fresh lemon rind, at the discretion of the drinker.

Chocolate.—Four table-spoonfuls of grated chocolate to each person, one and one half gill of boiling milk, and one and one half gill of boiling water, to each portion of chocolate.

Mix together the boiling milk and water, and let them boil up together.

Place the grated chocolate into a bowl, and stir it to a smooth paste with a little cold milk or water. Pour the chocolate into the boiling milk and water, and let all boil together for two minutes, stirring it constantly meantime.

NOTES.—If preferred, the sugar may be mixed with and boiled in the chocolate, and if this is done, half as much sugar should be used as there is chocolate.

Cream whipped to a froth is sometimes served with this beverage, and powdered sugar should be used in it instead of the cut loaf.

Cocoa is made by mixing it with the desired amount of sugar, this mixture being placed in the cup, and equal quantities of boiling milk and water poured over it.

MISCELLANEOUS DISHES.

Scotch Haggis.—One sheep's pluck, one stomach-bag, one half pound beef suet, two tea-cupfuls oatmeal, one tea-spoonful Jamaica pepper, one half tea-spoonful pepper, one half dessert-spoonful salt.

The haggis must be prepared the day before it is required for use.

The stomach-bag must be thoroughly washed in cold water, then plunge it into boiling water, scrape it well, but take great care not to break it.

When this is done, lay the bag into a basin, cover it with cold water, add a table-spoonful of salt, and let it lie over night.

Wash well the pluck and put it into a sauce-pan of cold

water, and allow it to boil for one hour; take it from the water and let it get quite cold.

When quite cold, grate one quarter of the liver on the carrot grater; chop very finely all of the lights, also the heart.

Place these ingredients in a large bowl, and mix with them the Jamaica pepper, the salt, and pepper.

Chop very finely the suet and add it to the mixture; dry in the oven for about ten minutes the oatmeal, add it also, and stir the whole to a consistency with half of the water that the pluck was boiled in. Fill the bag a little more than half full, sew up the aperture with a stout thread. Put the haggis now in a large pan of boiling water, prick the skin occasionally to allow the steam to escape as the mixture in the bag begins to cook.

Boil for three hours.

NOTE.—Chopped onion may be added to the haggis mixture if the flavour is desired.

Unboiled Pickle for Beef or Pork.—Three gallons of water, seven pounds salt, two ounces saltpetre, one quarter ounce black pepper, one quarter ounce Jamaica pepper, one quarter ounce cloves, one pound sugar.

Place the beef to be pickled for one night in strong salt and water, take it out and put it in the pickling-tub.

Mix well with the above three gallons of water the salt, pepper, sugar, and saltpetre, grind the cloves and Jamaica pepper, add them also, let the mixture stand a little to settle, then pour it over the beef or pork.

Keep the beef or pork under the pickle by placing on either a stone or two.

Do not cover the tub; merely throw a cloth over to keep out the dust.

Salt Beef (German way).—One and one half pound salt, one and one half pound sugar, one ounce saltpetre, five quarts cold water.

Rub well the beef to be pickled with salt, place it in a jar with a stone on it.

Place in a large sauce-pan the water, add the saltpetre salt, and sugar, stir until boiling, take the sauce-pan from the fire and let the contents cool.

When quite cold pour this pickle over the beef in the jar, and cover it with a cloth.

The beef may be used in three weeks.

Ginger Beer.—Three gallons water, three pounds lump-sugar, two large table-spoonfuls yeast, one lemon, four ounces ginger, two ounces cream of tartar.

Place the ginger in a very large pan, pour over it the water, and allow it to soak for twenty-four hours, place then the pan on the fire, and let it boil for three hours.

Dissolve the sugar in as much water as may have boiled in during the three hours, add it to the ginger and water in the pan, and allow all to boil for ten minutes longer.

Take the pan then from the fire, put into it the cream of tartar and the lemon thinly sliced; it must then stand until the mixture is nearly cold.

Pour the liquid gently from the ginger into another vessel, add the yeast, and let it ferment for twenty-four hours.

At the end of this time skim off the top, and strain it from the sediment, and bottle it for use. The bottles must be well corked and not filled too full.

Mutton Pies.—Two pounds lean mutton, one pound flour, one half pound suet, one tea-cupful of sweet milk, one tea-spoonful salt, one half tea-spoonful pepper.

Place the mutton on a board, remove from it all skin and bone, and cut it into neat square pieces; sprinkle over the pieces a little pepper and salt, and put them on one side.

Chop very finely the suet, put it in a bowl, and pour over it the milk, which must first be brought to the boiling-point.

Stir well together the suet and milk, add a little salt, and when they have stood for one minute stir quickly in the flour.

Flour well the board, turn the contents of the bowl on to it, knead the mixture quickly together, forming a firm dough.

Roll out the dough as quickly as possible, as the instant it cools it becomes very tough. Cut from the dough six rounds a little larger than breakfast saucers, and place them on one side. Knead together again what remains of the dough, and cut from it six more rounds.

Grease well six breakfast saucers, and place on them the last rounds· which were cut out; brush the edges of the dough with a little milk, place in each lined saucer a portion of the seasoned mutton, cover each with a round of the dough which was first cut, and press the two edges firmly together.

With the point of a skewer make a hole in the top of each, brush each over with a little milk, place the pies in a moderate oven, and bake them for three quarters of an hour.

Lemon Pickle.—Six lemons, one half pound of salt, four cloves of garlic, one quarter ounce cloves, one quarter ounce cayenne, one quarter ounce nutmeg, one quarter ounce mace, two ounces mustard, three pints of vinegar.

Cut the lemons into quarters, place them in a sauce-pan, add the salt, garlic cloves, cayenne, nutmeg, mace, and mustard; pour over the vinegar. Place the pan over the fire, and allow the contents to boil for fifteen minutes. Pour all then into a jar; allow the jar to stand for six weeks. During this time the contents must be stirred once every day, and the jar must be closely covered. Strain then the liquor through a sieve and bottle it for use.

Sauce for Gravies or Soups.—One pint vinegar, one pint mushroom catchup, one half tea-spoonful cayenne, one tea-cupful red-currant jelly, two smal shallots.

Shred finely the shallots, place them in a bottle, and add the cayenne, then the jelly, pour over the catchup and vinegar. Shake the bottle well, and let it stand for one week, when the sauce is ready for use.

Noodlins (German fashion).—Two eggs, one quarter pound flour, one half tea-spoonful salt, two ounces butter.

Mix well in a bowl the flour and salt, moisten them with the eggs, turn all out on a board and knead well together, adding more flour if necessary. When stiff enough to roll out, flour the board well, and roll out the dough very thinly. Allow the dough to lie on the board until firm; but do not let it lie long enough to get hard. Flour it then well and roll it up. This will now have the shape of a rolled jelly cake. With a very sharp knife cut some strips from the roll, about the third of an inch in thickness. When the half of the roll is cut into strips, cut the other half into strips about half the width of the former. Throw the broad strips into a pan of boiling water in which has been dissolved a good pinch of salt. Boil these strips for fifteen minutes. While they are boiling, melt in a frying-pan the butter; when it smokes, throw in the narrow strips, and allow them to take a pale brown colour. When both are ready, drain the boiled strips quickly on a sieve, and pile them on a hot dish. Lift from the butter with a fork the browned strips, and pile them high on the boiled ones.

This ought to be served with cream and any sort of preserve.

Clarified Fat.—Cut into pieces any convenient quantity of fat, either of beef or mutton. Place these in a sauce-pan, and covering them with cold water, stir all until the water boils. When boiling, skim the surface very carefully, and allow the preparation to boil thereafter very rapidly until the water has all been discharged in vapour.

The presence of remaining water may be determined by the liquid retaining its white colour; but when this has all evaporated the fluid will take on the colour and appearance of salad oil.

When free from water the fat should be strained, and is ready for any use to which it is to be put.

NOTE.—Fat so clarified will keep for any length of time.

Caramel.—One pound of coarse brown sugar, one pint of cold water.

Put the sugar into a dry sauce-pan, place this over a hot fire, and stir the sugar until it melts and turns to a darker brown colour. Draw the sauce-pan aside from the fire, and add to its contents by degrees the cold water.

Return the sauce-pan to the fire, and stir all together until the water boils.

Pour the mixture through a strainer into a bowl, and allow it to become quite cold, after which it should be placed in a bottle and kept uncorked, to be used as required.

Toffy.—One and one-half pound sugar, one pint cold water, one quarter pound butter, the juice of one lemon.

Place in a brass pan the sugar, pour over it the water, and stir the two over the fire till boiling. Then allow them to boil quickly for twenty minutes, stirring constantly all the time; add then the butter and lemon-juice; boil all for ten minutes longer, still continuing to stir. Grease well a flat dish with butter, pour this over, and allow it to get cold.

Raspberry Vinegar.—Three pints raspberries, one and one-half bottle vinegar, four pounds sugar.

Soak over night the rasps and vinegar in a large basin, press them slightly with a silver spoon, and strain through a piece of muslin. Pour the strained juice into a preserving-pan, and add the sugar. Place the pan over a brisk fire, stir well till boiling. Simmer this slowly for twenty minutes. When cold bottle it, adding, if desired, a wine-glassful of brandy to each quart bottle.

Ginger Beer.—One quarter pound whole ginger, one ounce cream of tartar, three gallons cold water, one lemon, three pounds sugar, two large table-spoonfuls of brewer's yeast.

Place the ginger in a coarse towel, and bruise it with a hammer. When bruised, place it in a large brown jar, and pour over it two pints cold water. Allow this to remain for twenty-four hours. Pour all then into a large sauce-pan, and place the pan over a quick fire. When the liquid boils, draw the pan on one side, and allow the liquid to simmer very slowly for three hours. At the end of three hours add the sugar, and boil all for ten minutes longer. Take the sauce-pan from the fire and add the cream of tartar; slice the lemon and add it also. When this mixture is nearly cold, pour the liquid very gently from the sediment, which is of no further use. Add to the liquid the yeast, and let all stand in a warm place to ferment for twenty-four hours. Skim off now the crust from the top, and strain it again from the sediment. Bottle this now for use, taking care not to fill the bottles quite to the top. Cork the bottles firmly.

Black Currant Cordial.—One quart of whisky, one quart black currants, one ounce whole ginger, one lemon.

Place the currants in a large basin, and pour over them the whisky. Grate over the rind of lemon, then squeeze over the juice; bruise the ginger, and add it also. Allow this to stand in a cool place for ten days. At the end of this time strain the liquid through a clean towel.

Measure the liquid, and for each pint allow a pound of lump sugar. Place the sugar and liquid in a preserving-pan, and stir all over the fire till the sugar is melted. Take the pan from the fire and set it on one side to cool. When quite cold, bottle for use.

Ginger Cordial.—Four pounds red or white currants, eight ounces whole ginger, two ounces bitter almonds, half an ounce sweet almonds, the rind of one lemon, the juice of three lemons, one gallon of whisky, four pounds sugar.

Bruise the ginger well with a hammer, place it in a large basin, and add to it the fruit, also the rind and juice of the lemons. Pour over the almonds as much boiling water as cover them, remove the skins, and place them also in the basin, then pour over all the whisky. Allow this to stand in a cool place for ten days. At the end of this time strain all through a towel. Place the liquid in a preserving-pan, and add the sugar. Stir all over a clear fire until the sugar is melted. Take the pan from the fire, and when quite cold bottle the cordial for use.

Cream Nectar.—Six pounds sugar, four ounces tartaric acid, two quarts water, the whites of two eggs, one teaspoonful essence of lemon.

Place the sugar in a preserving-pan, add the water and tartaric acid, stir over the fire until the sugar is melted. Whip to a stiff froth the whites of egg, add them, and stir all together till very hot; but do not let it boil. Remove the pan from the fire, and when the mixture is cool pour it through a piece of fine muslin; then add the lemon-juice, and bottle it.

Directions for use :—Place two table-spoonfuls of the syrup in a glass filled two-thirds with cold water. Add as much carbonate of soda as will lie on a sixpence, stir until it effervesces, and drink at once.

Raspberry Syrup.—Six pounds raspberries, one quart of water, two ounces of tartaric acid.

Place in a large jar the tartaric acid, and pour over it the cold water; add then the fruit, and allow all to stand for twenty-four hours. At the end of this time strain the liquid through a fine piece of muslin, taking care not to bruise the fruit. Add to the strained juice one pound and a half of powdered sugar to each pint. Stir this frequently until the sugar is quite dissolved; then bottle the syrup and keep it in a dark place, as if exposed to the light its bright colour fades.

Cherry Brandy.—One quart whisky, one quart cherries, one pound sugar, one dozen cloves.

Place in a jar the cherries, add the sugar and cloves, and pour over all the whisky. Cover the jar closely, and let it remain in a cool place four weeks. During this time the mixture must be stirred once every day. At the end of this time strain the mixture through a fine piece of muslin, when it is ready to bottle for use.

Lemon Syrup.—Five pounds of sugar, two ounces of citric acid, two table-spoonfuls essence of lemon, the white of one egg, one quart of cold water.

Place in a preserving-pan the sugar, pour over the water, and add the white of egg, which must first be beaten to a stiff froth. Place the pan over the fire, and stir the contents until boiling. Take the pan from the fire, strain the liquid through a towel, and allow it to cool. Dissolve in a small cup of boiling water the acid, and when the syrup is quite cold add also the lemon essence. Bottle for use. Proportions—one table-spoonful of syrup to one glassful cold water.

Apple Jelly.—Six pints of apple-juice, six pounds of lump sugar, three gills of cold water.

Place the sugar in a preserving-pan, pour over the cold water, and stir all over the fire until it boils. When boiling, draw the pan on one side, and let all boil very slowly till the water evaporates. Skim constantly during this time. To ascertain when the water has evaporated, dip a spoon in the boiling liquid, and then dip it at once in cold water; then touch the sugar which adheres to the spoon with the finger, and if the sugar cracks it is ready. Add now to the boiling sugar the juice, and stir till boiling. Skim well and boil slowly five minutes, when the jelly is ready to put in the pots.

NOTE.—Directions for preparing the apple-juice:—Take any quantity of green apples, rub them well in a clean towel, cut them in quarters, and throw them into cold water. Place them now in a preserving-pan, and cover them with cold water. Allow them to simmer till a pulp. Tie a flannel or felt bag over a large basin, pour into the basin through the bag a kettleful of boiling water. Pour the water away; then pour into the bag the apples, and allow the juice to drip through all night.

White Currant Jelly.—Prepared exactly as above, with this exception, that the juice and sugar ought only to come to the boiling-point, and then be at once taken from the fire. If allowed to boil but one minute, the jelly will take a pinky shade, which it ought not to have.

Cherry Plum Jam.—Six pounds of plums, six pounds of lump sugar, three gills of cold water.

Pick the stalks from the plums, and rub them in a damp towel. Place in a preserving-pan the sugar, pour over the water, stir till boiling, then add the plums. Stir all again till boiling, skim well, and boil quickly for thirty minutes. Draw the pan on one side, and allow the jam to cool ten minutes before putting it in the pots.

Apricot Marmalade.—Four pounds of apricots, three pounds and one-half of lump sugar.

Remove as thinly as possible the skins from the apricots, split them open, remove the stones. Pound now in a mortar the sugar, place the apricots in a large basin, sprinkle over the sugar, and allow them to stand for twelve hours.

Break the stones, remove the kernels, place the kernels in a basin, pour over enough boiling water to cover them, and remove the thin skin. At the end of twelve hours place the apricots and sugar in a preserving-pan, and stir them very gently over a clear fire till boiling. Add the kernels, skim well, and simmer all very slowly for three quarters of an hour. As the pieces of apricot get clear, remove them with a skewer and place them in small jars. Fill up the jars with the kernels and syrup; cut some pieces of tissue paper a little larger than the tops of the jars, brush them over with white of egg, and cover the jars with them.

Damson Jam.—Six pounds of damsons, six pounds of lump sugar.

Pick the damsons from the stalks, throw aside any that are at all damaged, place alternate layers of the sugar and damsons in a large preserving-pan, place the pan over a slow fire, and begin at once to stir gently. Continue stirring, and as the scum rises remove it. When quite boiling draw the pan on one side, and allow all to simmer very slowly for one hour. Take the pan from the fire, and let the jam cool for ten minutes before putting it in the pots.

Damson Cheese.—Four pounds sugar, five pounds damsons, one gill cold water.

Pick the damsons over, remove all damaged ones, place in a preserving-pan the water and damsons, stir gently till boiling, and allow all to simmer slowly for one hour. Place then a coarse wire sieve over a large basin, and with the back of a wooden spoon rub the damsons through the sieve. Weigh out four pounds of the pulp, place it in a preserving-pan, add the sugar, place the pan over a gentle fire, and stir the contents slowly until boiling. Draw the pan on one side, and allow the damsons to simmer slowly for two hours. Then place the pan over the fire again, and let them boil quickly for half an hour longer, continuing stirring all the time.

Marmalade.—Six oranges, five quarts cold water, five pounds lump sugar, two lemons.

Wash the oranges well in cold water, and if necessary scrub them well with a brush. With a very sharp knife slice them very very thinly. Remove the seeds and place the oranges in a large basin, pour over them the water, and allow them to stand for twenty-four hours. Pour then the oranges and water into a preserving-pan, place the pan over the fire, and stir the contents until boiling. Draw the pan on one side, and allow the oranges and water to boil for two hours; add then the sugar and juice of lemons, stir again till boiling, skim well, and boil slowly half an hour longer.

Citronell.—Six pounds vegetable marrow, three pounds and a half crushed lump sugar, three lemons, one tea-spoonful essence of ginger.

Pare the marrow, remove the seeds, and cut it in small square pieces. Place in a large basin alternate layers of sugar and the pieces of marrow. Allow this to stand over night. Pour then from the marrow the syrup, place the syrup in a preserving-pan, and stir it till boiling. Pour the boiled syrup over the marrow, and allow it again to stand over night. Grate over now the thin yellow rind of the lemons, squeeze over the juice through a strainer. Pour all into a preserving-pan, add the ginger, place the pan over the fire, and stir the contents till boiling. Draw the pan on one side, and allow all to boil slowly for half an hour.

Rhubarb Ginger.—Six pounds rhubarb, six pounds lump sugar, two ounces whole ginger.

With a damp towel rub well the stalks of rhubarb, cut them in inch lengths. Place the ginger between the folds of a kitchen towel, and bruise it with a hammer. Place the ginger in a large basin, and place over it alternate layers of the rhubarb and sugar. Allow this to stand twenty-four hours. At the end of this time pour the syrup from the rhubarb. Pour the syrup into a preserving-pan, stir it over the fire until it boils. Pour the boiling syrup over the rhubarb, and allow this to stand twenty-four hours longer. Pour all now into a large preserving-pan, place the pan over a brisk fire, and stir the contents until boiling. Skim well, draw the pan on one side, and let all simmer slowly half an hour, when the preserve is ready to pour into the pots.

NOTE.—September and the latter end of August are the best months for preserving rhubarb.

Rhubarb and Oranges.—Four pounds rhubarb, four pounds oranges, eight pounds sugar, one gill cold water.

Wash well the oranges, place them in a preserving-pan, cover them with cold water, and boil them gently for three hours. Take now four pounds young rhubarb (forced rhubarb is best), rub the stalks well in a damp towel, and cut them in pieces about three inches long. Take the oranges from the water with a silver knife, cut each in four pieces. Place now in a preserving-pan the gill of water and sugar, stir the two over a slow fire till boiling, add the rhubarb and oranges. Stir again till boiling, skim well, draw the pan on one side, and simmer all very slowly fifteen minutes.

Black Currant Jam.—Six pints of black currants, three pints of rhubarb-juice, nine pounds of lump sugar.

Pick all the stalks from the currants, place in a preserving-pan the rhubarb-juice and sugar. Place the pan over a brisk fire, and stir with a wooden spoon the juice and sugar until they boil. Add then the currants, stir again till boiling, skim well, and boil slowly twelve minutes. Take the pan from the fire, and stir constantly until the currants begin to sink in the syrup, then put the jam in the pots. This prevents the currants rising to the top of the pots when the jam is cold.

NOTE.—Directions for preparing rhubarb-juice :—Take a dozen stalks of rhubarb, rub them in a damp towel, cut them in inch lengths, and put the pieces in a preserving-pan. Cover them with cold water and boil them twenty minutes. Tie a clean towel over the top of a basin, and strain the rhubarb through.

Strawberry Jam.—Four pints strawberries, one pint red currant juice, five pounds lump sugar.

Place in a preserving-pan the sugar, pour over it the red currant juice. Place the pan over a clear fire, and stir the contents till boiling; add now the strawberries, and stir very gently till boiling; skim well, and boil slowly thirty minutes. Take the pan from the fire, and before potting the jam allow it to stand ten minutes, stirring occasionally during this time.

NOTE.—Directions for preparing red currant juice :—Pick the stalks from the currants, place them in a preserving-pan, cover them with cold water, and boil them slowly twenty minutes. Tie a flannel or felt bag over a basin, pour through the bag a kettleful of boiling water, pour away the water, then pour through the currant-juice.

Raspberry Jam.—Four pints of raspberries, one pint of currant-juice, five pounds of sugar.

Place in a preserving-pan the sugar, pour over the currant-juice, stir till boiling. Add the raspberries, stir till boiling, skim well, and boil briskly ten minutes. Take the pan from the fire, and allow it to stand ten minutes before potting it.

NOTE.—Directions for preparing juice will be found in previous recipe.

Green Gooseberry Jam.—Six pounds sugar, six pints gooseberries, one pint cold water.

With a pair of scissors remove the stalks and tops from the gooseberries. Place the sugar in a preserving-pan, pour over the cold water, and stir over the fire till boiling. Add then the gooseberries, stir again till boiling, skim well, and boil briskly twenty minutes. Take the pan from the fire, and allow it to stand ten minutes before pouring the jam into the pots.

Red Gooseberry Jam.—Follow in every particular the directions for green gooseberry jam.

Pea-Soup.—One half pound split pease, one half head of celery, one piece of soda (size of a large pea), three pints water, one quarter of a tea-spoonful salt, one pinch pepper.

Wash well the pease, and soak them over night in a large basin of cold water. Pour away the water, and place the pease in a sauce-pan; add the soda, pepper, and salt. Bring the water to the boiling-point in a kettle, pour the water over the pease, place the sauce-pan over the fire, and stir all together till boiling. Wash well now the celery, cut it in small pieces, add them; draw the pan on one side, and allow all to boil slowly two hours. Place a colander in a large basin, and pour the soup through it; rub the pease through with a wooden spoon. The soup is then ready for use.

NOTE.—If desired, a large table-spoonful of dried mint may be added.

Haricot Bean Soup.—One half pound haricot beans, one ounce dripping, one piece of soda (size of large pea), one pint milk, two pints water, one quarter of a tea-spoonful salt, one pinch of pepper, one small turnip, one small carrot, one onion.

Soak the beans over night in a large basin of cold water. Place also over night the onion in a small basin of boiling water. Pour in the morning the water from the beans and onion. Place the beans in a sauce-pan, and pour over the cold water, add the soda, pepper, and salt, and allow to come to the boiling-point. Pare very thickly now the turnip, slice it thinly, scrape and slice also the carrot, slice the onion, and when the water boils in the sauce-pan add them, and boil all very slowly two hours and a half. Place a colander in a basin, and pass the soup through, rubbing the beans through with a wooden spoon. Return the soup to the sauce-pan, add the milk, stir all over the fire till boiling. The soup is then ready for use.

Fish Soup.—One large haddock, two quarts water, two ounces whole rice, one table-spoonful finely-chopped parsley, one small onion, one blade mace, one half tea-spoonful salt, one quarter tea-spoonful pepper, one and one-half gill milk.

Wash the haddock well, clean it and place it in a sauce-pan, pour over it the cold water. Place the pan over the fire, and allow the water to boil five minutes. Remove then the haddock, take the skin from it, and remove the flesh from the bones in large flakes. Return the bones and skin to the sauce-pan, add the mace, onion, salt, and pepper, and boil all for one hour. Strain now the liquor through a clean towel or a sieve, and return it to the sauce-pan. Wash well the rice and add. Place the sauce-pan again on the fire, and boil slowly twenty minutes. Add the milk then, and when again boiling put in the pieces of fish, and cook two minutes. The soup ought then to be served at once.

Rabbit Soup.—One rabbit, one large onion, two ounces dripping, one dessert-spoonful curry powder, one half dessert-spoonful salt, one half tea-spoonful pepper, three quarts cold water, one ounce flour.

Wash well the rabbit, cover it in a basin with cold water, and soak it over night. Soak over night also the onion in sufficient boiling water to cover it.

Cut the rabbit in pieces, place it in a sauce-pan, pour over the water, and place the pan over the fire. When the water boils add the onion, pepper, and salt, draw the pan on one side, and let all simmer very slowly for two hours. Remove the rabbit, and take all the meat from the bones. Return the bones to the sauce-pan, and place the pan again on the fire, allow all to simmer slowly one hour longer. Strain the liquor now through a colander into a large basin. Place the pan on the fire, melt in it the dripping, stir in the flour and curry powder, and add the strained liquor. Stir all till boiling, then cut in small square pieces the rabbit meat, add them, and boil all ten minutes longer, when the soup is ready for use.

Bone Soup.—Three pounds bones, one small cabbage, one large onion, two carrots, one turnip, one leek, one half table-spoonful salt, one half tea-spoonful pepper, two and one-half quarts water, one tea-cupful of barley.

Wash well the bones and chop or saw them through (this the butcher will do). Place the pieces of bone in a large sauce-pan, pour over the water, and place the pan over a brisk fire till the water boils. Skim well, and then add the salt. Skim a second time, then draw the pan on one side, and let its contents simmer for two hours. During this time prepare the vegetables in the following manner:— Wash well, and remove from the cabbage the outer leaves, place the centre part on a board, and chop it finely, then place it in a large basin of cold water. Pare thickly the turnip, and cut it in small square pieces, add them to the water in the basin. Scrape and slice thinly one carrot, place it in the water also; wash and slice the leek and onion, and place them in the water. Place the barley in a basin, and cover it with boiling water. At the end of two hours, pour the water from the vegetables, and add them to the liquor in the sauce-pan; pour the water from the barley, add it also, then the pepper. Let all simmer slowly now for one hour and a half. Wash, scrape, and grate the remaining carrot, and fifteen minutes before the soup is ready add it. Before serving the soup remove the bones.

Rice Soup.—Two pounds back ribs of mutton, one tea-cupful of rice, two quarts of cold water, one half table-spoonful of salt, one salt-spoonful of pepper, one leek.

Place the ribs of mutton in a large sauce-pan, and pour over the cold water. Place the pan over the fire, and when the water boils, skim it well; add the salt, and skim a second time. Draw the pan on one side, wash well and slice the leek, add it and the pepper, and allow all to simmer very slowly one hour and a quarter. Wash well now the rice in several waters, add it to the soup, and boil for half an hour longer, when the soup is ready to serve. Serve the mutton on a large hot dish, and pour round it a couple of table-spoonfuls of the soup.

Potato Soup. — One pound potatoes, one onion, two ounces dripping, one and a half quarts water, one quarter of a tea-spoonful salt, one pinch of pepper, one small carrot, one gill of milk.

Remove the skin from the onion, place it in a small basin of boiling water, and allow it to soak over night. Pare thinly the potatoes, place them in a pan of cold water, place the pan over the fire, and the instant the water boils pour it away. Add now to the potatoes the dripping, salt, and pepper, pour over the cold water; return the sauce-pan to the fire, and when the water boils slice and add the onion, which must be taken from the water in which it has soaked. Boil now slowly for one hour, add the milk, scrape the carrot, grate it on the grater, add it, and boil all fifteen minutes longer.

Lentil Soup.—One half pound of lentils, two ounces dripping, three pints water, one ounce flour, one pinch pepper, one quarter of a tea-spoonful salt, one small turnip, one small carrot, one onion.

Soak the onion as for potato soup. Place the lentils in a basin, cover them with cold water, stir them well up, pour away the water; pour fresh water on the lentils six or eight times, until it pours from them quite clear. Place them now in a sauce-pan, pour over the water, and place the pan over the fire until the water boils. While the water is coming to the boiling-point, pare very thickly the turnip, and slice it thinly, scrape the carrot, and slice it thinly also, slice also the soaked onion. When the water boils, add the vegetables, pepper, and salt, and allow all to cook slowly one hour and a half. Melt now in a frying-pan the dripping, add the flour, stir both well together, then add a few table-spoonfuls of the liquor from the sauce-pan, stir well together, and add this to the contents of the sauce-pan. Boil ten minutes longer, and the soup is ready.

Milk Soup.—Two large potatoes, two ounces clarified fat or dripping, one pint and a half of water, one half pint milk, two ounces seed-sago, one tea-spoonful salt, one salt-spoonful pepper.

Pare thinly the potatoes, place them in a sauce-pan, cover them with cold water, and place the pan on the fire till the water boils. Pour then away the water, add the dripping or clarified fat, return the pan to the fire, and stir the contents till the dripping is melted. Add now the pepper and salt, and allow all to boil slowly half an hour. Place a colander in a large basin, pour the liquor from the sauce-pan through, and rub the potatoes through with a spoon. Pour all back into the sauce-pan, add the milk, and sprinkle in the sago, stirring all the time. Return the pan to the fire, and stir all till boiling; draw the pan on one side, and boil slowly ten minutes.

Sheep Head Broth.—One sheep head, one tea-cupful barley, two quarts and a half cold water, one turnip, two carrots, one onion, one half table-spoonful salt, one half tea-spoonful pepper, one small cabbage, two small leeks.

If the head is singed, place it in a large basin or jar, cover it well with cold water, and allow it to stand over night. In the morning scrape it well, and wash it in several waters. Place it in a large sauce-pan, pour over it the cold water, and place the pan over the fire till the water boils, when it must be well skimmed, the salt added, and skimmed a second time. Allow this to boil slowly two hours and a half, then remove the head. Prepare the vegetables in the following manner:—Take a thick paring from the turnip, cut the turnip in small dice, and throw them into a large basin of cold water; scrape well the carrots, and slice one of them thinly; wash and slice thinly the leeks; wash and chop finely the cabbage; slice also the onion; and place all these vegetables in the basin of cold water. Wash them well, and place them in the sauce-pan with the liquor when the head has been removed. Soak now the barley for two minutes in boiling water, pour away the water, and add the barley to the liquor; add also the pepper. Draw the pan on one side, and let all boil slowly two hours, when the soup is ready.*

SIMPLE MILK PUDDINGS.

Rice Pudding.—One quart milk, one half pound rice, one egg, one ounce raisins, two table-spoonfuls sugar.

Wash well the rice and place it in a sauce-pan, pour over it the milk, and place the sauce-pan by the side of the fire. Allow the contents to simmer for twenty minutes very slowly. Beat well in a basin the egg and sugar together, and when the rice has cooked twenty minutes add it, and stir all well together. Grease a basin or mould with dripping; take the seeds from the raisins, and stick them over the basin. Pour gently in the mixture from the basin, and cover the basin with a piece of paper. Place the basin in a sauce-pan, and pour round it as much boiling water as will come half-way up the sides. Place the pan over the fire, and allow the water to boil for one hour. Turn then the pudding out on a very hot dish.

Ground Rice Shape.—One pint milk, three ounces ground rice, three ounces sugar.

Place the rice in a basin, and pour over it one gill of the milk, stir them well together until the rice is quite smooth. Place in a sauce-pan the remainder of the milk, place the pan over the fire, and let the milk get very hot, but not

* Directions for sheep-head pie, see page 268.

boiling; pour in then the moistened rice, stir constantly with a wooden spoon until boiling, draw the pan on one side, and let all boil slowly for fifteen minutes longer. Take the pan from the fire, and add the sugar, stir well together until the sugar is melted. Dip a mould or basin in cold water, pour in the mixture, and when cold and set, turn it out on a flat dish.

Corn-Flour Shape.—Two table-spoonfuls corn-flour, one pint milk, one large table-spoonful of sugar.

Place in a sauce-pan nearly all of the milk, and place it over the fire to heat. Place in a basin the corn-flour and sugar, and moisten them with the remainder of the milk; stir until the corn-flour is very smooth. When the milk is very hot, pour into it the corn-flour and sugar, stir it very quickly; and when boiling, allow it to boil ten minutes, stirring all the time. Dip a mould or basin in cold water, pour in the mixture, and when cold, turn out on a flat dish.

Barley Pudding.—One tea-cupful barley, one pint and a half milk, three table-spoonfuls of sugar.

Place in a basin the barley, pour over enough cold water to cover it, and allow this to soak over night. In the morning pour away the water, and pour over the milk, and let it soak two hours. Grease well a pie-dish with dripping, pour in the barley and milk, add the sugar, and let this cook in a slow oven for two hours.

Sago Pudding.—Two ounces of sago, one pint of milk, two table-spoonfuls of sugar, one egg, one half ounce of dripping.

Place the sago in a basin and soak it for an hour in as much water as cover it. Pour away the water and pour over the milk, put both in a sauce-pan and stir over the fire till boiling; draw the pan on one side, and let the contents simmer for twenty minutes. Beat well in a basin the egg and sugar together with a fork. At the end of twenty minutes take the pan from the fire and let the sago cool a little, then pour in the egg and sugar; stir well together. Grease well a pie-dish with the dripping, and pour in the mixture. Place the pie-dish in a moderate oven, and bake for half an hour.

Bread Pudding.—Four slices of bread, three table-spoonfuls currants, three gills milk, two table-spoonfuls sugar, one ounce dripping.

Cut the bread about half an inch in thickness, and place one slice in a pie-dish, sprinkle over a few of the currants; place over another slice of bread, and so on till bread and currants are used up. Beat well in a basin the egg and sugar, add the milk, and pour this over the bread in the pie-dish. Let this soak for an hour, then place the pie-dish in a quick oven for twenty minutes.

NOTE.—A great improvement is to butter the bread.

Rice Pudding without Eggs.—Four ounces of rice, one quart of milk, two ounces of suet, two large table-spoonfuls sugar.

Wash the rice well in cold water, place it in a pie-dish, and pour over it the milk; add the sugar. Remove from the suet all skin, and chop it finely, add to the ingredients in the pie-dish. Place the pie-dish in a moderate oven, and let the pudding bake very slowly for two hours.

Corn-Flour Pudding.—Two table-spoonfuls corn-flour, one pint milk, one ounce butter, one egg.

Moisten the corn-flour in a basin with two or three table-spoonfuls of the milk. Place on the fire the remainder of the milk, and allow it to get very hot, then stir into it the moistened corn-flour; stir all together till boiling, then take the pan at once from the fire. While the corn-flour is cooling a little, beat well with a fork in a basin the egg and sugar, then stir them well into the corn-flour. Pour this now into a well-greased pie-dish, and bake twenty minutes in a quick oven.

SIMPLE PUDDINGS, ETC.

Apple Pudding.—Two pounds apples, three table-spoonfuls of sugar, four ounces of suet, eight ounces of flour, one tea-spoonful baking-powder, one half pint cold water.

Pare, core, and cut in small pieces the apples. Remove from the suet all skin, place it on a board, and chop it very finely. Place the suet in a basin, add the flour, salt, and baking-powder; stir all well with a spoon, then moisten all to a dry dough with the cold water. Turn this dough quickly out on the board and knead it slightly together. Cut off the third part. Roll out the remainder the third of an inch in thickness, and line a greased basin with it; put in the pieces of apples, and add the sugar; then pour over two table-spoonfuls of water. Roll out the remainder of the dough exactly the size of the top of the basin, place it over the apples, and press well together the two edges of crust. Dip a pudding-cloth in boiling water, sprinkle over a little flour, tie this over the top, and place the basin in a large pan of boiling water to boil for two hours. Turn out this on a flat hot dish.

Sago and Apples.—Six apples, one quarter pound sago, two table-spoonfuls sugar, one pint and a quarter cold water.

Pare and core six large cooking apples; do not cut them up. Place them in a large pie-dish, and place in each apple an equal quantity of sugar; place now round the apples the sago, and pour over the cold water. Let this soak for two hours, then place the pie-dish in a quick oven for three quarters of an hour.

Plain Plum Pudding.—One pound bread crumbs, one quarter pound flour, one quarter pound sugar, one half pound suet, one quarter pound raisins, one quarter pound currants, one tea-spoonful ground ginger, one tea-spoonful ground cinnamon, one half of a nutmeg, one tea-spoonful baking-powder, one half pint milk.

Place on a board the suet, remove the skin, and chop it

very finely; place it in a basin, and add the bread crumb and flour; stir all well together, then add the sugar, ginger, cinnamon, and baking-powder. Wash well and dry the currants, add them; seed the raisins, add them also; then grate over the nutmeg. Moisten all with the milk, and stir thoroughly together. Dip a pudding-cloth in boiling water, sprinkle over a little flour, and place the cloth over a basin, pour in the mixture, tie up the cloth rather loosely round with a piece of twine. Plunge this now into a large pan of boiling water, and boil it for four hours.

Apple Fritters.—Four large apples, three table-spoonfuls of flour, one gill water, one half ounce butter, one table-spoonful sugar.

Pare the apples, remove the cores; but do not cut them up. Cut the apples in round slices about half an inch thick. Place in a basin the flour, melt over the fire in a small sauce-pan the butter, and pour it into the centre of the dry flour. Heat the water also in the pan, and when tepid pour it over the butter, then with the back of a wooden spoon beat and stir all well together. Place on the fire to heat a stew-pan half filled with clarified fat, and when the smoke rises lift, one by one, the pieces of apples with a skewer or fork, dip each piece in the batter in the basin, and then drop each one into the clarified fat. Cook each for three minutes, then lift them out one by one on to a sheet of paper. Drain them one minute on the paper, then place them on a hot dish, and sprinkle over the sugar.

Pancakes.—Four table-spoonfuls of flour, one half pint milk, one egg, two table-spoonfuls of sugar, two table-spoonfuls of dripping.

Place in a basin the flour, make a little hole in the centre, drop in the yolk of egg, and place the white on a plate. Add to the flour and yolk of egg by degrees half of the milk. With the back of a wooden spoon beat this mixture till it begins to rise in bells; add then the remainder of the milk. Whip with a dry knife the white of egg to a stiff froth.

Mix the white very lightly to the other ingredients. Melt now in a small frying-pan a very little of the dripping, pour in half a tea-cupful of the batter, cook it over a moderate fire until a pale brown on the under side, turn it quickly on the other side. When the second side is browned turn the pancake out on a plate, sprinkle over a little of the sugar, roll it up quickly, then place it on a hot flat dish, and prepare the other in the same way.

Fried Rice Balls.—One quarter pound rice, three gills milk, one table-spoonful sugar, two table-spoonfuls bread crumbs, one egg.

Wash well the rice in several waters, place it in a small sauce-pan, and pour over enough water to cover it, place the pan over the fire, and the instant the water boils pour it away. Add the milk, and return the pan to the side of the fire, and allow the contents to simmer very slowly for twenty minutes. Take the pan from the fire, drop in the yolk of egg, add the sugar, and stir all over the fire for three minutes. Turn the mixture out on a plate and allow it to get quite cold. Flour slightly then a board, and roll the mixture into small balls. Beat slightly on a plate the white of egg, roll the balls in it; place the bread crumbs on a sheet of paper, and roll each ball in them. Heat over the fire in a stew-pan as much dripping or clarified fat as will cover the balls; when the smoke rises drop the balls in one by one, and allow them to brown for two minutes. Take them out one by one and place them for a minute on a sheet of paper. To be eaten with jam, or with milk and sugar.

Currant Dumpling.—One half pound bread crumbs, two table-spoonfuls of flour, one quarter pound currants, one quarter pound sugar, one quarter pound suet, one gill and a half milk.

Remove from the suet all skin, place it on a board and chop it finely, place it in a basin, add the bread crumbs, sugar, and flour. Wash well the currants and dry them.

Add the currants to other ingredients, then moisten all with the milk. Dip a pudding-cloth in boiling water, sprinkle over it a little flour, place it over a basin, then pour in the mixture. With a piece of twine tie the cloth loosely round the mixture, and plunge the dumpling into a large pan of boiling water. Add to the water half a table-spoonful salt, and boil the dumpling two hours. Turn it then very carefully out of the cloth on to a very hot flat dish.

Suet Dumplings.—Twelve ounces of flour, five ounces of suet, one half pint cold water, one tea-spoonful salt, one half tea-spoonful baking-powder.

Remove from the suet all skin, place it on a board, and chop it very finely. Place the chopped suet in a basin, add the flour, salt, and baking-powder. Stir all together with a spoon, then moisten all to a dry dough with the water. Turn the dough out on the board, knead it very slightly together, cut it into eight or ten pieces. Flour the fingers well, and roll each piece into a ball. Have in readiness a large pan of boiling water, add to it a dessert-spoonful salt. Drop in one by one the dumplings, taking care not to add too many at once, as it cools the water. Boil the dumplings twenty minutes, take them out one by one, drain the water from them, and serve on a very hot dish. To be eaten with treacle or sugar.

Treacle Roly-Poly.—One quarter pound suet, one half pound flour, one half tea-spoonful baking-powder, one pinch salt, one gill and a half cold water, four table-spoonfuls of treacle.

Grease well one large jelly-jar. Remove from the suet all skin, chop it very finely on a board. Place the suet in a basin, add the flour and baking-powder, also the salt. Stir all well together with a spoon, and moisten with the cold water to a dry dough. Turn the dough out on a board, knead it very lightly together. Cut it into five pieces, and roll each piece out nearly the size of the mouth of the jar. Place one piece in the jar, then pour over a little treacle;

place in another round of dough, then a little more treacle; and continue to do this until all is used up. Twist over the top of the jar a piece of paper, and place it in a sauce-pan in which there is enough boiling water to come half-way up the sides of the jar. Cover the sauce-pan closely, and boil for one hour and a half. Remove the paper from the top of the jar, and turn out the pudding on to a very hot dish.

Sheep-Head Pie.—One sheep-head, one quarter pound bacon, two eggs, one half table-spoonful salt, one half teaspoonful pepper, one half pint of the liquor in which the head was boiled.

After the head has been boiled (directions for which see page 260), remove the meat from the bones, and cut it in small pieces; remove the skin from the tongue and cut it in slices. Take the skin from the bacon and slice it thinly. Boil the eggs for ten minutes, put them in a basin of cold water, remove the shells and slice the eggs. Place now in a pie-dish a layer of the meat and tongue, over them place a little bacon and a little egg. Sprinkle over a little pepper and salt. Continue putting these layers until all the quantities are used up.

Pour over the liquor, and cover with a dripping crust (directions for which see page 229).

Ham and Eggs.—One pound ham, four eggs.

Remove the skin from the ham, slice it thinly, place the slices in a cold frying-pan. Place the pan over a moderate fire, and cook the ham for four minutes on each side. Remove the slices and place them on a very hot dish. Break an egg into a tea-cup, and pour it into the frying-pan, taking care not to break the yolk. Let the first egg set a little before putting in the second. Cook the eggs each three minutes, and lift each carefully with a broad knife and place on the slices of ham.

Frizzled Bacon.—One half pound bacon.

Remove the skin from the bacon, slice it thinly. Place a

hot dish before a clear fire. Place on the dish the slices of bacon, lift them one by one with a fork, and hold each close to the fire for three minutes, allowing the dripping to fall on the hot dish.

Macaroni and Meat Shape.—One half pound cold meat, one quarter pound macaroni, two table-spoonfuls bread crumbs, one tea-spoonful salt, one quarter tea-spoonful pepper, one half gill milk.

Chop on a board very finely the cold meat, when chopped add to it the bread crumbs, pepper, and salt. Mix all well together. Wash the macaroni, place it in a small sauce-pan and cover it with cold water. Place the pan over the fire and allow the water to boil for fifteen minutes. Pour away every drop of water, and allow the macaroni to get cold. Cut it then in pieces about an inch in length. Take now a small dry basin, and grease it well with dripping; then place in it a layer of the cut macaroni, then a layer of the cold meat and bread crumbs, then another layer of macaroni, and so on, till the basin is filled. Pour over the milk, and twist over the top of the basin a sheet of paper. Place the basin in a sauce-pan, and pour round enough boiling water to come half-way up the basin, and let the water boil for an hour and a half. Remove the paper, and turn out the shape on a hot dish.

Fish Cakes.—One pound boiled potatoes, one pound salt fish, one egg, three table-spoonfuls of bread crumbs, one half tea-spoonful of pepper, two table-spoonfuls of milk, one ounce of dripping.

Cover the salt fish well with cold water, and allow it to soak over night. Take it from the water, place it in a sauce-pan and cover it with cold water; place the pan by the side of the fire, and allow the water to heat slowly till boiling-point, then boil slowly twenty minutes. Separate the skin and bone from the fish with two forks, and put the fish into a large basin. Boil and mash the potatoes. (See directions, page 108.) Add the potatoes to the fish, then the pepper, dripping, and yolk of egg; mix well together, then add the milk. Flour the baking-board, and with a knife form the mixture into flat round cakes. Beat very slightly now on a plate the white of egg, roll each of the cakes in it; then place on a sheet of paper the bread crumbs, roll each cake in it. Melt now in a frying-pan about two ounces of dripping; when the smoke rises place in the cakes, and cook them five minutes on each side.

NOTE.—Cold boiled fish of any kind may be used up in this way.

Twice Laid.—One pound salt fish, one pound potatoes, one ounce dripping, two table-spoonfuls of milk, one salt-spoonful of pepper.

Soak over night the fish in a large basin of cold water; take it out of the water and place it in a sauce-pan of fresh water. Place the pan by the side of the fire and allow the water to heat slowly till boiling, then boil it for twenty minutes. Take the fish from the water, and remove all bone and skin. Boil and mash the potatoes (see directions, page 108), add to them the pepper, dripping, and milk. Stir all well, then place a layer of the potatoes in a pie-dish, then a layer of the pieces of fish; continue doing this until all are used up. Place a layer of potatoes on the top, smooth them well with a knife. Place the dish in a moderate oven, and bake one half hour.

NOTE.—Cold fish of any kind may be used up in this way.

Fish and Sauce.—One pound salt fish, two ounces of dripping, one ounce of flour, one half pint milk, one gill water, one salt-spoonful pepper.

Soak the fish over night in a large basin of cold water; take it from the water, place it in a sauce-pan and cover it with fresh water. Place the pan by the side of the fire and let the water heat up very slowly till boiling, then boil slowly twenty minutes. Melt in a separate sauce-pan the dripping, add the flour, and stir till well mixed; add then the water by degrees, then the milk also by degrees; stir till boiling, add the pepper, and draw the pan from the fire. At the end of twenty minutes take the fish from the water, remove all bone and skin, and place the fish in rough pieces in the sauce-pan, with the flour, dripping, and milk. Return the pan to the fire, and let all simmer slowly for five minutes.

Baked Fish.—One large plaice or flounder, one table-spoonful chopped parsley, two table-spoonfuls bread crumbs, two ounces dripping, one tea-spoonful salt, one half tea-spoonful pepper.

Place in a small baking-tin half of the bread crumbs, dripping, parsley, pepper, and salt. Wash well the fish, clean it and cut off the fins; place it over the bread crumbs on the tin, sprinkle over the remainder of the parsley, bread crumbs, pepper, and salt. Place the remainder of the dripping over in very small pieces. Place the tin in rather a quick oven for half an hour. Lift the fish very carefully, and place it on a very hot flat dish, when it is ready for use.

Baked Fish.—Two pounds cod fish, four table-spoonfuls of bread crumbs, two table-spoonfuls of flour, one half pint milk, one tea-spoonful salt, one salt-spoonful pepper, one table-spoonful of vinegar.

Wash the fish well, cut off the fins, and cut it in slices about half an inch thick. Place in a pie-dish half of the bread crumbs and half the pepper and salt. Place over the bread crumbs the slices of fish, and pour over the fish the vinegar. Sprinkle over the remainder of the bread crumbs, pepper, and salt. Place now the flour in a basin, and moisten it with two or three table-spoonfuls of milk. Add the remainder of the milk, and stir all till the flour is quite smooth. Pour the milk and flour over the fish and bread crumbs, and place the pie-dish in a quick oven for half an hour.

Stewed Fish.—Two pounds cod fish, two ounces clarified fat, one large table-spoonful of chopped parsley, one ounce flour, one tea-spoonful of salt, one salt-spoonful of pepper, three gills milk or water.

Wash well the fish, cut off the fins, cut it in slices about an inch thick. Melt now in a sauce-pan over the fire the dripping, add the flour, stir both well together, and add by degrees the milk or water. Stir all till boiling. Add the salt and pepper, then the pieces of fish. Draw the pan on one side, cover it, and allow the contents to simmer for ten minutes. Add the parsley, and cook two minutes longer. The dish is now ready, and ought to be served at once.

NOTE.—A tea-spoonful of vinegar is a great improvement when the water is used.

Fried Fish.—Two slices of cod fish, two table-spoonfuls of bread crumbs, one table-spoonful of flour, one tea-spoonful of salt, one salt-spoonful of pepper, two table-spoonfuls of dripping, one egg.

Cut the fish about an inch in thickness. Place on a sheet of paper the flour; place on another sheet the bread crumbs. Beat well on a plate the egg. Season the bread crumbs with the pepper and salt. Lift the fish with a fork. Roll it well in the flour, then dip it in the beaten egg. Roll it now in the bread crumbs. When both pieces are prepared in this way, heat in a frying-pan the dripping; when the smoke rises, place in the pieces of fish; cook them for seven or eight minutes on both sides. Place the slices on a very hot dish, and garnish with a little parsley.

Fried Fish.—Two large haddocks, one table-spoonful flour, one tea-spoonful salt, one salt-spoonful pepper, two table-spoonfuls dripping.

Mix well on a sheet of paper the flour, pepper, and salt. Wash well and clean the haddocks. Cut off the fins; and roll them in the seasoned flour. Melt in a frying-pan the dripping; when the smoke rises, place in the haddocks, and cook them seven or eight minutes on both sides. Serve on a very hot flat dish, and garnish with parsley.

MEATS.

Hot Pot.—One pound cold cooked meat or one pound lean mutton, two pounds potatoes, one large onion, one half pint cold water, half an ounce dripping, half a table-spoonful salt, one half tea-spoonful pepper, one table-spoonful flour.

Soak over night in a small basin of boiling water the onion, then cut it in thin slices. Pare the potatoes very thinly, place them in a sauce-pan, cover them with cold water, and allow the water to boil. While the water is coming to the boiling-point, place on a plate the flour, pepper, and salt. Mix them well together. Cut in small pieces either the mutton or cold meat. Roll each piece in the seasoned flour. Take the potatoes from the boiling water, dry them in a towel, and slice thinly about half. Place a layer of the slices in a pie-dish, then a layer of the meat, then a little of the onion, and so on, until all is used up. Cut the remainder of the potatoes in half. Place them on the top, with the round sides uppermost. Melt the dripping in a cup or tin, and with a feather brush the potatoes over. Place the pie-dish in a moderate oven, and bake half an hour. If mutton has been used cook one hour.

Sea Pie.—One pound steak, one quarter pound suet, one half pound flour, one half tea-spoonful baking-powder, one large tea-spoonful salt, one salt-spoonful pepper, three gills cold water, one carrot, one turnip, one onion.

Cut in small pieces the steak. Place the pieces in a stew-pan. Pour over half of the water, half of the salt, and all of the pepper. Place the pan over the fire, and allow the water to boil. Pare thickly the turnip; slice it thinly. Scrape the carrot; slice it also. Pare and slice also the onion. When the water boils, draw the pan on one side. Add the vegetables; and let all simmer slowly one hour and a quarter. While this is simmering, remove the skin from the suet, and chop it finely. Place it in a basin. Add the flour, the remainder of the salt, and the baking-powder. Stir all well together, and moisten the mixture with the remainder of the cold water. Turn it quickly out on the board, knead it lightly together, cut it into eight pieces, roll each piece into a ball. When the meat has cooked one hour and a quarter, place the balls on the top, and let all cook slowly for half an hour longer. When ready, serve the meat and vegetables in the centre of a hot flat dish, and the balls of pastry round them.

NOTE.—The onion for this must be soaked over night in boiling water.

Poor Man's Goose.—One pound liver, one quarter pound bacon, one half table-spoonful salt, one half tea-spoonful pepper, two pounds potatoes, one large onion, one half pint cold water.

Soak the onion over night in a small basin of boiling water. Take it out of the water, and slice it. Place the potatoes in a pan, cover them with cold water, and allow the water to boil. Cut the liver in thin slices, and put them in a basin of cold water. Remove the skin from the bacon, and slice it also. Take the potatoes from the boiling water and slice them. Place now in a Yorkshire pudding-tin a layer of potatoes, then a layer of the liver, then a little of the onion, a little pepper and salt, then a little of the bacon. Continue to do this until all those ingredients are used up. Place over the top a last layer of potatoes. Pour in the water at the side. Place the tin in a hot oven, and bake one hour and a half.

Toad in the Hole.—One pound sausages, four table-spoonfuls of flour, three gills of milk, one egg, one tea-spoonful salt, one salt-spoonful pepper.

Prick the sausages all over with a fork, place them in a pie-dish, place the pie-dish in a quick oven, and bake the sausages for fifteen minutes. Place in a basin the flour. Add the salt and pepper. Drop into the centre of the flour the yolk of egg. Pour over the yolk of egg a very little of the milk, and begin to stir in the flour from the sides. Continue to do this until all the flour is moistened and about half the milk is used. Beat this mixture well with a wooden spoon until it begins to rise in little bells. Add then the remainder of the milk, and stir all well together. Place on a dry plate the white of egg, and with a dry knife whip it to a very stiff froth. Stir in very lightly the white of egg to the mixture in the basin. When the sausages have baked fifteen minutes, pour the mixture in the basin over them, and bake the whole for fifteen minutes longer.

NOTE.—Cold meat may be used instead of the sausages, or one pound of lean mutton.

Stewed Steak.—One pound steak, one carrot, one onion, one small turnip, one half pint cold water, one half ounce dripping, one tea-spoonful salt, one salt-spoonful pepper, one half table-spoonful flour.

Melt in a stew-pan the dripping. Cut the steak in small square pieces. When the smoke rises from the dripping, put in the pieces of steak and brown them well. Place in a basin the flour, pepper, and salt. Moisten them with a very little water. Stir till the flour is very smooth, then add the remainder of the water. Pour this over the browned steak, and stir all over the fire till boiling. Skim well, and draw the pan on one side. Pare the turnip thickly, cut it in small pieces, scrape and slice the carrot, take the skin from the onion. Add these vegetables to the steak, and allow to simmer very slowly for an hour and a half.

NOTE.—The onion ought to be soaked over night in boiling water.

Stuffed Ox Heart.—One ox heart, one table-spoonful chopped parsley, two table-spoonfuls milk, four table-spoonfuls bread crumbs, one half table-spoonful salt, one half tea-spoonful pepper, one ounce dripping, one pint cold water, three ounces of suet.

Wash well the heart in several waters. Cut across the centre, so as to make the cells into one large cavity to hold the stuffing. Remove from the suet the skin. Place it on a board, and chop it finely. Place in a basin the bread crumbs, parsley, and half the pepper and salt. Mix well together. Add the suet, and moisten all with the milk. Place this stuffing in the heart; sew it in with a strong needle and twine. Melt in a large sauce-pan the dripping. Put in the heart, and brown it over the fire. Turn the heart frequently, until it is browned all over. (This takes nearly one hour.) Take then the heart from the pan. Pour out of the pan the dripping. Return the pan to the fire, and sprinkle in the flour; add by degrees the water; stir till boiling. Skim well. Add the remainder of the pepper and salt. Return the heart to the pan; draw the pan on one side, and allow all to cook very slowly for one hour and a half.

NOTE.—To the stuffing may be added a small onion, which must be first peeled and soaked over night in boiling water, then chopped finely.

Boiled Stuffed Heart.—One ox heart, five ounces of suet, twelve table-spoonfuls of flour, one tea-spoonful baking-powder, one half table-spoonful salt, one half pint cold water.

Wash well the heart in water several times. Cut it across the centre, so as to make one large hole. Remove from the suet the skin. Place it on a board, and chop it finely. Place it in a basin. Add the flour, powder, and salt. Mix it to rather a dry dough with the water. Turn it out on the board, and knead it slightly. Take quarter of this dough and place it as a stuffing in the heart. Roll out the remainder of the dough about half an inch thick. Dip a large pudding-cloth in boiling water, sprinkle over a little flour, place it on the table, place on it the dough, place on the dough the heart, draw up the pudding-cloth and tie it round. Plunge this into a large sauce-pan of boiling water. Add about one table-spoonful of salt, and let this boil for three hours. Should the water reduce in this time, add a little boiling water. Cut the string, and turn the heart carefully out of the cloth on to a hot dish.

Shepherd's Pie.—One pound cold meat, one pound boiled potatoes, one tea-spoonful salt, one quarter tea-spoonful pepper, one onion, one table-spoonful milk, one ounce clarified fat or dripping.

Boil and mash the potatoes. (See directions, page 108.) Add to them the pepper, salt, milk, and dripping. Stir well together. Chop finely the cold meat. Soak the onion over night in a basin of boiling water. Take it from the water, and place it in a small sauce-pan. Cover it with cold water, and boil it fifteen minutes; then chop it finely. Place now in a pie-dish a layer of the potatoes, then a layer of the cold meat, then a little onion. Continue to do this till all is used up. Place a last layer of potatoes on the top. Dip a knife in milk and make them very smooth. Place the pie-dish in a moderate oven, and bake half an hour.

Meat Roll.—One pound steak, one half pound flour, one quarter pound suet, one half tea-spoonful baking-powder, one and one-half gill cold water, one onion, one tea-spoonful salt, one salt-spoonful pepper.

Soak the onion over night in a small basin of boiling water. Cut the steak in small square pieces, and sprinkle over it half the salt and all of the pepper. Remove all skin from the suet. Place it on a board, and chop it finely. Place the suet in a basin. Add the flour, baking-powder, and remainder of the salt. Moisten this to rather a dry dough with the cold water. Turn the dough out on a board, and knead it lightly together. Roll the dough out about half an inch in thickness; place over it the steak. Then take the onion from the water, and slice it over. Roll up the dough. Dip a pudding-cloth in boiling water; sprinkle over a little flour. Place it on the table. Lift the roll carefully into the centre, roll the cloth round it, and tie the ends with a piece of twine. Plunge the roll into a large pan of boiling water. Add about half a table-spoonful salt, and boil the roll two hours.

NOTE.—A small plate ought to be put in the bottom of the sauce-pan to prevent the cloth burning.

Brazilian Stew.—Two pounds middle cut shin of beef,

one large turnip, two carrots, one large onion, one leek, two table-spoonfuls vinegar, one half tea-spoonful pepper, one half table-spoonful salt.

Place the vinegar in a basin. Cut the meat from the bone. Dip each piece of meat in the vinegar. Put them closely together in a stew-pan. Sprinkle over the salt and pepper. Slice over the onion. Pare very thickly the turnip, and slice it over also. Scrape the carrots, and slice them over. Slice the leek over. Cover the stew-pan closely. Place it by the side of the fire, and let the contents heat gradually through. Shake the pan frequently, and allow all to simmer very slowly for three hours and a half. Turn the pan occasionally from side to side, as (there being no liquid but the vinegar), unless cooked with great care, it is apt to scorch.

NOTE.—The onion must be soaked over night in a small basin of boiling water.

Irish Stew.—One pound neck of mutton, two pounds potatoes, two large onions, one large tea-spoonful salt, one salt-spoonful pepper, one half pint boiling water.

Cut the neck of mutton in small pieces, wash the pieces, and place them in a stew-pan, sprinkle over the salt and pepper, and pour over the cold water. Place the pan over the fire, and when the water boils skim it well. Soak the onions over night in a basin of boiling water, slice them, and add them to the mutton in the stew-pan. Draw the pan on one side, and cook the contents very slowly for one hour and a quarter. Pare thinly the potatoes, place them in a separate sauce-pan, cover them with cold water, and allow the water to boil. Take the pan at once from the fire, remove the potatoes, and place them over the mutton in the stew-pan. Allow all to cook for half an hour longer, when the dish is ready for use. Serve the mutton and onions in the centre of a hot dish, and place the potatoes round.

Fried Sausages.—One pound sausages, one half table-spoonful flour, one half tea-spoonful salt, one quarter tea-spoonful pepper, one gill and a half cold water.

Prick the sausages well with a fork, place them in a cold frying-pan, place the pan over a slow fire, and turn the sausages frequently for fifteen minutes. Place the sausages on a hot dish, and add to the dripping which has drawn from the sausages in the frying-pan the flour, pepper, and salt. Stir all well together, and add the cold water; stir till boiling; let it boil for two minutes, and pour it over the sausages.

NOTE.—If desired, a piece of dry toast may be served under each sausage.

Rice and Cheese.—One quarter pound rice, one quarter pound cheese, one half pint milk, one tea-spoonful salt, one quarter tea-spoonful pepper, one ounce dripping or clarified fat.

Wash well the rice in several waters, place it in a sauce-pan, cover it with cold water, and place the pan over the fire till the water boils. Pour away then every drop of water, and pour over the milk, return the pan to the fire, and let all simmer very slowly twenty minutes. Take a piece of dry, hard cheese, grate on the carrot-grater four ounces of it. Place on a flat dish in small pieces half of the dripping, place over a layer of the rice, sprinkle over a little cheese, then a little pepper and salt. Continue to put these layers until all is used up. Place over the top the remainder of the dripping in small pieces, and bake in the oven or before the fire until browned nicely on the top.

Macaroni and Cheese.—One quarter pound macaroni, one quarter pound grated cheese, one half pint milk, one tea-spoonful salt, one quarter tea-spoonful pepper, one ounce dripping or clarified fat.

Wash the macaroni well in cold water, but do not soak it. Place it in a sauce-pan, cover it with cold water, place the pan over the fire, and boil the macaroni for fifteen minutes. Pour away every drop of water, and add the milk; place the pan by the side of the fire, and simmer very slowly for half an hour. Place on a flat dish half of the dripping, and then place over the boiled macaroni; sprinkle over the salt, then sprinkle over the grated cheese; sprinkle over the cheese the pepper, and then over all place in small pieces the remainder of the dripping. Place the dish in a quick oven for ten minutes, or brown in a Dutch oven before the fire.

Baked Cheese.—Three ounces grated cheese, three table-spoonfuls bread crumbs, one gill milk, one quarter tea-spoonful pepper, one half tea-spoonful salt, one ounce dripping or clarified fat.

Grate on a carrot-grater three ounces dry, hard cheese; place it in a basin, and add to it the bread crumbs, pepper, and salt. Moisten with the milk, and stir all well together. Grease well a flat dish with the dripping, pour this mixture on, and bake in rather a quick oven fifteen minutes, or place it in a Dutch oven before the fire for half an hour.

NOTE.—A little dry mustard may be added, if desired.

Cheese Pudding.—One quarter pound cheese, one ounce dripping or butter, one and one-half gills milk, one pinch pepper, one half tea-spoonful salt, two eggs.

Place in a sauce-pan the butter or dripping, and slice into it the cheese, add the milk, then stir all over the fire until the cheese is melted. Draw the pan from the fire, and drop into it the yolks of egg. Stir all well together. Place the whites of egg on a dry plate, and whip them with a knife to a stiff froth. Stir the whites of egg very lightly to the mixture in the sauce-pan, and pour all into a small pie-dish.

Place the pie-dish in a quick oven, and bake for ten minutes; then serve at once.

Simple Omelette.—One egg, one tea-spoonful corn-flour, one table-spoonful milk, one pinch baking-powder, one pinch salt, one pinch pepper, one ounce butter.

Place in a basin the corn-flour, and moisten it with the milk, stir till very smooth, add the salt and pepper. Drop in the egg, and beat slightly together; add a pinch of baking-powder. Melt in a frying-pan the butter, and pour in the mixture from the basin; stir over a moderate fire until the egg begins to set; draw it with a spoon to one side of the pan, and then hold the pan before a clear fire until the omelette browns slightly on the top. Turn out quickly on a hot plate, and serve at once.

Goose Pudding.—One quarter pound scraps of bread, one large onion, one quarter tea-spoonful powdered sage, two ounces suet, two table-spoonfuls milk, one half tea-spoonful salt, one salt-spoonful pepper.

Break the scraps of bread into rough pieces, place them in a basin, and pour over enough water to cover them. Cover the basin with a plate, and let the bread soak for ten minutes. Pour then away every drop of water, and beat the bread very smooth with a fork. Add the milk, sage, salt, and pepper. Chop the suet very finely, and add it also. Stir all well together. Soak the onion over night in a small basin of boiling water, take it from the water, then place it in a small pan of cold water, and boil it half an hour. Chop it finely, add it also to other ingredients, pour all into a pie-dish, and bake for half an hour.

SICK-ROOM COOKERY.

Arrowroot Pudding.—One dessert-spoonful of arrowroot, one tea-spoonful of sugar, one half pint milk, one half salt-spoonful grated nutmeg, one half ounce butter, two eggs.

Place in a small basin the arrowroot, moisten it with a table-spoonful of the milk, stir both together till very smooth. Place the remainder of the milk in a sauce-pan over the fire to boil; when quite boiling pour it over the moistened arrowroot, and stir quickly until the mixture thickens. The eggs must now be broken, and the whites separated carefully from the yolks. Place on a dry plate the whites, and whip them to a very stiff froth with a dry knife. When the arrowroot has cooled a little, drop into it one by one the yolks, and stir all well together; add the sugar, then stir in as lightly as possible the whites. Grease a small pie-dish with the butter, pour in the mixture, and grate over the top the nutmeg.

Place the pie-dish in rather a quick oven, and bake the pudding ten minutes.

Note.—Arrowroot ought to be kept in a tin or closely-stoppered bottle, as, if too long exposed to the air, the mere pouring of boiling water or milk over it will not thicken it.

Clear Arrowroot with Port Wine.—One dessert-spoonful of arrowroot, one tea-spoonful of sugar, one half pint of boiling water, two table-spoonfuls of port wine.

Place the arrowroot in a small basin, add the sugar, and moisten them with a table-spoonful of cold water. Bring the remainder of the water to the boiling-point, pour it very quickly over the arrowroot, and stir all quickly until the arrowroot thickens. Pour over the port wine, and the arrowroot is ready for use.

Arrowroot and Milk.—One dessert-spoonful arrowroot, one half pint milk, one tea-spoonful sugar.

Moisten the arrowroot with a table-spoonful of the milk, add the sugar, and stir all thoroughly together.

Place the remainder of the milk in a sauce-pan, and place it over the fire until quite boiling. Pour the boiling milk over the arrowroot, and stir well till quite thick, when it is ready for use.

Note.—Arrowroot ought only to be used in the sick-room as a medium for giving nourishment or stimulant, as in itself it contains a very small amount of nourishment.

Milk Gruel.—One table-spoonful oatmeal, one half ounce butter, one tea-spoonful sugar, one half pint milk.

Place in a small basin the meal, pour over it by degrees, stirring all the time, the milk. When well mixed, pour this into a sauce-pan, and place the pan over a slow fire; stir the contents until boiling, then add the butter and sugar. Draw the pan on one side and allow the contents to simmer very slowly for five minutes. This must then be strained through a fine piece of muslin into a well-heated basin, when it is ready.

Water Gruel.—Two table-spoonfuls oatmeal, three gills boiling water, one gill cold water, one half ounce sugar, one half ounce butter, one wine-glassful port wine.

Place the oatmeal in a large basin, pour over the cold water, and stir it well. Allow the meal and water to soak for twenty minutes, then pour over the boiling water, and stir all well together. This mixture must now be allowed to stand for three minutes, so that the meal may sink to the bottom. Pour from this now very gently the liquid into a sauce-pan, taking care to leave the sediment in the basin. Place the sauce-pan over the fire, and stir all till boiling; add the sugar and butter, and boil all slowly for ten minutes. Add at the last minute before serving the port wine.

Clear Barley Water.—One ounce pearl barley, two ounces lump-sugar, the rind of one lemon, two quarts boiling water.

Place the barley in a strainer, put the strainer under the water-tap, and let the water run for three or four minutes. Place the barley now in a basin, and pour over it enough boiling water to cover it. Allow this to soak for ten minutes, then pour away every drop of water. Rub now the pieces of lump sugar on the lemon, and then add them to the barley. Pour over now two quarts boiling water, and allow this to become quite cold. Strain the liquor now through a fine piece of muslin, when it is ready for use.

Lemon Peel Tea.—The rind of one lemon, ten grains of cream of tartar, one pint of boiling water, one ounce of lump-sugar.

Remove very carefully from the lemon the rind, using a sharp knife, and taking care to take none of the white part. Place the rind in a jug, add the sugar, pour over the boiling water, and when almost cold add the cream of tartar.

NOTE.—The quantity of sugar may be increased or diminished at will.

Savoury Jelly.—Three pounds shin of beef, one tea-spoonful salt, one salt-spoonful pepper.

Cut the meat from the bone, break up the bone with a hammer, place the pieces in a jar; cut the meat in very small pieces, place them in the jar also. Cover the jar, then tie over it a strong piece of brown paper. Place the jar in a large pan of boiling water, and allow the water to boil slowly round it for six hours. Remove the cover from the jar, strain the liquor into a basin, and season it with the pepper and salt. A pint of nourishing soup may be made from the meat by adding to it a sliced carrot and turnip, covering it with a pint and a quarter of cold water, and allowing all to simmer slowly two hours. Strain and season it, when it is ready for use

Quickly-made Beef Tea.—One half pound of steak, one half pint cold water.

Procure the steak from the top of the round, remove all fat and skin, place it on a board, and with a sharp knife cut it in very thin, small pieces. Place the pieces in a dry stew-pan, place the pan over a very slow fire, and with the back of a wooden spoon stir the pieces of steak for five minutes. At the end of this time the steak will be nearly covered with a very strong gravy; add now the cold water, stir all till boiling. Cover the sauce-pan, and simmer the contents very slowly for ten minutes. Strain the tea into a basin, when it is ready for use. Season to taste.

Economical Beef Tea (for long illness).—One knuckle bone of veal, four pounds middle cut of the shin of beef.

Break the knuckle bone with a hammer, place it in a large jar. Cut the meat from the beef-bone, remove the marrow from the bone, break the bone and place it in the jar also. Cut the meat in small pieces, add them to the bones in the jar. Cover the jar, and then tie over the top a strong piece of brown paper. Place the jar in a large pan of boiling water, and let the water boil round the jar for ten hours.

At the end of ten hours uncover the jar, and strain the

liquor from the meat into a large basin. When cold, this will form a strong jelly, containing a large amount of nourishment. To make a cupful of beef-tea, place a table-spoonful of the jelly into a cup, and fill up the cup with boiling water. Stir till the jelly is melted, and season to taste.

Uncooked Beef Tea.—Two ounces of steak, four table-spoonfuls of cold water.

Procure the steak from the top of the round. Remove all fat and skin, place it on a board, and with a sharp knife scrape it until the fibre begins to show. Turn the steak on the board and scrape the other side also. All the part which the knife removes must be placed in a cup, and over it must be poured the cold water. Allow this to soak for fifteen minutes, when it is ready for use.

NOTE.—If desired, this may be a strained through a very fine piece of muslin.

Easily-digested Beef Tea.—One pound steak, one pint cold water.

Procure the steak from the top of the round. Remove from it all skin and fat. Place it on a board and cut it in very small pieces; place the pieces in a sauce-pan, and pour over them the cold water. Cover the sauce-pan, and place it by the side of the fire for twenty minutes, at the end of which time it ought almost to be at boiling-point. Place the pan then on the fire, and allow all to boil once. Take the pan at once from the fire, and strain the liquid from the meat. Allow the liquid to cool, when all the sediment will have fallen to the bottom. The top part, which will have the colour of very pale sherry, must be carefully poured off, then heated and seasoned for use.

Restorative Jelly.—One ounce pure isinglass, one quarter of an ounce gum arabic, two ounces of sugar, the rind of one lemon, six cloves, one half pint port wine.

Place the isinglass in a jug, add the cloves and sugar; remove the rind from the lemon with a sharp knife, taking care to take none of the white part. Place the rind in the jug, add the sugar, and pour over all the port wine.

Cover the jug with a thick piece of paper, and allow it to stand over night. Place then the jug in a large pan of boiling water, and stir the contents with a wooden spoon until the isinglass is quite melted. Pour the mixture then through a strainer on to a plate. When cold, cut the jelly in small square pieces. This will keep for a very long time, and ought to be given to the patient in very small quantities.

Claret Jelly.—One pint bottle of claret, one half pound of lump sugar, one ounce and a quarter of gelatine, one pound pot of red currant jelly, one wine-glassful of brandy, the rind of one lemon.

Place in a preserving-pan the sugar and gelatine, and pour over them the claret and brandy. Allow this to soak for ten minutes. Remove very carefully with a sharp knife the rind from the lemon, and place it in the pan; add the currant jelly. Place the pan over rather a brisk fire, and stir all till boiling; draw the pan on one side, and let all simmer slowly five minutes. Dip a mould in cold water, strain into it the jelly, and put on one side to cool.

NOTE.—Half of this quantity makes a good-sized shape.

Custard Toast.—One slice of bread, one egg, one ounce of sugar, one half pint of milk, one ounce of butter.

Cut the bread about half an inch in thickness, remove the crust, and toast it to a nice pale brown on both sides; butter it with about half of the butter. Place in a basin the egg, and whip it till very light. Place in a sauce-pan the butter, sugar, and milk, and stir them over the fire till boiling. Draw the pan on one side, and let the milk cool a little, then pour it over the egg in the basin, stirring all the time. When well stirred together, pour this over the toast, and serve at once.

Rice Water.—One quarter pound rice, one ounce lump sugar, one inch stick-cinnamon, two pints cold water.

Place the rice in a strainer, place the strainer under the water, and allow the water to run through it for five minutes. Place now the rice in a sauce-pan, and add the sugar and cinnamon-stick. Place the pan over a quick fire, and boil all for twenty minutes. Strain now into a large jug the water, and as it cools shake the jug frequently, to prevent the water forming to a very thin jelly.

Lemonade.—Two lemons, three ounces of lump sugar, one pint of boiling water.

Rub the lemons in a clean towel, then with a sharp knife remove the thin yellow rind, taking great care to take none of the white part. Place the rind in a jug. Then remove very carefully from the lemons the thick white skin, which is very bitter, and must not be used. Cut now the centre part of the lemon into very thin slices, remove all pips, and place the slices in the jug. Add the sugar, pour over the boiling water, cover the jug, and let it stand over night. When required, strain into a glass in which has been put a piece of ice as large as a walnut.

Appleade.—Two pounds green apples, the rind of one lemon, one ounce of sugar, one quart boiling water.

Rub well in a towel the apples, cut them in round thin slices. Place the slices in a basin, add the lemon rind and sugar, and pour over the boiling water. Cover the basin with a plate, and let it stand over night. Strain in the morning, when it is ready for use.

Arrowroot Drink.—One tea-spoonful arrowroot, two breakfast-cupfuls of boiling water, one tea-spoonful lemon-juice, one tea-spoonful sugar.

Place in a basin the arrowroot and sugar, moisten them with a table-spoonful of cold water. Stir well together; then pour over the boiling water, still continuing to stir. Add the lemon-juice, allow it to get cold, when it is ready for use.

Soda Water Drink.—One tea-cupful milk, one half bottle soda water.

Put the milk in a glass, fill the glass up with the soda water. This ought to be given to the patient at once after the soda water is added.

Egg Flip.—One egg, one tea-cupful of milk, one half tea-spoonful sugar, one tea-spoonful brandy.

Place the egg in a basin and whip it till very light with a fork; add the sugar; stir well together. Pour this into a glass, and add to it by degrees, stirring all the time, the milk. Add the brandy, and give it at once to the patient.

NOTE.—The milk may be heated a little, if desired.

Lightest way to give an Egg to an Invalid.—One egg, one ounce dripping.

Melt the dripping in a frying-pan, break the egg into a cup, then pour it gently into the frying-pan, taking care not to break the yolk. Keep the pan over the fire for three minutes, then pour over the egg as much boiling water as cover it. Let it stand one minute; then lift the egg out of the water, place it on a very hot plate, and serve it at once.

NOTE.—The boiling water draws the oil from the egg.

Bread Berry.—One half slice of bread, one tea-spoonful sugar, one half pint of milk.

Cut the bread about half an inch in thickness, cut off the crust, then toast it to a pale brown on both sides. Cut the toast in small square pieces, place them in a basin, and cover them with boiling water; cover the basin with a plate, and let it stand by the side of the fire or in a very cool oven for half an hour. Pour away every drop of water, add the sugar, pour over the milk, cover the basin again, and place it by the side of the fire or in a very slow oven for two hours longer.

NOTE.—This must not at any time reach boiling-point.

Cup Custard.—One egg, one gill milk.

Grease well with fresh butter a tea-cup. Beat well in a basin the egg, pour it into the greased cup, fill up the cup to the top with the milk. Place the cup in a sauce-pan, and pour round it enough boiling water to come up half-way. Place the sauce-pan over the fire, and allow the water to boil slowly for twenty minutes. Turn the custard out on a hot plate, and serve at once with sugar to taste.

Invalid Shape.—One half ounce gelatine, one pint milk, two eggs, one ounce sugar.

Place the gelatine in a basin, and pour over the milk; allow the gelatine to soak for ten minutes. Pour then the milk and gelatine into a sauce-pan, place the pan over the fire, and stir the contents till boiling, then take the pan at once from the fire. Beat well in a basin the sugar and yolks of egg, and pour over them the milk, stirring well meanwhile.

Pour all back into the sauce-pan, and stir over the fire until very hot; but do not let the mixture boil, as the yolks of egg will curdle. Pour the mixture into a basin, and let it get cool, but not set. Place on a plate the whites of egg, and with a very dry knife whip them to a very stiff froth. Mix them in very lightly to the other ingredients in the basin. Dip a mould in cold water, pour in the mixture, and when set turn it out in a glass dish.

Invalid Pudding.—One sponge-cake, two apples, one ounce of sugar.

Crumble a stale sponge-cake into small pieces, pare thinly and core the apples. Grease a tea-cup well with fresh butter, place in the bottom of it a little of the cake crumb, then a piece of apple, sprinkle over a little sugar. Continue to do this until all the apples, sugar, and sponge-cake are used up. Place the cup in rather a quick oven, and bake the pudding for half an hour. Serve in the cup in which it was baked.

Rusk.—One rusk, one tea-cupful milk.

Place the rusk in a small jelly-jar, pour over the milk. Place the jar in a pan in which there is enough boiling water to come half-way up the jar. Allow the water to boil three quarters of an hour. The rusk must then be turned out of the jar on to a hot plate and served with sugar to taste.

Minced Steak. — One quarter pound steak, two tea-spoonfuls water, one tea-spoonful catchup, one pinch pepper.

Place the steak on a board, remove the skin, and chop it very finely. Place the chopped steak in a stew-pan, add the water, pepper, and catchup. Place the pan over a slow fire, and stir the contents until just at boiling-point; but do not let it quite boil, as the steak would then become tough. Serve at once on a very hot plate.

NOTE.—If the flavour is not desired, the catchup may be left out and a little salt added.

Steak Broiled. — One quarter pound steak, one pinch pepper, one pinch salt, one half ounce butter.

Have the steak cut an inch in thickness. Place before a clear fire a plate, lift the steak with a fork, and hold it before the fire for five minutes on each side. Place it quickly on the plate, sprinkle over the salt and pepper; place on the butter, and with the point of a knife press it well into the steak. This will draw out sufficient gravy. The steak ought to be served at once.

Chop.—One loin chop, one pinch of pepper, one pinch salt.

Trim nearly all the fat from the chop. Place a plate before a hot clear fire, lift the chop with a fork, and hold it before the fire for four minutes on each side. Put the chop quickly on the plate and serve at once.

Sweet-Bread (White Sauce). — One sweet-bread, one tea-spoonful arrowroot, one gill and a half milk, one pinch pepper, one pinch salt.

Soak the sweet-bread for an hour in a basin of cold water. Take it from the water, place it in a sauce-pan, cover it with cold water, place the pan over the fire, and allow the water to boil slowly for half an hour. Take the sweet-bread from the water and plunge it into a basin of cold water, wash it well, trim all the fat from it, and cut it in small pieces. Moisten now in a basin the arrowroot with a little of the milk; when smooth add all the milk, and pour this into a fresh sauce-pan; stir over the fire till boiling. Add the sweet-breads, pepper, and salt, and simmer all very slowly for ten minutes. Serve at once on a hot dish.

Sweet-Bread (Brown Sauce). — One sweet-bread, one half tea-spoonful Liebig's extract of beef, one gill cold water, one pinch pepper, one pinch salt, one half tea-spoonful arrowroot.

Soak the sweet-bread in a basin of cold water for an hour; take it from the water, place it in a small sauce-pan of cold water, and boil it for half an hour. Pour away the water and put the sweet-bread in a basin of cold water; wash it well, trim the fat from it, and cut it in pieces. Place the arrowroot in a basin, moisten it with a very little cold water, and when quite smooth add the remainder of the water. Pour this into a fresh sauce-pan, and stir it over the fire till boiling; add the Liebig extract, and then the pieces of sweet-bread. Simmer all slowly for ten minutes, and serve at once on a hot dish.

Sweet-Bread (Fried).—One sweet-bread, one table-spoonful bread crumb, one pinch pepper, one pinch salt, one egg.

Soak the sweet-bread for an hour in a basin of cold water; take it from the water, place it in a sauce-pan, cover it with cold water, and allow it to boil for half an hour; pour away the water, and place it in a basin of cold water; wash it well, and cut it in slices. Beat well on a plate the egg, and roll each slice in it. Place the bread crumb on a paper, and add the pepper and salt. Roll each slice in the bread crumb. Melt in a frying-pan about two ounces dripping; when the smoke rises, place in the slices of sweet-bread, and brown them to a pale brown on each side. Have in readiness a sheet of kitchen-paper on a plate; as the slices brown, place them on it, and place the plate before the fire for a minute or two to drain the grease from them. Serve on a hot dish, and garnish with parsley.

Breast of Chicken.—One side from the breast of a chicken, one half ounce butter.

Cut the breast carefully with a sharp knife from the chicken, spread the butter over a small piece of kitchen-paper, roll the piece of chicken in the paper. Lift the piece with a long skewer or fork, and hold it before the fire for ten minutes, turning it once. Remove the paper, and serve on a very hot plate.

NOTE.—A leg of fowl may be done in the same way. It is necessary to have a very clear fire for this.

Rabbit for Invalid.—One leg or small piece of the back, one quarter tea-spoonful Liebig's extract of beef, one and one-half gill cold water, one pinch salt, one pinch pepper, one half tea-spoonful arrowroot.

Soak the piece of rabbit for one hour in a basin of strong salt and water. Take it from the water, place it in a sauce-pan, pour over the water, place the pan over the fire, and when the water boils draw it on one side. Skim well, and let all simmer slowly together for one hour and a quarter. Moisten now in a small basin the arrowroot with a table-spoonful of cold water, pour it into the sauce-pan, stir well, and then add the Liebig. Simmer ten minutes longer, when it is ready. Serve the rabbit on a hot dish, and pour the sauce over.

Rabbit and White Sauce.—One leg or piece of the back of a rabbit, one ounce butter, one half ounce flour, one gill water, one gill milk, one pinch pepper, one pinch salt.

Soak the piece of rabbit one hour in strong salt and water. Take it from the water, place it in a sauce-pan, and cover it with cold water. Place the pan on the fire, and when the water boils pour it away; cover it again with water, and when it boils pour it away also. Take out the piece of rabbit, melt in the sauce-pan the butter, add the flour, stir both well together, and then pour in by degrees the water and milk. Stir all till boiling; draw the pan on one side, add the pepper and salt, and simmer slowly for one hour and a quarter. Serve the piece of rabbit on a very hot dish, and pour the sauce round and over.

Boiled Fish.—One small sole, or the tail-end of a cod fish, one small table-spoonful of salt.

Place a large sauce-pan of boiling water over the fire, add the salt, and, when rapidly boiling, wash well the piece of cod and plunge it in. Boil for seven minutes. Serve on a folded napkin placed on a very hot dish; garnish with fresh parsley.

To prepare the sole, wash it well and clean it, but keep on both skins; plunge it into plenty of boiling water in which has been dissolved a little salt. Boil for five minutes, and serve in same way as cod fish.

Fried Sole.—One fillet of sole, the white of an egg, one pinch salt, one pinch pepper, one table-spoonful bread crumbs.

Beat well up the white of egg on a plate. Place on a sheet of kitchen-paper the bread crumb, pepper, and salt. Roll the piece of fish well in the egg; do not handle it, but turn it over and over with a fork; roll it in the bread crumb. Have in readiness in a stew-pan as much clarified fat* as cover the fish; place the pan over the fire, and when the fat begins to smoke, plunge in the fish, and cook for three minutes. Lift the fish out with a fork, and place it to drain before the fire on a piece of kitchen-paper. Place it on a hot dish, and garnish with fresh parsley.

White Wine Whey.—One wine-glassful port wine, one half pint milk, one tea-spoonful sugar, one pinch grated nutmeg.

* Directions for clarified fat, see p. 247.

Place in a sauce-pan the milk, place the pan over the fire, and when the milk boils add the sugar and wine. Stir twice, then pour instantly through a fine piece of muslin into a small basin; grate in the nutmeg, and serve very hot.

Fried Tripe.—One quarter pound boiled tripe, one tablespoonful bread crumb, one pinch salt, one pinch pepper, two ounces dripping.

Take the boiled tripe,* dry it well in a clean towel. Beat well on a plate the white of egg; mix well on a sheet of paper the bread crumb, pepper, and salt. Roll the piece of tripe well in the egg, then well in the seasoned bread crumb. Heat well in a frying-pan the dripping, and when the smoke rises place in the tripe, and fry it to a pale brown on both sides. This will take about six minutes. Drain it for a couple of minutes before the fire on a sheet of kitchen-paper. Serve on a very hot plate, and garnish with parsley.

Tripe in White Sauce.—One quarter pound tripe, one ounce butter, one half ounce flour, one half pint milk, one pinch pepper, one pinch salt.

Take one ounce of butter and melt it in a sauce-pan, add the flour, stir well together, then add by degrees the milk. Stir till boiling, add the pepper and salt, then the boiled tripe. Simmer all for fifteen minutes, when it is ready. Serve on a very hot dish.

* See directions for boiling on page 238.

INDEX.

Aberffrau Buns, 226.
Albert Pudding, 142.
Alexandra Pudding, 165.
Almond Gaufres, 220.
Amber Pudding, 150.
Anchovy Croquettes, 131.
Anchovy Eggs, 227.
Appleade, 287.
Apple Dumplings, 155.
Apple Fritters, 133, 265.
Apple Hedgehog, 173.
Apple Jelly, 251.
Apple Pie, 198.
Apple Pudding, 264.
Apple Sauce, 177.
Apple Transparency, 193.
Apricot Marmalade, 252.
Arrowroot Drink, 237.
Arrowroot and Milk, 282.
Arrowroot Pudding, 281.
Asparagus Purée, 21.
Aunt Martha's Pudding, 144.

Baked Cheese, 280.
Baked Fish, 271.
Baked Onions, 111.
Baked Tripe, 239.
Bakewell Pudding, 163.
Banana Fritters, 134.
Barley Pudding, 262.
Beef Olives, 90.
Beef Salad, 124.
Beefsteak Pie, 50.
Belvoir Castle Buns, 225.
Berlin Pudding, 169.
Black Currant Cordial, 249.
Black Currant Jam, 254.
Blanquette of Veal, 53.
Boiled Asparagus, 105.
Boiled Beef, 47.
Boiled Beefsteak Pudding, 49.
Boiled Beets, 115.

Boiled Cabbage, 107.
Boiled Carrots, 108.
Boiled Cod-fish, 33.
Boiled Custard, 172.
Boiled Fish, 293.
Boiled Fowl, 48.
Boiled Haricot Beans, 109.
Boiled Heart, 276.
Boiled Mutton, 46.
Boiled Oatmeal, 237.
Boiled Onions, 110.
Boiled Parsnips, 113.
Boiled Potatoes, 108.
Boiled Rice, 237.
Boiled Tripe, 238.
Bone Soup, 258.
Boudins, 81.
Brain Cakes, 240.
Braised Fillet of Veal, 59.
Brandy Sauce, 179.
Brazilian Stew, 277.
Bread Berry, 288.
Bread and Butter Pudding, 146.
Bread Pudding, 263.
Bread Sauce, 176.
Breakfast Coffee, 242.
Breast of Chicken, 292.
Broiled Beefsteak, 77.
Broiled Chicken, 77.
Broiled Haddock, 36.
Broiled Kidney, 76.
Broiled Mackerel, 34.
Broiled Oysters, 27.
Browned Calf's Head, 65.
Browned Rabbit, 60.
Browned Sweet-Breads, 101.
Brown Sauce, 176.
Brown Soup, 12.
Brown Stock, 9.

Cabbage à-la-Mode, 112.
Cabinet Pudding, 144.

INDEX.

Calf's-foot Jelly, 191.
Calf's Liver, 228.
Caper Sauce, 174.
Caramel, 247.
Casserole Chicken, 238.
Cauliflower au Gratin, 103.
Chantilly, 173.
Charlotte Russe, 186.
Chaud-froid of Chicken, 94.
Cheese Fritters, 132.
Cheese Pudding, 280.
Cheese Soufflé, 139.
Cherry Brandy, 250.
Cherry Plum Jam, 252.
Chestnut Soufflé, 140.
Chicken Croquettes, 95, 126.
Chickens' Livers, 235.
Chicken Salad, 119.
Chicken Soufflé, 140.
Chocolate, 243.
Chocolate Pudding, 153.
Chocolate Soufflé, 138.
Chop, 290.
Citronell, 253.
Claret Jelly, 286.
Clarified Fat, 247.
Clear Arrowroot, 282.
Clear Barley Water, 283.
Clear Soup, 10.
Colcannon, 109.
Cold Boiled Mutton, 69.
Cold Cabinet Pudding, 164.
Cold Chicken, 75.
Cold Meat Shape, 74.
Cold Turkey, 72.
Corned Beef Hash, 69.
Corn-Flour Cake, 214.
Corn-Flour Pudding, 263.
Corn-Flour Shape, 262.
Corn Fritters, 134.
Cornish Pasties, 70.
Corn Lunn, 205.
Corn Starch Pudding, 156.
Crab Croquettes, 128.
Crab Pie, 29.
Cream Cake, 208, 218.
Cream Nectar, 250.
Cream Pudding, 162.
Croquettes of Macaroni, 130.
Croquettes of Salmon, 129.
Croquettes of Shad-Roe, 129.
Cucumber Salad, 123.
Cup Custard, 288.

Currant Cake, 217.
Currant Dumpling, 266.
Curried Eggs, 232.
Curried Lobster, 30.
Curried Rabbit, 61.
Curry, 68.
Curry with Boiled Rice, 88.
Custard Pie, 199.
Custard Sauce, 180.
Custard Toast, 286.
Cutlets à-la-Maréchal, 100.

Damson Cheese, 253.
Damson Jam, 252.
Derby Pudding, 169.
Deviled Turkey, 229.
Devonshire Junket, 167.
Dresden Patties, 234.
Dressed Cauliflower, 117.
Dressed Lamb's Head, 66.
Dried Herb Omelettes, 231.
Duck with Green Pease, 63.
Dutch Sauce, 178.

Easily-digested Beef Tea, 285.
Economical Beef Tea, 284.
Eel Pie, 31.
Egg Flip, 288.
Egg Sauce, 174.
Eggs au Plat, 231.
Eggs on Toast, 232.
English Plum Pudding, 149.

Fairy Butter, 170.
Family Dumpling, 161.
Fig Pudding, 142.
Fillet of Beef, 99.
Fillet of Sole, 32.
Fish Cakes, 38, 269.
Fish Chowder, 23.
Fish à-la-Russe, 37.
Fish and Sauce, 270.
Fish Soup, 257.
Flaky Crust, 195.
Folded Rolls, 205.
Forcemeat Balls, 65.
French Beans, 114.
French Pudding, 171.
French Rolls, 202.
Fricassée of Chicken, 54.
Fricassée of Lobster, 32.
Fricassée of Oyster, 25.
Fricassée of Sweet-Breads, 91.

INDEX.

Fried Chicken, 79.
Fried Fish, 272.
Fried Oysters, 25.
Fried Rice Balls, 266.
Fried Sausages, 278.
Fried Smelts, 35.
Fried Sole, 293.
Fried Tripe, 294.
Frizzled Bacon, 268.
Frozen Pudding, 182.
Fruit Cake, 212.

Galettes, 206.
German Pudding, 172.
German Sweet Sauce, 179.
Giblet Soup, 13.
Ginger Beer, 245, 248.
Ginger Bread, 217, 225.
Ginger Cordial, 249.
Ginger Pudding, 160.
Glacé Pudding, 163.
Goose Pudding, 231.
Green Codling Ice-Cream, 194.
Green Gooseberry Jam, 256.
Green Pease, 106.
Grenadines of Veal, 97.
Ground Rice Shape, 261.

Ham and Eggs, 268.
Ham Omelette, 230.
Hard Sauce, 180.
Hare Soup, 15.
Haricot Bean Soup, 256.
Haricot of Mutton, 53.
Haunch of Venison, 80.
Hotch-potch, 14.
Hot-pot, 51, 273.

Iced Pudding, 181.
Iced Soufflé, 184.
Invalid Pudding, 289.
Invalid Shape, 289.
Irish Seed Cake, 223.
Irish Stew, 278.
Italian Cream, 188.
Italian Pudding, 154.

Jam Sauce, 179.
Jellied Tongue, 241.
Jelly Sauce, 180.
Jugged Hare, 80, 82.

Kedgeree, 40.

Kidney Omelette, 229.
Kidney Soup, 11.
Kromesquies Russe, 87.

Larded Sweet-Breads, 92.
Leeks au Gratin, 113.
Lemonade, 287.
Lemon Cake, **222.**
Lemon Jelly, **190.**
Lemon Peel Tea, **283.**
Lemon Pickle, 246.
Lemon Pie, 198.
Lemon Pudding, **145.**
Lemon Sauce, 179.
Lemon Soufflé, 136.
Lemon Sponge, **192.**
Lemon Syrup, 251.
Lemon Water Ice, 183.
Lentil Soup, 259.
Lettuce Salad, 124.
Light Egg for Invalid, 288.
Lima Beans, **112.**
Liver and Bacon, **79.**
Llanberries Pudding, 147.
Lobster Cutlets, **30.**
Lobster Salad, **121.**
Lobster Sauce, **177.**
Lothian Pudding, **167.**
Lowell **Pudding, 143.**
Lunch **Cake, 219.**

Macaroni and Cheese, 116, 279.
Macaroni and Meat Shape, 269.
Maître d'Hôtel Potatoes, 118.
Marmalade, 253.
Marmalade Pudding, 160.
Marrow Pudding, 159.
Meat Roll, 277.
Méringues, 194.
Méringue Pudding, **162.**
Merveilles, **224.**
Mock Turtle Soup, 11.
Milk **Biscuit,** 203.
Milk **Gruel, 282.**
Milk Rolls, **202.**
Milk Soup, 260.
Minced Chicken, 73.
Minced Cold Veal, 76.
Minced Collops, 66.
Minced Steak, 290.
Mince Pie, 199.
Mint Sauce, 175.
Muffins, 203.

Mullagatawny Soup, 18.
Mushrooms, 233.
Mutton Cutlets, 67.
Mutton Pies, 245.
Mutton Soubise, 57.

Noodlins, 246.

Omelette Soufflé, 138.
Onion Sauce, 176.
Orange Cake, 209.
Orange Cream, 186.
Orange Jelly, 190.
Overton Pudding, 148.
Ox-tail Soup, 19.
Oyster Balls, 29.
Oysters à-la-Créme, 27.
Oyster Croquettes, 28.
Oyster Fritters, 132.
Oyster Sauce, 174.
Oyster Soup, 24.
Oyster Soup à-la-Reine, 23.

Pancakes, 157, 265.
Partridge Pie, 83.
Pea Soup, 256.
Peach Pie, 199.
Peach Sago, 156.
Pie Crust, 197.
Pigeon and Tomatoes, 63.
Pigeon with Peas, 85.
Pig's Feet, 236.
Plain Currant Cake, 226.
Plain Fruit Cake, 219.
Plain Plum Pudding, 264.
Plain Suet Pudding, 165.
Poor Man's Goose, 274.
Popovers, 213.
Pork Sausages, 78.
Potato Croquettes, 126.
Potato Fritters, 131.
Potato Purée, 22.
Potato Sauté, 233.
Potato Soufflé, 135.
Potato Soup, 259.
Potted Halibut, 40.
Pound Cake, 210, 223.
Puff Paste, 195.
Purée à-la-Condé, 19.
Purée of Green Pease, 20.

Queen Cakes, 218.
Quenelles of Veal, 96.
Quickly-made Beef Tea, 284.

Rabbit for Invalid, 292.
Rabbit Pie, 62.
Rabbits Stewed, 61.
Rabbit and White Sauce, 202.
Rabbit Soup, 18, 257.
Ragout of Rabbit, 58.
Railway Pudding, 153.
Raspberry Jam, 255.
Raspberry Syrup, 250.
Raspberry Vinegar, 248.
Red Gooseberry Jam, 256.
Rhubarb Ginger, 254.
Rhubarb and Oranges, 254.
Rice and Cheese, 279.
Rice Cream, 187.
Rice Croquettes, 127.
Rice Méringue, 163.
Rice Pudding, 158, 261, 263.
Rice Soup, 258.
Rice Water, 286.
Rissoles, 67.
Rissoles of Veal, 89.
Roast Beef, 42.
Roast Grouse, 84.
Roast Heart, 45.
Roast Pheasant, 82.
Roast Pork, 44.
Roast Turkey, 43.
Rock Cakes, 211.
Rolled Shoulder of Mutton, 55.
Rough Puff Paste, 197.
Rusk, 289.
Rusks, 212.
Russian Pancakes, 171.

Sago and Apples, 264.
Sago Pudding, 262.
Salad à-la-Russe, 125.
Salmon Pie, 39.
Salmon Pudding, 41.
Salt Beef, 244.
Sauce for Gravies, 246.
Sausage Rolls, 71.
Savoury Hash, 74.
Savoury Jelly, 284.
Scalloped Oysters, 27.
Scones, 216.
Scotch Haggis, 243.
Scrambled Eggs, 232.
Sea Pie, 273.
Seed Cake, 214, 220.
Seven-Cup Pudding, 161.
Sir Watkin Wynne's Pudding, 146.

INDEX. 299

Sheep Head Broth, 260.
Sheep Head Pie, 228, 268.
Sheep's Trotters, 227.
Shepherd's Pie, 71, 276.
Short-Bread, 224.
Short Crust, 196.
Shrimp Salad, 120.
Shrimp Sauce, 177.
Simple Omelette, 230.
Snow Cake, 209, 215.
Snowden Pudding, 159.
Snow Jelly, 189.
Soda Cake, 215.
Soda Scones, 204.
Sole au Gratin, 34.
Sole in Jelly, 36.
Sole à-la-Normandie, 36.
Solid Custard, 170.
Soup à-la-Reine, 17.
Spinach with Eggs, 102.
Sponge Cake, 210, 221.
Sponge Sandwich, 216.
Steak Broiled, 290.
Stewed Beef, 52.
Stewed Celery, 115, 119.
Stewed Cod Fish, 41.
Stewed Fish, 271.
Stewed Kidney, 59, 240.
Stewed Pigeon, 86.
Stewed Steak, 275.
Stewed Tomatoes, 115.
Strawberry Ice-Cream, 184.
Strawberry Jam, 255.
Strawberry Jam Pudding, 166.
Strawberry Short Cake, 222.
Strawberry Water Ice, 183.
Stuffed Haddock, 35.
Stuffed Heart, 275.
Stuffed Potatoes, 234.
Suet Crust, 196.
Suet Dumplings, 267.
Sultana Cake, 207.
Sweet-Bread, 290, 291.
Swiss Apple Pudding, 168.
Swiss Rissoles, 155.
Syrup Cake, 219.

Talleyrand Cutlets, 98.
Tapioca Cream Soup, 16.
Tapioca Pudding, 148.

Tartare Sauce, 175.
Tea, 242.
Tibble Shiel's or Girdle Scones, 204.
Timbales, 98.
Tipsy Cake, 172, 213.
Toad in the Hole, 274.
Toffy, 248.
Tomato **Farci,** 104.
Tomato **Purée,** 20.
Tomato Sauce, 178.
Treacle Roly-Poly, 267.
Trifle, 152.
Tripe with Onion Sauce, 239.
Tripe in White Sauce, 294.
Turban, 167.
Turbot à-la-Créme, 39.
Turkey and Chestnuts, 64.
Turkish Soup, 17.
Turnip Purée, 21.
Turnip **Radishes,** 118.
Turnips, 106.
Turnips in White Sauce, 117.
Twice Laid, 270.

Unboiled Pickle, **244.**
Uncooked **Beef** Tea, **285.**

Vanilla Ice-Cream, **185.**
Vanilla Soufflé, 137.
Veal Balls, 72.
Veal Pie, 62.
Vegetable Marrow, 118.
Velvet Cream, 188.
Venoise Pudding, 151.
Vermicelli Pudding, 166.
Victoria Buns, 226.
Vol-au-Vent of Sweet-Breads, 92.

Wakefield Pudding, 149.
Walnut Ice-Cream, 193.
Water Gruel, 283.
Welcome Guest Pudding, **141.**
Wheat Bread, 201.
White **Currant** Jelly, 251.
White **Sauce, 181.**
White Stock, **16.**
White **Wine** Whey, 293.
Wild Ducks, 84.
Windham Cutlets, 56.
Wine Sauce, 181.
Woodcock on Toast, **85.**